Resurrection in Cannes

Wes Herschensohn was born in Milwaukee, Wisconsin, on December 14, 1928, and at the age of eleven moved with his family to Los Angeles, where he has resided ever since. Herschensohn studied at Chouinard Art Institute and the Los Angeles Art Center.

An artist and storyman for five years at the Walt Disney Studios, Herschensohn developed a lust for animation that has since carried him to dazzling heights. Having animated and co-produced *The Picasso Summer*, Herschensohn is now engaged in the preparation of a feature film on the life of Beethoven, where he expects to take the art of animation to an even more dazzling plateau of creativity.

Herschensohn is divorced and has two children, David and Brigitte.

RESURRECTION IN CANNES

The Making of
The Picasso Summer

WES HERSCHENSOHN

South Brunswick and New York:
A. S. Barnes and Company
London: Thomas Yoseloff Ltd

A. S. Barnes and Co., Inc.
Cranbury, New Jersey 08512

Thomas Yoseloff Ltd
Magdalen House
136-148 Tooley Street
London SE1 2TT, England

Library of Congress Cataloging in Publication Data

Herschensohn, Wes, 1928-
  Resurrection in Cannes.

  Includes index.
  1. Picasso summer (Motion picture) 2. Herschensohn,
Wes, 1928   3. Moving-picture producers and
directors—United States—Biography. I. Title.
PN1997.P4783H47   1979   791.43′7   76-24621
ISBN 0-498-01942-X

Printed in the United States of America

By some miraculous circumstance, I'm convinced that before I was born I must have been allowed to choose my parents from all the world; and with more love and gratitude than that world can hold I dedicate this book to them:

Dr. Herbert L. Herschensohn
and
Mrs. Ida E. Herschensohn

"If only," she said, "you liked other painters."

Others? Yes, there were others. He could breakfast more congenially on Caravaggio still lifes of autumn pears and midnight plums. For lunch: those fire-squirting, thick-wormed Van Gogh sunflowers, those blooms a blind man might read with one rush of scorched fingers down fiery canvas. But the great feast? The paintings he saved his palate for? There, filling the horizon like Neptune risen, crowned with limeweed, alabaster, coral, paint-brushes clenched like tridents in horn-nailed fists, and with fish-tail vast enough to fluke summer showers out over all Gibraltar—who else but the creator of *Girl Before a Mirror* and *Guernica*?

"Alice," he said patiently, "how can I explain? Coming down on the train, I thought, Good Lord, it's *all* Picasso country!"

—Ray Bradbury, "In a Season of Calm Weather"

Contents

An Urgent Preface

Having just reread my own manuscript of this, my personal journey to Picasso and his world as I found it in 1964 through 1967, I found myself at first surprised, then a little appalled, by an unmistakable thread of egomania that seems to wend its way through the narrative. This is not by way of apology, since what is said must speak for itself, and to rewrite it in order to delete my own feelings and to create a false sense of humility would be, of course, a complete lie.

However, all through these adventures and encounters I was so totally overwhelmed by a feeling of joy and discovery, and (despite countless negative admonishments and assurances to the contrary) a feeling of positive inevitability that I *would* not only meet Picasso but interest him in my idea, that some great thrusts of egomania were absolutely necessary if I were to succeed. Thus, in recalling my feelings and motives during these times, to subdue them in the telling would be more than dishonest and hypocritical—it would render the telling a complete absurdity.

Since early childhood, through the unbelievable encouragement of my beloved parents, I had steeped myself in drawing and in art history, so that the lives of all the great artists and periods in art became as much a part of me as the act of breathing, and I devoured it all with an ever-increasing appetite. And, like anyone brought up in this background, I had always *assumed* as a natural birthright that I would one day write my own chapter in this endless epic, so that what might emerge as egomania is actually a guileless sort of accumulated identification with and love of all those other lives and episodes in art history.

Preparing for my journey to Picasso, I felt such confidence and warm, pleasurable assurances of the outcome, that it was as though I were languishing in the comfort of a great womb, waiting, as it were, to be born. And when suddenly the brilliant sunlight and colors of southern France were enveloping me and nourishing me, I was, in fact, *resurrected*. To abruptly find myself surrounded on every side by the bright world of

The four photographs in this Preface depict the man whose monumental works of art inspired all that is told herein, the great Pablo Picasso. The pictures were taken in the late spring or early summer of 1966, following Picasso's gall-bladder operation. He is accompanied by his fast friend Luis Miguel Dominguin, world-famous matador and international playboy. The scene is an unidentified local restaurant in Cannes. (COURTESY OF BRUCE CAMPBELL)

Picasso, only miles from the fields where Van Gogh had roamed and created under this same dazzling sunlight; to encounter the bright-eyed little French beauties I had come to know in the eighteenth century canvases of Boucher and Fragonard, clothed in the modern sensuality of today; and in Paris, to roam the very streets in Montmarte and Monparnasse where Modigliani and Lautrec and Picasso himself had roamed, where George Gershwin had found himself dazzled into new creations—who was I to resist?

The woman in the background is a friend of Picasso's. The shape in the foreground is the back of the head of Jacqueline, the Master's wife. (Courtesy of Bruce Campbell)

And in Spain, under the guidance of the great matador Dominguin, I saw the land not as a tourist or a mere visitor, but as a lifetime disciple of the great Goya—and being submerged in the dark mystery, mysticism, and sensual rhythms of the land.

Further, to be surrounded at once by such warm friends and to be admitted without hesitation into the circle of such world-famous figures offering their enthusiastic assistance to me in my "mission," I was staggered into a sense of a certain destiny that does, surely, manifest itself in the writing as nothing less than egomaniacal.

Much, however, is left unsaid—since this narrative was not intended as an "exposé" of anyone—therefore, in order to spare some good people (and some not-so-good people), certain things have been deleted; but the astute reader may possibly discern these for himself between the lines. On

11

the other hand, there were many things that perhaps I should have deleted; but had I done so, I might as well have been writing about some other planet, and would have failed entirely in re-creating the atmosphere in which I met Picasso, and of his world at that time. A world, incidentally, which I found to be totally steeped in the mythology of this century's greatest creator, over which he reigned like a great god of ancient times; *that* was incredible, and there will never be anything like it again.

So, with unforgiveable shamelessness, I took an absolute joy in myself and whatever small part I might be playing in this unbelievably bright spot on the map of art history where Picasso and Chagall were still charting their courses; and I played my role to the hilt—my sole purpose being, with the help and/or sponsorship of Picasso, to advance the technology and art

Picasso and Dominguin are apparently watching some form of entertainment, probably Flamenco. (COURTESY OF BRUCE CAMPBELL)

of painting from the canvas to the motion picture screen, where it would spring to life in a *new kind of movement*—where for the first time rhythm would be a delight of the *eye*, rather than the ear only! Where form would metamorphosize into form; wild, dancing shapes and colors moving ever forward in an unstoppable flow of progressive change, with the rhythmic inevitability and excitement of a Beethoven symphony: a living world of dazzling beings in a continuous activity of demonic, uninhibited energy, pulsating to the ebb and flow of a predetermined *rhythm*.

The story tells of Picasso's enthusiastic, almost frightened response to this idea; on through to the completion and aftermath of the resultant film *The Picasso Summer,* with all its thrills and agonies.

Enjoy it; and this week, take an egomaniac to lunch.

Picasso seems to have moved in order to get a better view of the proceedings—that angle of vision which in all the world is uniquely his. (COURTESY OF BRUCE CAMPBELL)

13

Acknowledgments

I would like to give heartfelt thanks to a number of people for their help and encouragement in the making of this book.

First, to Mr. Thomas Yoseloff, its publisher, for his faith and encouraging words upon his first receipt of the unfinished manuscript and his continuing enthusiasm throughout the many busy months that followed, my gratitude is endless.

To my editor, Mr. Ronald B. Roth, I express special thanks for his kindness and understanding, and for the magnificent job of editing he did on the manuscript. His wise and tasteful comments were invaluable, both to me and to the flow and content of the book. His tireless efforts and empathetic patience are deeply appreciated.

And, as a bonus throughout the lengthy exchange of long-distance phone calls with managing editor Dena Rogin, I fell head over heels in love with a voice. And I am endlessly grateful for her help and advice.

For the typing of the manuscript I am indebted to Mr. Roy Wallenstein, and to his lovely wife, Sophia, for the proofreading. Roy not only typed and corrected, but provided me with much-needed comments of professional confidence and enthusiasm throughout the long periods of the book's creation.

Many thanks to dearest Nancy for her generous help along the way, assisting in the tedious tasks such as running errands that supplied me with priceless extra time, and for her unswerving and loyal support.

Special thanks also to Ginger St. Pierre for her wise counsel and cheerful encouragement; to N., who knows why she is forever included; to Bruce Campbell, for reasons that will be apparent in the text; and to Don Christensen, Lou Scheimer, Norm Prescott, and everyone at Filmation for cheering me on.

There is no way I can ever thank my beloved family for the way in which they continually provided me with everything in the way of love, warmth, and encouragement: my parents, Dr. And Mrs. Herschensohn (Herbert and Ida); my sister Vi and her husband Mort Logan; my brother Bruce and his wife Bunny; my dear children, David and Brigitte; to all of these loved ones—Turksey, and of course Pablo and Misty—my eternal thanks.

Finally, thanks beyond words to David Douglas Duncan, Luis Miguel Dominguin, and Pablo Picasso—without whom this book simply would not exist.

W.H.

Resurrection in Cannes

1

Cannes

Ah, I shall never be able to convey my impressions of some faces I have seen here. Certainly this is the road on which there is something new, the road to the South [of France], but men of the North find penetrating it difficult.

> —Vincent van Gogh, letter to Theo,
> St. Remy, September 10, 1889

Cannes was catapulated toward me like a thousand rockets, and I charged forward willingly to be hit by all of them—God Almighty, what a blaze of daylight colors fanned themselves outward to greet me, knowing why I had come and elated that the waiting was over!

Because they knew, as I knew, and now you know, that at that very moment of my entrance to Cannes, I was George Gershwin in Paris, Thomas Wolfe in Vienna, Eugene Delacroix in Morocco, T. E. Lawrence in Arabia, Vincent van Gogh in Arles, Santa Claus at the North Pole—anybody who was ever anywhere he was destined to be!

And that is how it was to be from that moment on, doors swinging open, arms outstretched to embrace; "Henceforth I ask not good fortune," Walt Whitman said, *"I myself am good fortune!"* For the next three months, anyway.

Well, I saw those twin gleaming domes of the magnificent Hotel Carlton, the palm-lined Croisette, the joyous blue of the Mediterranean, the yellow sun brimming over into the warm transparency that was the air of Cote D'Azur, the Riviera of the senses! Are you there with me now? Then look away discreetly for five minutes only, allowing me a brief plunge into utter insanity, while I make Cannes pregnant with my acknowledgment of what is very definitely to be.

★   ★   ★

I've just arrived in Tangier. I have rushed through the town. I am quite bewildered by all that I've seen. I can't let the mail boat go—it's leaving shortly for Gibraltar—without telling you something of my amazement at all the things I've seen. We landed in the midst of the strangest crowd of people. The Pasha of the city received us, surrounded by his soldiers. One would need to have twenty arms and forty-eight hours a day to give any tolerable impression of it all. The Jewesses are quite lovely. I'm afraid it will be difficult to do more than paint them: they are real pearls of Eden. We were given a superb reception by local standards. They treated us to the most peculiar military music. At the moment I'm like a man in a dream, seeing things he's afraid will vanish from him.

—from the letters of
Eugène Delacroix

Cannes is a winding line, on which one side is that sea of mystic blue and on the other side that little town where your eye flies over the charming little stores and elegant hotels, up, up, into the mountains, building by building amid the splendorous greenery. That winding line is called the *Croisette*, the palm-lined main thoroughfare that travels the length of the city separating beach from street. The air is always clear and bright, bright blue, bright yellow sun.

So dominated was the entire Cote d'Azur at the time of my visit by the incredible presence of Picasso, one could never comprehend, unless *there*, how similar was this legend to that of Zeus on Olympus. His home in Mougins, on the mountains behind Cannes, was as potent as Olympus, and all logic was absent to the observant visitor in Cannes; myth and fantasy swarmed through the very air to an extent even the inhabitants failed to realize. What a joy prevailed everywhere, to be in the citadel of an immortal who had reshaped the entire world and made this portion of it his home.

And, too, a less conspicuous god, Eros, chose to make his home nearby, endowing his gifts of love upon this chosen golden coin of earth called Provence, and he was known as Chagall and lived in Vence at the time of my visit, and afterward moved to St. Paul de Vence. His gifts of love were great paintings of fantasy and color, and pottery that captured the feeling of the earth and sea of Provence. The texture of his pottery had the roughness of earth and the color of sea and sky with paintings of fantastic winged lovers and animals that floated through the dream-air over the

Mediterranean, with the buildings of Nice or Cannes far below in the mountains, yellow lights glowing from their distant windows through the earth-textured blues and purples of this dream-sky, and yet capturing, like an arrow on target, the *reality* of the scene.

In the Madoura gallery the aunt of Picasso's wife took me to a back room and showed me two of these Chagall vases, and holding one in my hand I could smell the sea more strongly than I ever did standing on the shore. Our life, after all (that is, our *reality*), is really no more or less than an experience of a compilation of man's imagination and the results of it—therefore, Chagall's vase was as powerful an evocation to the touch as whatever mysteries the sea itself evokes.

But more potently, the real dancing, prancing, loving, playing nymphs and fauns and satyrs and centaurs and lovers of Picasso's Mediterranean were becoming more than myth and fantasy, and dominating the pattern of life with such a powerful explosion of great health and joy that mythology, with a logic of its own, became reality, and somewhere in the mountains above Cannes mortals in hushed reverence approached, with a logic of their own, a new Olympus—and Picasso, through the sheer vitality of his creative magic, was everywhere, and became Zeus.

Can you, then, imagine my uproarious happiness at being there, *then*—at that time? Not as a tourist, but (as what?) there to see Zeus himself, confident to the core of my every cell that he would see me, even though he had just concluded the first year of the ten-year seclusion that was to take him to the end of his life.

Soon Cannes, sunny and starry Cannes, was entirely mine, in this way: I knew it for what it was, a town in the throes of a silent celebration for the point in history that it at this moment occupied. I saw, smelled, sketched, and loved every corner of it till I was the most familiar figure on the streets and was expected to be seen as surely as a white sail on the Mediterranean. I knew every shop, sales girl, department store, open-air market, grocery, fish-stall, restaurant, prostitute, tourist, smell, hotel, bird, plant, car, street, road, alley, and avenue to the point that if you had pricked me and put a sample of my blood under a microscope you would have seen this incredible reflection of Cannes in every corpuscle.

I take it with me everywhere now, part of my racial memory that will haunt me in reincarnations to come as a vague, distant, uncertain, but *urgent memory* of long years gone. I know that if I live again the memory of Cannes will haunt me with brief and momentary glimpses, flashes, that stop me short in a swelling of feeling that will be gone as soon as it comes; just as we all have these waves of mist-covered memories of something beyond our recollection, barely adrift of our grasp. But I knew, even at the time I was devouring Cannes in the immediate *present,* that it was no more real than the ancient memory it was to become.

The twin dazzling domes of the Carlton Hotel gleam in the sunlight like the two glorious breasts of Cannes herself, that unattainable beauty who languishes tauntingly along the vast stretch of beach by the sea of her lover, Zeus.

The men of Cannes—well, I wanted to give them the incredible faces one finds in the canvases of Van Gogh and Picasso, but set in the motion of an *animation* the likes of which had never before been seen or imagined, with undreamed-of rhythms of their own, swirling across the giant screen.

The women of Cannes—the delicious little Cannesiennes—they were already flesh and blood Fragonards set to the music of Ravel and Debussy, but I wanted to give them more, much more.

Every bright-eyed girl became to me the embodiment, the materialization, the localized figuration through which the great goddess Cannes revealed herself, and I was in love with all of them, in love with a town, with myself, and with love itself. I could identify with Van Gogh, who became enraptured with that very sun above, which poured down and devoured him in nearby Arles, little more than three-quarters of a century earlier. My imagination was home, and all the thrilling images of a wild new kind of motion in animation that were but seeds in my mind when I left Los Angeles now sprouted to fruition in the fertile soil of Picasso country, and I knew that I had come to the right place at the right time for the right reason.

2

Flashback—To the Desperate Beginning

There are women like a Fragonard and like a Renoir. And some that can't be labeled with anything that's been done yet in painting. The best thing to do would be to make portraits of women and children. But I don't think that I am the man to do it. I'm not enough of a Monsieur Bel Ami for that.

—Vincent van Gogh, letter to
Theo, Arles, May 5, 1888

THE ANGEL OF DESPAIR WAS MY MISTRESS FOR ONE MONTH IN MARCH AND FOR one week in April of 1964, and the more intimate I became with her the more I despised her—but how does one shake an unwanted lover? My wife had found it easy, and divorced me, so I took this most available and willing mistress and very quickly felt rotten about her.

She made me look out of a window on the twelfth floor of the tower on Sunset and Vine where I was working as an animator on "Tom and Jerry." (*They* did not cheer me up at all—they only accented what seemed to be the senselessness of everything.)

So I stood there, looking out, and down; the others had long since gone home, and it was dark—early evening. I was really down, in a frightening way that was foreign to me, and I felt that I was at the end of my rope—wrenched away by divorce from the warm domesticity of home, wife, and children that I had come to expect as my birthright, and that I loved so thoroughly. Below, on the boulevards of Hollywood, people were driving home from work oblivious to the dark, lonely figure looking down

23

at them in despair until he noticed his own reflection in the glass looking back at him.

When a man is sad his own reflection is of little comfort to him, and so I turned away and went to the men's room. There, in the large mirror, I caught my reflection again, but this time more clearly, so I went quickly into the toilet booth, closed the door, closed the toilet seat, and sat down on top of it.

I am always bored by people wondering "who they are" and "where they're at," and it would be with great reluctance that I would volunteer my name to that endless list of those who, in their darkest moments, suddenly *found* themselves. But I did! Yes, I reflected on my entire life to that point, found it to have been unusually happy and very fruitful for the most part—except for one very singular thing. My "fantasy" consisted of myself as a great artist, when in reality, all along I had been, at best, an imaginative and creative painter and a practicing cartoonist in the field of animation, with four valuable years from 1953 to 1957 with Walt Disney, and with really nothing more than a sort of impulsive and restless cleverness that surfaced now and then. I do not say that at times I was not *very* clever, and *very* creative, and in fact, really unusual if not feverishly terrific—but so were thousands of other brilliant young souls, and what did it all mean? Nothing; totally and absolutely. I did not want *that*. Not *that*.

But animation! Here was a whole new world that for over sixty years had been used, often with genius, merely for the entire purpose of "yukking it up." Talk about your *Wasteland!* Here was the greatest medium for visual expression in the entire history of art, and not one major artist—not *one*—had ever touched or even approached it.

I did not resolve anything, sitting on top of that toilet seat, but I began slowly to receive involuntary mental glimpses, each coming in a separate flash, like two frames on a movie screen, then seven, then twelve—of a warm, sunny view of the French Riviera! Well, naturally, what better escape when you have sunk to the lowest depths? But they were *uncontrolled* flashes—they appeared by themselves: the French Riviera, sun, warmth, "Come, come, come, sun, joy, life, come!" Yes, all right, I had money from my share of the sale of our house, not much, but enough—I could go—yes, all right, why not?

The first step in making a dream a reality is to tell others, contrary to what anyone tells you, because then you have consigned it to this world, and you must back it up or be the fool. As for me, I felt such joy in my resolution, rather such *strength,* that instead of going to the drab hotel room that since my divorce had become my unlikely home—I drove toward my parents' home in Westwood, with the intention of announcing my new plan.

What I did not realize was that the plan had not yet fully revealed itself to me, but as I drove toward Westwood, the pieces of my jigsaw mind began dropping into place. What kind of a "plan" would it be to go to another part of the world to lie in the sun? There was something more, something very much more.

I remembered a year or so earlier I had written a vow to myself on a card, and looked at it every day; and it said something to the effect that I would be true to the potential for art that I saw in animation—not much more than that—a vow I really only half understood myself. I had made that vow because I sensed that something could be done with it similar to that which the great composers had done with symphonic music, where the artist works in the dimension of *time,* as one does (or should do) in animation. I saw the possibility of great parallels between the two mediums that thrilled me, but which I did not totally comprehend yet.

Because of my fascination of working in "time," and my great and fierce love for the music of Beethoven, I had for a time considered giving up visual for audial art to become a composer of music, until I realized the great parallel between the two mediums of symphonic music and animation, and made my "vow" to see it through until I could understand it all more clearly. I had always thought it strange that Picasso had not experimented with animation, since he had worked in literally every other artistic medium known to Man—

PICASSO!

The French Riviera! Of *course!* I almost crashed my car into the curb, so thunderingly did the last piece of my jigsaw thump into place!

By the time I got to my parents' house I was able to tell them this:

That I was going to France to meet Picasso in order to teach him the craft of animation, and that I visualized, as I was confident *he also* would visualize, a *new kind of movement*—a movement that was its own reason for being—images that flowed, metamorphosized, and flowed again onward in their own inevitable rhythm, making endless variations of themselves in this new kind of organic movement that found its only parallel in symphonic music. Colors and forms and images *unlimited,* but all caught up in this onward rush, this irresistible force of forward movement, through change and visual rhythm that would open up an entire new universe and *way of seeing!*

My reasoning was that only through the incredible fame and genius of Picasso would I be able to open the door to this new kind of movement, allowing animation to live up to its name and expand to its rightful place at the head of the arts, alongside music. Were I, an unknown, to attempt it solely on my own, I would be struggling fruitlessly against insurmountable financial and commercial obstacles.

I could not have found a better or happier reception than that which I found that night in my parents' beaming smiles and joyous words of encouragement, and I knew at that moment that my true life had begun.

That night, in my depressing little hotel room on the Sunset Strip, the first night of my new life, I was perusing with new interest two books that I had recently purchased and treasured greatly. The first was a thin book called *The Private World of Pablo Picasso,* and the second was a big blockbuster of a book called *Picasso's Picassos.* What these two books had in common other than their subject matter was that they were both authored by David Douglas Duncan. Probably the greatest photo-journalist of all time, he photographed for *Life* magazine what was undoubtedly the single most horrendously poignant and powerful record of war ever captured on film. This was the conflict in Korea. In Michelangelo's *Last Judgment* there is a *face* of one of the damned, being pulled down toward hell by demons. The eyes that burn unforgettably from this dark face were seen again, five centuries later, in Duncan's most heart-searing portrait of an American Marine, in brief respite from combat, wrestling with his own demons in his own hell.

But Duncan is more than a photo-journalist. He is a man. Adventurer, romantic, author, poet, liver of life, and a compassionately warm individualist who seems to typify what we have come to think of as the Rugged American, with steel-gray hair, strong features, and thick dark brows over eyes that reflect a sincere and passionate idealism. He has been everywhere, met the truly great of the world, consorted with them as their sure equal, and looks forward to more adventures, to record in words and photos the world as he finds it.

I read that he was living with his wife Sheila in southern France in a luxurious and beautiful spot called Castellaras, about two miles from Picasso's home in Mougins, in the hills behind Cannes. It occurred to me that if anyone could help me in my plan to meet Picasso it would certainly be this man—a fellow American who knew Picasso intimately, had lived with him, in fact, for a couple of months while doing his book *Picasso's Picassos.* I slept that night—not at all.

The next day I placed a call to *Life* magazine in New York, in the hope that they could tell me how I could contact Duncan. And they did. They had his postal address only, a small locality called Mouans-Sartoux, the nearest post office to Castellaras. *Life* told me that I could contact Duncan by placing a call to Mouans-Sartoux. This I did about half an hour or so after midnight, in the dismal loneliness of my hotel room. The operator in Mouans-Sartoux knew Duncan by name and said that she would try to contact him at home in Castellaras and then call me back and connect me. She referred to him as "M'sieur Dooncan" in an accent that I knew was soon to become a part of my existence.

Placing this call was not easy for me, because it was the first real step of what was to become a long, very personal journey to Picasso, and I had to take a few deep breaths before actually placing the call. Waiting for it to come through, I was in a fit of silently hysterical agony, as though I were waiting at the precipice of a cliff I had to leap across; and in a quiet state of panic for having followed my impulse, and now waiting for the first return.

At 1:00 A.M. the phone rang, and my heart jumped. "We 'ave M'sieur Dooncan for you," the operator said. Good God, I thought, I'm not really that sure just what it is I'm going to say to him, so impulsive was this whole thing. It was ten in the morning, Duncan's time, and his voice came through clear and warm and friendly, and I was encouraged by that alone. With the sound of his voice, all the bright sunshine of a warm morning in southern France, green trees and bird-songs included, seemed to pour through the phone and fill my small dark room, transfiguring everything.

I told him my idea, and he listened patiently and warmly. We talked for a long time, and he told me that there were droves of people that came to see him *every day* simply because he knows Picasso; some with good ideas, some with crackpot ideas, but all with the hope of cashing in on the name of Picasso, or just simply to meet the great man. He said that Picasso himself had been in seclusion for over half a year (this was the beginning of the ten-year seclusion that lasted until his death on April 8, 1973), working on no one knows what, and had not appeared in public for more than a year. Duncan told me that he drove by Picasso's house every night and saw the light burning in his studio window just last night, in fact. He said that I caught him at a good time, for he had just returned yesterday from a short trip. I asked him for advice, or any little help he could throw my way. He said, "The only advice I can give you, Wes, is not to waste your time and money coming over here. The chances of your ever meeting Picasso aren't even one in a million—they're *minus zero!*"

As discouraging and defeating as this statement was, as crushed as I felt after hanging up, I felt nevertheless as though I had made the leap over that precipice. And I went to sleep with the musical sound of that French operator's voice singing in my ears, and I knew I would be hearing a lot more of that accent soon.

The next day at work I again took my heart in my hands and went to see my boss, Walter Bien, about a leave of absence. Walter was an ambitious, likable, good-looking guy who also happened to be my cousin-in-law, and who ran the whole operation of SIB Productions for the parent company of Metro-Goldwyn-Mayer. The initials SIB. stood for Steven Ira Bien, Walter's young son. The animation portion of SIB Productions was called "Tower Twelve" since it was on the twelfth (and fourteenth) floor of the tower at Sunset and Vine in Hollywood. Tower Twelve was involved in the production of "Tom and Jerry" for MGM, under the able direction of the famous Chuck Jones. Walter had wisely put Chuck Jones in charge of

27

animation, a man of vast experience in the motion picture cartoon who had created "The Road Runner," and cocreated "Bugs Bunny" for Warner Bros., among other notable achievements in animation.

The fact that Walter was my cousin only made the idea of asking him for a leave of absence more difficult, since the last thing I wanted was for him to think I was taking advantage of our relationship. At any rate, when I walked into the executive office of the studio, Walter was talking to his assistant, Sonny Klein. I told them that I wanted a leave of absence for a few weeks to go to France. They looked at each other, then back at me and asked me why. When I told them why, they seemed at a loss for words, then Sonny Klein said, "Leave of absence, hell! Why don't we finance the thing?"

That night and the following day were the beginning of many excited discussions, in which Walter decided to send a cameraman with me and make a special film of my "journey to Picasso," an idea that I firmly rejected on the grounds that it would give Picasso the wrong idea of my intentions and scare away whatever possibilities for an animated film that might exist. I asked Walter to give me two or three weeks to make a storyboard in Picasso's style—in this case, a complex series of large paintings to show the way his work might look in animation, and something I could use as a springboard for discussion when I met Picasso. As my subject I used the bullfight, since it was one of Picasso's favorite subjects and something that would lend itself beautifully to animation. Walter asked me to work the thing entirely through Chuck Jones, who, as I said, was head of animation, doing the "Tom and Jerry" cartoons for MGM., who, in turn, would supposedly come through with the financing of this Picasso project.

Though I said nothing, I balked a little at the suggestion of working with Chuck, or in fact with anyone else, on this very personal idea that was by now a part of my being. Chuck is a quiet, intellectual man, a tall red-haired fellow with a pleasant, sensitive face. He called me into his office, took me over into a corner, and with an almost misty-eyed look, spoke softly to me. This man, who had his own dreams, seemed quite taken with mine, and so I was much relieved. He told me how rare it was for someone to dream a bold dream and then to *do* something about it. He said that he admired and envied me, and wanted to take a part in it, *however* small, saying I had real guts and that there were few men like me around anymore—that this sort of thing only happened in the old days, long ago. It was a strange, quiet, and oddly disconcerting meeting, and it was really all we had to say until the day I left for France.

About a week later I called David Duncan again. I told him I was coming to France soon to see the Cannes Film Festival as one of the representatives for MGM. I wanted to be able to see him when I got to Cannes, but I could not tell him that I was ignoring his advice and coming anyway, so I told him this white lie. Once again his warm manner put me at ease—he said that it would be great to meet me and to call him as soon as I arrived in Cannes.

There was lots of excitement around the studio due to the "Picasso project," and I got all puffed up when Walter's secretary, Lorri, said, "I understand we have a hero in our midst," referring to me—praise from a pretty girl being always sweeter than any other source, foundless as it might be.

Yet at that point, more than a week after my first meeting with Walter and Sonny, I had still done absolutely nothing on my storyboard, except in my head (constantly), and I knew that at the very last minute, with all the importance it had for the success of my mission, I would put it together exactly as I had envisioned it, and that all who saw it would look at it as a labor of several weeks—which was, in fact, exactly how the whole thing went.

One day Walter and I were casually discussing who should do the music for the film, and he said that we should get the *best*—Leonard Bernstein. I told him the "best" was Igor Stravinsky, and he smiled wryly, telling me not to be carried away. I had often thought of Stravinsky doing the score, not only because he was considered the greatest composer of this century and therefore the one most qualified to work in this way with Picasso, but also because they had worked together in 1920 on the Diaghilev ballet; and the thought that I could be in any way instrumental in reuniting these two giants of the art world thrilled me.

Dad was able to get Stravinsky's unlisted address and phone number for me, through a friend, and so I learned that he lived on Wetherly Drive in West Hollywood, in the hills just north of Sunset.

One bright afternoon I called his home and Mrs Stravinsky answered the phone. I told her the idea. She was not happy about it and told me that Stravinsky was about to make a tour of Europe (this was in the middle of April 1964), and in any case was very busy, as well as tired, and would not be interested. She hung up, literally, in my face. Once again I was momentarily crushed, but in my own head I said to her, "*You're* not Stravinsky!" and got in my car and drove to Stravinsky's white home on Wetherly Drive. The sun was shining so beautifully I knew that it must be shining for me as well as anyone. And it was! I knew that if Stravinsky's wife answered the door, I was dead for good, insofar as any hopes of a Stravinsky score were concerned. But I *sensed* all kinds of better things.

Anyway, no sooner did I pull up across the street from Stravinsky's home than an elderly little lady walked down the stairs, to the garage, into a Cadillac, and drove away! Who else?—it had to be Mrs. Stravinsky—the timing was so powerfully geared *to the very second* that I literally yelped my way out of the car in a surge of confidence, across the street, and up the stairs of Stravinsky's home.

The front door was slightly ajar, and I stood there on the porch debating certain things with myself; I then noticed to my right that another door was wide open, and through the screen door I could see that it was obviously Stravinsky's study, with books, musical scores, and a bust of Stravinsky himself. I walked over and looked in. A man in his late 30s was inside folding a tuxedo, apparently preparing for a trip since there were several other things already folded, as well as a general disarray. We said "Hi" to each other, and he said "Come on in" as if we had been old friends. I introduced myself and told him my idea and of my conversation with Mrs. Stravinsky. He laughed and said, "Don't ever talk to *her* about doing business with Stravinsky—she mothers over him and would prefer he go into complete retirement!"

He was very excited about my idea and said that if I get Picasso to do this he could guarantee a Stravinsky score. It was only then I discovered I was talking to Robert Craft, Stravinsky's associate, biographer, and conductor, as well as a brilliant composer in his own right, who has since become almost notoriously famous in the literary and musical world as Stravinsky's "Boswell." I had seen him recently conduct Stravinsky in the Hollywood Bowl on the same program in which Stravinsky himself was conducting ("The Rite of Spring" and "The Firebird Suite"), but did not recognize him until he told me who he was. Then I apologized and shook his hand and he laughed. He took my name and number down in his address book and said to keep in touch.

As I was about to leave he told me that there was a little bad feeling about Picasso on Stravinsky's part, because eight years earlier on Picasso's seventy-fifth birthday Stravinsky sent him a telegram of congratulations. When Picasso failed to acknowledge this telegram, Stravinsky tried to ignore the whole thing, but Mrs. Stravinsky was angry. Then, a year later when the world was celebrating Stravinsky's seventy-fifth birthday, he expected that Picasso would now respond with a like wire of congratulations to him—but when it did not come he finally succumbed to his sensitivities and joined Mrs. Stravinsky in her anger for Picasso. Craft said that this, too, was part of the reason for Mrs. Stravinsky's reaction to me, but that it could all be worked out and smoothed over; no doubt of it whatsoever.

I asked Craft where Stravinsky was at the moment, and he said that he was in the next room, asleep.

It gave me chills.

As my storyboard neared completion one evening, I picked up my itinerary and really *read* it rather than merely browsing through it as I had done on those rare occasions when I had picked it up for a leisurely glance. It was arranged by Jet Age Travel Service through Chuck Jones. I was to leave Los Angeles on Sunday, April 26 on American Airlines flight #6 to New York. From New York I was to take Air France flight #702 to Nice,

France, with a short stopover in Paris. From Nice it would be a quick hop by bus or auto to Cannes. The reality of it all was beginning to sink in, and though I began to feel a little nervous, I was more than ready for it.

My storyboard could not have been a bigger hit. Everyone at the studio seemed to go wild over it and heaped praise on it and on me, and I must say that I was surprised and overwhelmed at the extent, if not the extravagance, of the reaction. I think that a lot of the people never actually realized what it was I really had in mind until seeing the storyboard, with everything spelled out pictorially. And yet still they knew nothing of the ultimate purpose—to visually capture the swelling and ever-changing rhythms of motion in a virtuosic display of animation that would make an adult of the medium, on a level with music itself.

Walter was still insisting on having a cameraman following me every step of the way, photographing me leaving the L. A. International Airport, arriving in Nice, checking in at the Carlton Hotel in Cannes, and so on, with the idea of making a short movie that could run as a possible companion feature to the film, showing how my idea was born and carried through. Flattering as hell to my ego, but I really balked at the idea of a cameraman following me around, for it would definitely cramp my freedom of movement, so necessary in a project of this sensitive nature—especially since I had no idea of how I was going to go about the whole thing—I knew only that I was going to do it. We argued the point (pleasantly), but Walter insisted that the cameraman be there. I suggested, by way of alternative, that the whole thing could be restaged after it was all over, and Sonny Klein agreed with me that this might be the better way.

On the morning of April 22 I got a phone call from Stravinsky's lawyer, William Montapert. He said that Robert Craft had told him about me and my idea and that he wanted to talk to me. So that afternoon he came over to see me, and told me that he doubts very strongly that I could ever meet Picasso. He said he was *positive* that Picasso would never agree to actually animate his own work, but that if I even got permission from Picasso to let me do animation based on his works that I would have the biggest artistic coup of the century; and, Montapert said, that furthermore if I were able to do this, he himself would have lots of work for me when I got back, for he has to deal, in his work, with so many famous people in the arts, most of whom are very difficult to work with. All this, I assumed, was said sincerely, but framed in an obvious air of skepticism.

I told him that the whole point of my idea was to have Picasso create something *new* in animation. He said that even if I got permission from Picasso to do the animation myself, based on his works (which he doubted I could), that he would guarantee *an original Stravinsky score* for the film. He expressed much admiration for me and my plan, and said he was amazed and inspired to actually see someone setting out to tackle such a great dream and so forth.

3

Arrival in Cannes, April 1964— David Douglas Duncan

AFTER SPENDING A BEAUTIFUL FAREWELL EVENING WITH MY LOVED ONES, I was on my way. It was April 27, 1964. The plane on which I traveled was as a great bird transporting me to a realm as yet unknown and yet known so well, as though it were, in reality, taking me *home* after an eternity of being away. I loved everything, like a trusting schoolboy on the way to his first circus, and the Air France stewardesses were angels, down to their immaculately manicured red fingernails.

My first view of Paris in the bright morning as the plane flew very low toward Orly Airport filled me with indescribable sensations. How unique was the landscape—the trees, the rooftops, the light, everything! And how much more powerful were my feelings, knowing *why* I was there and remembering looking at myself in despair out of that *other* window on Sunset and Vine.

After a brief stopover at Orly, we flew on to Nice, where I rented a Volkswagen for the drive into Cannes. I met a French girl at the Nice airport who drove most of the way with me, and she pointed out many interesting things en route. The trees all along the journey were thick with the greenest foliage, and the early afternoon sun was bright and yellow. The entire mood was joyously happy.

Cannes was catapulated toward me like a thousand rockets, and I charged forward willingly to be hit by all of them—God Almighty, what a blaze of daylight colors fanned themselves outward to greet me, knowing why I had come and elated that the waiting was over!

There was, underlying all the seeming madness of it all, something very, very sane and strong. I checked in at the luxurious Carlton Hotel, landmark of Cannes, then returned immediately to my little Volkswagon and drove up and down the Croisette, the main thoroughfare of Cannes, which runs along the entire stretch of beach, with the long string of elegant hotels, little shops, and restaurants on the opposite side. At night I walked through every square inch of Cannes—just walked, walked, walked; observing, exploring, and loving everything—all the holiday activity and added crowds and diversions brought about by the annual Film Festival. It was extremely crowded, but what a beautiful diversity of crowds! I made several interesting friends including a sweet young girl from Paris named Jacqueline Bordares who looked like the Mona Lisa. More about her later.

The following day, at about 1:30 in the afternoon, while lying on my soft, downy bed in the dazzling brightness of my room at the Carlton, I called David Douglas Duncan to tell him I was in Cannes. It was eery hearing his voice, knowing that it was no longer halfway across the world. He was happy to know I had arrived, and though he was leaving in half an hour for Switzerland by car he told me to come over anyway, suggesting I take a cab, Castellaras being difficult for a newcomer to find.

On the ride to Castellaras I found myself once more open to those exquisite sensations I had felt upon my arrival—a feeling, more precisely, of *timelessness*, as though this were all happening centuries ago, and simultaneously as though it were eons in the future. The taxi took me along a winding country road through hills of trees that knew every shade of green and yellow and blue, partially hidden rooftops of red and orange, occasional passing motorists in tiny cars, or pretty girls on bicycles or motor scooters. The driver pointed out to me the road that led up the hill to Picasso's home in Mougins. "Yes," I said to myself, looking back as we drove by, "I'll be going up that road."

I arrived at Duncan's home in about twenty minutes. It was a fascinating structure, a blend of ultramodern and ancient that I had never seen before. Duncan came down the long, wide flight of stairs that led to the house to greet me as I got out of the cab. I recognized him immediately from the pictures I had seen of him with Picasso. His handsomely rugged features, with iron-gray hair and thick dark eyebrows belied an essentially open and gentle-voiced man, and he wore a warm grin as he approached. He laughted when he saw that I had brought with me a large portfolio case, which told him immediately my real reason for coming to France. We were instant friends.

Inside Duncan introduced me to his wife Sheila, a strikingly attractive woman with bright, intelligent eyes and a warmth and friendliness that matched David's. She had a sort of sensuous New York sophistication, and I felt immediately at home. Then I was introduced to a little dachshund named Lumpy, who I also knew on sight as Picasso's dog! I had seen so many paintings in which Lumpy was included—specifically, that fantastic series called *Las Meininas—Variations On Velasquez's Maids of Honor*.

33

David Douglas Duncan's magnificent home
in Castellaras. (PHOTO BY THE AUTHOR)

The walls were covered by original unframed Picasso oils, and I felt as
though I had entered an exclusive domain that I had heretofore relegated
to art history, as opposed to the living moment. For me, there was a sort of
staggering strangeness to it all, a sense of healthy inevitability. The sun
flowed through the Duncan home—he had built it that way. The interior
architecture was composed of a series of imaginatively curved walls built of
light gray ancient stone or concrete, leading to an upstairs mezzanine,
where the Picassos hung. There were four large oils and a big color print,
all very recent. I had seen them first from downstairs and walked up, heart
pounding, for a closer look. My favorite of the four was from Picasso's
Dejueners series, the *Picnickers* (after Manet). The paint was applied with a
thick deliciousness that for some reason reminded me of the "salt"
paintings we used to make in grammar school—I always wanted to eat the

34

paintings after I finished them. As it turned out, according to Sheila, this particular painting happened to be a wedding present from Picasso to the Duncans, two years earlier. She told me that Picasso had his chauffeur, Janot, take the present from the trunk of his car, and Picasso put his arm around her, and pinched her, and presented her and David with this painting. I remarked on the unframed condition of these paintings, and how this added to their impressiveness, and David replied that the wall itself served as an adequate frame.

David was amazed at how Lumpy (or "Lump" as he was also called) took to me, and said that I was the very first person he had not barked and growled at, even including those familiar to him. Lump was originally a present from Duncan to Picasso several years earlier, and then recently Lump had become so sick and paralyzed that Picasso (with the fatalism of the Spaniard, as Duncan said) was going to have him "put to sleep." However, Duncan felt that he could be saved, and a stormy argument followed, with Duncan stalking out of Picasso's home, Lumpy in arm. Sure enough, David nursed the dog back to health, though he was left with a slight limp, and a rather heavy way of moving about.

While Sheila was in the kitchen preparing hot chocolate I showed Duncan my storyboard. I never expected such a reaction! He went *wild*, and called Sheila in from the kitchen. She came running, and her reaction matched his. He said that if Picasso were to see my work it would *scare* him, and that my stuff actually had more fluidity than Picasso's. I could not believe my ears. I could not believe this was all happening. Duncan said that Picasso *had* to see this, that this was something different, something that *should* be done, that *had* to be—and that I was the one to do it!

Then he sat in deep, deep thought for a very long time, seemingly oblivious of his intended departure for Switzerland. Sheila would look at me during this time of David's intense concentration and smile or raise her eyebrows quizzically. Finally David said that it was important that Picasso *definitely* agree to do this and that he be approached with as much chance as possible in my favor. He explained that were he to take me to Picasso the chances might be 50/50, or even if they were 60/40 in my favor it would not be good enough, as Picasso is quite changeable. He further explained that there is only *one man* who Picasso himself idolizes, and for whom he would do anything in the world—the bullfighter, Luis Miguel Dominguin. It was like a sacred father-son relationship. Sheila reminded me that this was the great, intensely handsome matador about whom Ava Gardner was so crazy several years earlier, and whom she followed everywhere—Dominguin, the romantic idol of all Europe, the subject of much of the writings of Ernest Hemingway. Duncan felt that if Dominguin himself were to approach Picasso with the idea the chances would be as good as 100 percent. What he *did not* tell me, until several months later, was that the reason he could not take me to Picasso himself was that he was still on the "outs" with Picasso because of the incident with Lumpy. Perhaps the real reason went deeper, but in any case the rift, happily, was a temporary one.

At any rate, Duncan told me that in order to contact Dominguin it was necessary for him first to contact a mutual friend of his and Dominguin's, the American screenplay writer and novelist Peter Viertel, who was living in Klosters, Switzerland, with his beautiful actress wife, Deborah Kerr. Duncan said that he would see Viertel when he got to Switzerland and have him call me as soon as possible to let me know what the next step would be.

Before I left, Duncan took me downstairs to see his workshop, and excitedly showed me his new experimental photos with his original techniques and gave me an issue of the *Saturday Evening Post* that carried a cover article about him and his new type of photographs. A recent book, published in 1973 and titled *Prismatics: Exploring A New World*, will give the reader an idea of this technique of multiple images. Personally, I preferred his incredible examples of "straight" reportage—his unequalled portraits of people, where his camera seems to get inside the souls of those he photographed, as well as his masterful pictures of war, wherein he captures, for all to see, the flaming essence of hell itself. However, his enthusiasm for his "prismatics" was irresistible, and one had to be rather taken by it.

On the walls of this downstairs workshop were immense color photographs of Picasso and his wife, Jacqueline, the sharpness and clarity of which were amazing. One photograph in particular, of Picasso alone, life-size and lifelike, looking directly into the camera with those burning eyes blazing right into you—it gave me chills knowing that Picasso himself was so near, but as yet, so far.

Then Duncan took me out on the porch to show me the magnificent view of Cannes and the Mediterranean far below, several miles distant, and I knew why he had built his home here. He told me that he had designed the home himself, and that it served very well as a convenient stopping-off point for his European photographic jaunts, one of which he was just about to depart for when I called to say that I was in Cannes.

He asked me where I was staying, and when I told him I was at the Carlton he laughed and said, "Well, it's *your* expense account!" Then he suggested a more inexpensive but very beautiful little hotel called the Walsdorff-Victoria. It was located a couple of blocks behind the Carlton, with the patio-garden overlooking a delicious tree-shaded area, and the front of the hotel overlooking the Rue d'Antibes, the main business thoroughfare of Cannes. Duncan himself had lived there for two years while waiting to meet Picasso and to begin his marvelous outpouring of photographs and text that resulted in his two beautiful books on Picasso. So before I left he called his friend Monsieur Borello, director of the Walsdorff-Victoria, and told him he was sending him a new tenant—me.

Wishing to delay David no further I left, with a promise to keep in

36

constant touch through Sheila, who said she would call me in a day or so, for she seldom, if ever, accompanied David on his jaunts. It was a memorable visit.

.

4

Dream Hotel—The
Walsdorff-Victoria

IT WOULD BE IMPOSSIBLE FOR ME TO IMAGINE THE MENTION OF THE HOTEL
Walsdorff-Victoria not evoking a smile on the lips of anyone who has ever
stopped there. Nor could I imagine a hotel more aptly named. Not a pun,
as I first thought, on New York's Waldorf Astoria, it was named after the
owners, the Walsdorffs and their daughter Victoria, and run by the
venerable Madame Walsdorff herself. And so thoroughly was it pervaded
by a sort of French Victorian charm that this in itself seemed the reason for
its name.

Not one of the larger luxury hotels that were strewn along the bustling
glamour of the Croisette, it was nevertheless an extremely desirable place
to stay, and boasted an array of famous guests. Off the beaten path, still it
was situated in the center of town, for though its front door stepped out
onto the Rue d'Antibes, the main business thoroughfare of Cannes, its
main entrance was in the rear, through a delightful pebble driveway that
led to a beautifully delicious patio-garden, secluded within a sanctuary of
large, shade-giving trees. It was famous for its cuisine, considered the
finest in Cannes, and had a great staff of people of whom I became most
fond, and who returned my affection with a sort of Dickensian warmth and
friendliness. This charmingly old-fashioned place, situated in my dream-
city of Cannes, was therefore a dream within a dream, the womb within a
womb.

A large number of the regular guests were wealthy, elderly visitors from
the various European countries who could be counted on to reappear each
summer, and who could occasionally be found sleeping or chatting or
reading in the large, comfortable, quiet lounge that was the lobby, with its

The author's first home in Cannes—the
Walsdorff-Victoria. (Photo by the author)

heavy, sleep-inducing furniture and Victorian carpeting, or outside at the
tables on the terrace or in the garden, indulging in an aperitif or late-
afternoon snack. Someone always seemed to be eating, and a waiter in
white was forever on his way somewhere with a tray of something delicately
appetizing.

Just off the lobby, toward the foot of the stairway near the switchboard,
was a small combination writing-room and library where one could isolate
oneself amid a collection of old books in every language, to refresh oneself
in study or to catch up on a backlog of letter-writing.

Dominating all was the intense, dapper little figure of Monsieur Borello,
the hotel director of Spanish descent, as well as the equally dapper and
distinguished Monsieur Pierre, the little concierge with an abundant head
of white hair combed straight back, framing a ruddy face with a little
turned-up mustache; then there was Maguy, the protective and sexy little
switchboard operator; and Agnes, the affectionate hotel dining-room

39

Monsieur Borello, director of the Walsdorff-Victoria. (PHOTO BY THE AUTHOR)

Monsieur Pierre, concierge of the Walsdorff-Victoria. (PHOTO BY THE AUTHOR)

manager from Germany; and Henri, the concerned and friendly waiter. There was the luxuriously massive dining room itself, which encompassed both indoors and outdoors, and which, as I said, boasted the most famous cuisine in Cannes. There was the Rude family, consisting of Jack Rude, the bitter, once-divorced American businessman and his second wife, Victoria, a darkly luscious beauty from Brazil who had such tempting and captivating ways, and their brilliant little son Richard; and Rose Wang, the tiny, exquisitely proportioned and exotic Eurasian beauty with long black hair, who worked as an acrobatic dancer at the Casino and who was the cause of a near-rift in a priceless relationship I was to form; and the friendly, middle-aged English couple who took me under their wing; and the beautiful blond countess from Brussels.

Many were the serene afternoons relaxing in the warm, protective atmosphere of the hotel's large and picturesque lobby, with its old-fashioned European naturalness and pleasant smells and aromas, day-dreaming, watching television, or, best of all, watching the tourists from Germany, Paris, America, and everywhere in Cannes for the internationally celebrated film festival; and hearing the many stories of celebrities who in the recent past had carried on clandestine affairs within the discreet confines of the hotel.

My room was on the second floor—very small but charming. After a week or so, when Monsieur Borello had a larger room available (the film festival had been the cause of crowded facilities), I told him I preferred to stay where I was, and I had in fact become quite attached to my bright little cell. It had a bed as narrow as a cot, a writing table with chair, a reading light on the wall next to the bed as well as the overhead light, a clothes closet and a shelf closet, a telephone on the wall, a washbasin with mirror, a bidet, and an old carpet. Toilet and shower facilities were down the hall. From the large shuttered window that dominated the room one could step out onto the vast, pebble-covered rooftop and see the Rue d'Antibes directly below. It was perfect for my needs.

I felt a great and special affection for this hotel, almost as a home within some long-lost dream, whose staff hovered over me with the warmth and attentiveness of a band of specially appointed guardian angels. The very sad fact that this wonderful place has since been torn down to make room for a large, modern apartment complex, and that return to it is therefore impossible, lends to its memory all the more a nostalgic sense of dreamlike timelessness.

5

New Friends

ON THE MORNING OF MAY 4 SHEILA DUNCAN CALLED TO INVITE ME TO DINNER at the Club at Castellaras, saying she had a friend she wanted me to meet. That evening she picked me up at my hotel about 7:30 in her little red Austin. The Club was quite a place, built only a few years earlier but made to look ancient. So cleverly done, it was actually constructed out of bits and pieces of real castles and chateaus of ancient times, with an atmosphere that epitomized everything of supreme elegance that I had thus far seen. It was nestled in a very dark wooded area that seemed, to me at least, quite secluded and remote from everything.

There were only a few other people there, some elderly couples, and Sheila and I had a drink while waiting for her friend, Connie. I told Sheila how, that morning after she called me, I had asked my hotel director, Monsieur Borello, if he could get me three tickets to the Cannes Film Festival for the evening, and he said he would try. Many of the people at the hotel were in Cannes for the festival only, and if there was anyone who could not go to that evening's performance they sometimes left their tickets with Monsieur Borello for someone else to use. By late afternoon he was not having much luck, so I went to the festival building to see what luck I would have there. It was necessary for one to have a special producer's pass in order to obtain tickets, which of course I did not have. However, I told the girl at the desk that I was a producer, and that I would cry if I could not get tickets. She laughed and told me to come back at five o'clock. I did, and she gave me three tickets. Sheila was delighted.

Sheila Duncan (David's wife) on the beach at
Cannes, May 1964. (PHOTO BY THE AUTHOR)

While we waited for Connie, Sheila was called to the phone. She came
back all smiles, saying it was David and that she had been anxiously waiting
his call. He had just arrived in Switzerland, and told her to tell me that he
was keeping his fingers crossed for me, and not to get impatient. Lump was
along for dinner also, and was a big hit with the waiters at the Club—and at
one point actually found his own way, lumberingly, into the kitchen!

Finally Connie showed up, and we ordered dinner. She was a most
refreshing blond lady, pretty and very chatty, but not at all my type—even
though Sheila told me that she was divorced from a multimillionaire and
was quite a catch. We had great fun at dinner, and I could not have
imagined a more romantically exclusive place than this Club, with its
deeply hued atmosphere of rich purples, golds, and reds.

After dinner we went to the film festival, leaving Lumpy safely locked in
Sheila's car. It seems that although I was wearing a dark suit, most of the
men were in tuxedos, so one of the people at the festival had to pin a bow tie

on me before we could get in. Sheila and Connie thought this was very funny and were laughing hysterically "over nothing." The movie was unbearable—a Swiss film with French subtitles, *all* dialogue, no action, filmed in a variety of subdued grays that plunged one, visually, to the depths of depression. In spite of it, we enjoyed ourselves, laughing most of the way through the picture.

After the show we had some refreshments at one of the little sidewalk cafes along the Croisette, watching the swarming crowds of beautiful and weird people, who were all breaking their necks straining to get a look at each other, and to be seen themselves.

The next morning, on May 5, Sheila called again with someone else she wanted me to meet! She told me to meet her on the Carlton beach at two in the afternoon. And there I was introduced to Marie Christine Desouche—known simply as Christine, and without doubt one of the most delightful young women one could imagine. What impressed me most about her was a quality to which I had heretofore never given much thought—*style*. Instantly one saw that this girl had great style, which reflected itself in her broad, charming smile that brought warmth to all who fell under its irresistible spell. Her hair (newly blond, as she was quick to point out) was straight, and fell to just above her shoulders. She had the deepest golden tan I had ever seen, a fact that she was quick to attribute to Coppertone, and which for long afterward was to be a standing joke with us. Did I say that it was her style that first impressed me most? Perhaps I said this in the safety and coolness of retrospect. What first impressed me, as it did every other male on the beach, was her smooth, slim, golden body. She spoke perfect English, and, as do all French people who learn English from Americans, she spoke it with an American accent. She was a Paris fashion model, daughter of very wealthy parents who were, in fact, the owners of the Club at Castellaras where we had dined the night before! She was in Cannes for the season, staying by herself in her parents' summer home in Castellaras—and directly across the road from the Duncans' home. We became friends on sight, and the three of us (with Lump) spent a happy afternoon on the beach. Because of Christine's sensuously shaped mouth I gave her the nickname "Sexy-Mouth," and she in turned call me "Mister Son of a Deer," the literal translation of the name Herschensohn.

While we were lying on the beach I began to massage Christine's back, and then did the same to Sheila. A very fat French lady who happened to be sitting alone nearby smiled and said something in French. Christine said the lady was saying that she considered Sheila and Christine very lucky to have their backs rubbed. Then Christine and the lady began a conversation in French in which Christine mischievously told the fat lady that I was a *healer* who had a fantastic clientele in Brittainy! This greatly impressed the fat lady, who said that by coincidence her *leg* had had a continual cramp

Christine—*style* personified. (Photo by the author)

plaguing her for months, and Christine told her that I would be glad to heal it for her! When Christine told us what she had said, Sheila had to hide her face to keep from getting hysterical, and I felt like burying myself in the sand: the thought of massaging this very fat woman's very fat leg was not the most appetizing thing I could think of. Of course, I was obliged to do it, nevertheless—much to the amusement of Christine and Sheila. The lady said it was *amazing*—that I had actually healed her leg—then told me (through Christine) where I could find her (her hotel and room number!) for further treatments, as well as giving me references to friends of hers who could use my services as a healer. She even offered me money, and althought I did not take it, Christine kept telling me to accept it and that I have a whole new future opened up to me, which made Sheila laugh all the harder.

That evening in my hotel room I answered the phone, and a girl's voice said something I could not quite understand. After several repetitions it turned out to be Christine saying "Hi, this is 'Sexy-Mouth'!" It was funny

Lump originally belonged to Picasso, who gave him to David Douglas Duncan. (PHOTO BY THE AUTHOR)

how perfectly she spoke and how easy she was to understand in person; yet on the phone her accent seemed to increase to a great degree. She was inviting me to have dinner with herself and her girlfriend Armel, who just got in from Paris to stay at the Castellaras home with Christine for one week. Armel's husband Nissan was to arrive the following day.

When the two girls drove up an hour later in Christine's little rented sports car I had no idea who they were, even though I had been waiting there in the hotel garden for them. Of course, I had never seen Armel before, but the reason I did not recognize Christine was that she was now wearing her hair pulled back behind her neck, tied with a black ribbon, and had on a pair of horn-rimmed glasses for driving. So I just stood there while these two beautiful blonds sat smiling and honking at me.

Armel was gorgeous, with a peaches-and-cream complexion and a kind of quiet dignity and beauty reminiscent of the young Ingrid Bergman—and, like Christine, she seemed blessed with an intelligent nature. We went to a charming little restaurant in Cannes, and I found out that Christine has been carrying a torch (for five years) for Serge Bourgignon, the young academy-award winning director of *Sundays and Cybele.* She asked me if I knew Yvette Mimieux, because Serge was now in the United States, and was supposedly dating her. Christine was jealous and worried and hoped to join Serge in the U.S. the following September, but Armel shook her head knowingly at me, and I assumed that it was all quite hopeless for Christine. No, I said, I had never met Yvette Mimieux.

The next day was another bright, happy day at the beach. Sheila Duncan and Christine were there, as well as Armel and Armel's husband, Nissan—and, my cup runneth over, a shapely little full-bosomed beauty

Christine, Nissan, and Armel on the beach at Cannes. (PHOTO BY THE AUTHOR)

47

Claudine on the beach at Cannes. (PHOTO BY
THE AUTHOR)

with long, raven-black hair named Claudine! At the risk of sounding
repetitious, Claudine had what can only be described as a stupendous little
figure. She had just come down from Paris (where she worked as a reporter
for Paris' largest newspaper) to spend the week at Christine's home in
Castellaras. Although it was not visually discernible, Claudine was an
intellectual and spoke perfect English.

Armel's husband Nissan was instantly likable, with handsome, intelligent features and a rather slight frame. He was a painter, and came
originally from Israel. Everyone was already at the beach when I arrived,
and when I was introduced to Nissan and Claudine it was as though we
were already old friends.

A very singular thing happened during the afternoon as we all lay half
sleeping in the brilliant sunlight. Very softly, someone began to whistle the
opening bars of Beethoven's fourth piano concerto. The almost mystically

gentle music seemed to fit naturally in the peaceful surroundings of the Mediterranean, and I raised myself by the elbow to see who was whistling. It was Nissan, the only one of our group who was sitting up, silhouetted against the sun as I squinted to see him. I commented to him on the music, and he said he did not know why it came into his mind, and I told him that Beethoven was my favorite composer. He agreed that it blended very well with the sea, and we subsequently had several interesting discussions about music, though nothing of any great significance. Yet I can never listen to those opening bars of Beethoven's fourth concerto without remembering with great nostalgia Nissan's plaintive little whistle, as he sat silhouetted against the sun and the sea.

We all used one big beach basket for all our belongings and piled into the one little car for the ride to Castellaras, where, it appeared, I too was to be a temporary houseguest. Claudine sat next to me and told me that she liked me, and that in fact she liked me the instant we met. Upon overhearing this, Nissan, showing an alarming degree of astuteness, observed: "Claudine likes Wes, Wes likes Christine, and Christine loves Serge!" I laughed, albeit forlornly, but Claudine and Christine only pouted, and Armel gave Nissan a look that Nissan wisely chose to ignore—all to Sheila's quiet amusement.

The ride was glorious! We were enjoying each other immensely, and the countryside was sublime. What a landscape! The colors were uproariously joyful and yet at the same time serene. It is no wonder that so many painters attained their greatness while reacting to this beauty. The home of Christine's parents was very large, yet warm, friendly, and bright—done, as everything else in Castellaras, in the new "old world" style. It seemed funny, somehow, to see the Duncans' home right across the road.

In the evening we all went to the Club at Castellaras and sat together at a long table in a room that looked like something from a sumptuous old castle. After a remarkable dinner, while the others were still at the table, Sheila and I took Lump for a long walk behind the Club. Being a moonless night, everything was in total darkness, which was more than a little distracting, giving one a sensation of sudden blindness—but Sheila really knew her way around. As we walked, she told me that Christine had been pining away for years for Serge, to whom she was once engaged (and still imagined herself to be) and that, though still bright and witty at times, she had become increasingly withdrawn. Sheila said that she thought I would be just the right guy to "sweep Christine off her feet." I assured Sheila that no one would like that more than myself, but not to hold her breath.

Back at the table, Sheila told everyone about a story I had told her, which she called my "Mona Lisa" story, and which she had made me tell Connie two nights earlier at dinner, and then again to Christine the day I first met her on the beach. I begged Sheila not to make me tell it again, especially since Christine had already heard it; but this only caused Christine to join forces with Sheila in coaxing me to tell it to everyone, that in fact she was dying to hear it again, and that she agreed with Sheila that it was a pretty weird tale.

This, then, was the story: The day I arrived in Cannes, Monday, April 27, I raced up and down the Croisette in my little rented Volkswagen, and in and out of every side street, hungrily taking it all in. While I was driving along the Croisette I passed a little sidewalk cafe on a corner (the Cafe Royal) and saw a beautiful girl with long brown hair resting her cheek on her hand, sitting all alone at a table with a cup of coffee. She looked startlingly like the Mona Lisa. Just as I was driving by she lifted these immense, sad, dark eyes and looked at me, and our eyes locked in a look I'll never forget. I whipped around the corner, almost causing an accident, and parked. I walked over and sat down at the table next to hers. At a table on the other side were two young American businessmen with crew cuts, observing the whole thing. They began to smile, knowing why I was there. The girl looked over at me and smiled, and I was about to talk to her when I noticed these two men laughing and talking to each other as they watched to see my next move. Being a total newcomer, having been in Cannes little more than an hour, this shook me up more than it ordinarily would have and I was completely "chicken" to make my move. The girl finished her coffee, paid her bill, and then just sat there! Soon she began to sigh, and I was paralyzed. The two American fellows were hysterical. Then the girl got up and walked off quickly toward the street that led away from the Croisette. I then realized what an ass I was for letting these two clowns ruin what could possibly turn out to be something great, and ran after her. But when I got to the street she was gone! I was furious and dejected to have let such a beauty slip through my fingers, and tortured myself by recounting her many attributes—the obvious high quality and intelligence that shone through those large, sad, heavy-lidded dark eyes, and an all-pervading sweetness of expression.

That night I walked the streets of Cannes looking for her. Crowded as the town was, it nevertheless covered a relatively small area, and nobody stayed inside on these beautiful evenings. Several times I thought I saw her but it was always someone else. Then after two hours of searching I saw the long brown hair, the cheek resting on the hand—alone with coffee at a table—at a sidewalk cafe only a block away from the one at which I'd first seen her—and it *was* her! This time I vowed not to be such a fool and walked directly up to her and sat down. She looked up at me and smiled in a surprised way. I asked her if she spoke English and, indeed, she spoke it very well. She was here in Cannes on a two-week vacation of which this was her second day, having arrived the day before I did. She worked for a dressmaker in Paris, and though she was here alone she was visiting the mother of her boss, a very old woman who lived close to the hotel at which she was staying. This was her second visit to Cannes, having been here the previous year as well. And her name was Jacqueline Bordares. She promised to meet me the following morning on the public beach (which comprises a small stretch of beach at the end of a long string of private beaches) at 11:00 A.M.

I got there at ten o'clock the next morning, but when eleven o'clock came I had a feeling I wouldn't be seeing her and I was right. She didn't show up. So I looked for her up and down the streets of Cannes, then went back to the Carlton and flopped down to rest. That afternoon I had gone to meet David Duncan, but in the evening I resumed my search for Jacqueline, even having sort of a private joke with myself in the form of a little query, "Ou est Jacqueline?" ("Where is Jacqueline?"), which I found, to my dismay, began repeating itself over and over in my head till it began to drive me nuts.

Then, sure enough, coming toward me, half a block down, along the railing that overlooked the sea, was Jacqueline—arm in arm with an old woman, and walking along very slowly, at the old woman's pace. I told Jacqueline how I had waited for her so long and she told me that she was there but that I must not have recognized her lying in her bikini, with her hair up, and with dark glasses, and told me to ask the old woman (to whom she had just introduced me) for verification, but the old woman couldn't speak a word of English, anyway. After Jacqueline spoke to her in French, the old woman looked at me and nodded vigorously, verifying Jacqueline's story to me—in French. Then Jacqueline said she would see me the following morning at the public beach at 11:00 A.M.

Again I couldn't find her, but this time I only looked for a few minutes and left. Around noon I was walking through the streets of Cannes and just as I was rounding a corner I bumped into Jacqueline, who was coming around the other side. She was dressed in jeans and the typical French T-shirt and a huge purse dangled from a strap around her shoulder. She was looking sadder and lonelier than I had yet seen her, but so beautiful. She seemed happy and surprised to see me, saying she had just come from the beach where she arrived late, and not having seen me there, decided not to stay. I asked her if she would have lunch with me and she said yes, and as we walked she took my hand and held it tightly.

We looked in one restaurant that was very funereal inside, and Jacqueline decided instantly that it was not "sympatique," but soon we found a bright little place that suited my forlorn little Mona Lisa just fine. We went inside and ordered lunch, and then Jacqueline told me her sad little story. She had been raised in an orphanage, her parents having been killed by the Nazis. When she was fourteen a boy of the same age named Robert came to live at the orphanage and they grew very close. At age seventeen they left the orphanage and Robert went to college to study to be a doctor. Jacqueline and Robert were in love, and Jacqueline promised to wait for Robert to become a doctor and then they would marry. They saw each other only from time to time, but Jacqueline loved him very much. Then,

51

after eight years went by, came time for Robert to graduate and marry Jacqueline. She waited for his call but it never came. Finally, after a month or so she called Robert's home and an old man with whom Robert had been staying answered. The old man said, "But Jacqueline, haven't you heard? Robert was married months ago!" Jacqueline looked up at me as she spoke these words, then she gave a little smile and the tears gushed from her eyes and poured down her cheeks. Then she put her head on my shoulder and sobbed quietly, and everyone in the restaurant looked at me accusingly.

That night we had dinner together in a happy little restaurant with a waiter who sang when he talked and performed all kinds of tricks with the trays and glasses and joked with all the customers. It was good to see Jacqueline laughing, and we had a wonderful time and began to feel very close. We had planned on seeing a movie after dinner but couldn't find one that looked any good, so we went for a long, slow walk instead.

At the evening's end I walked her to her hotel, and it was on the street to which she had walked and disappeared the first time I had seen her, at the Cafe Royal. She said, "Here it is, the Hotel Florian!" and then for some silly reason we both shouted it slowly together—"the Hotel Florian!" Just then a drunken old tramp, with his clothes in shreds, walked by us and spoke to us, though I of course couldn't understand him. Instead of ignoring him, or acting frightened or disgusted as most young girls would have done, Jacqueline spoke to him, much to *his* astonishment, and after a short conversation the tramp walked away, overwhelmed and sober, with a new-found air of dignity. Jacqueline looked after him and said, "He had a good face." So did Jacqueline.

She went into the darkened little hotel and I walked slowly across the street and saw a light flick on upstairs, and I knew she was safe inside and walked home. Jacqueline had asked me to meet her the following day, a Wednesday, at the public beach at 11:00 A.M., then said, "No, let's make it at ten o'clock tomorrow."

The next day, when she wasn't there, I knew somehow I would never see her again. I went to her hotel and asked the manager for Jacqueline Bordares. He said that there was no one there by that name and showed me the registry to prove it. He said furthermore that there had been no young girl staying at the hotel for over two months, neither alone nor accompanied. I told him that I had escorted her back to the hotel the very night before and had watched her light turn on upstairs immediately afterward. He said only a middle-aged couple lived upstairs in the room I had indicated, and then the hotel director, an elderly lady, came out and I told her my story. She showed me the same registry and told me, as did the manager, that it had been two months since a young girl had stayed at the hotel, and that she had short blond hair, and that in fact she had never seen a girl resembling the Mona Lisa, as I had described her. Both the manager and the director seemed somewhat distressed on my behalf, offering many suggestions by way of solution or explanation, but the puzzle remained.

There was no chance of my being in the wrong hotel—the Hotel Florian—how could I forget the silly way we had both shouted it out together just the night before? Furthermore, it was the only small hotel of its kind in the immediate area. All I could think of then was that little query that kept going through my head over and over again that night shortly after I met her:

"*Ou est Jacqueline?*"

This was the sleeping arrangement in Christine's house: Christine's bedroom was on the first floor, next to the huge living room/dining area. The second floor consisted only of one large open bedroom with adjoining bath. This was the bedroom of Nissan and Armel. Downstairs, below ground level, were two more bedrooms and a bathroom. Claudine occupied one of these bedrooms and Christine assigned the second one to me. From the ground-level floor there was a winding stairway curving up to the second floor, and a winding stairway curving down to the basement floor. This basement floor, however, was actually at ground level at the rear of the house; the house being situated on a hill. And so the bedrooms overlooked the most exquisite assortment of backyard nature, in its fullest coloring.

When I awoke the following morning I was filled with a pleasurable sense of delight at the thought of where I was, and I had spent the night in contented slumber. My little room was bathed in delicious sunshine and outside my window was the most beautiful greenery. After dressing, I checked in on Claudine, whose raven-black hair was tossing about on the pillow in a groggy attempt at avoiding the sunlight. Christine was in the shower, and Nissan and Armel were sitting up in bed talking.

I strolled outside and began walking slowly down the road amid all sorts of little bird songs. Then I heard someone call my name. It was Sheila, standing somewhat down the road from her house talking to her gardener. She asked me if I had my breakfast yet, and when I told her I had not, she invited me in and made me a couple of eggs and a cup of cocoa. We talked a long time, mostly about Christine, and after a while Christine herself came over to find out where I was.

Then we all piled into Christine's little rented car once again, to go to the beach, this time without Sheila, who had things to do at home.

We had lunch at one of the tables of the outdoor eating area of our beach and were joined by several of Christine's friends including a gorgeous little movie actress named Anne Gabriel, who was very popular at the time in France. When she heard I was an animator, she said that I looked like a cartoon character myself with the funny little white hat I was wearing. Her husband was a quiet little guy, always smiling.

After lunch we took off, Nissan at the wheel, for St. Tropez, which was about a two-hour drive. What a wild, crowded place! This, until recently, had been the hangout of Brigitte Bardot, and seemed to be the gathering place of all the beautiful young wild ones of the smart set from southern France, and all points north, east, and west. It is a fascinating port town with dozens of open restaurants strung along the harbor, as well as exclusive little shops, which was the reason the girls gave for going to St. Tropez. While we were all doing our individual shopping and browsing, Christine ran up to a tall, good looking fellow with an open face whom she called Gicky (pronounced "Jheeki") and kissed him on the cheek. They were apparently old friends and were very happy to see each other. Gicky said that he was there with his wife but could not find her at the moment. Later, I saw a girl—a petite, brown-faced girl with large, bright dark eyes and long brown hair parted in the middle of her forehead—darting through the crowd to join Gicky, and this was his wife.

While we were sitting at a table eating ice cream, Christine jumped up and ran over to another fellow, and they threw their arms around each other and spoke for a long time. When she came back to the table she told us that it was her old friend Sammi Frey, Brigitte Bardot's recent ex-lover and a very popular movie star, whose picture I remembered seeing in several shop windows in Cannes.

We decided to eat dinner there in St. Tropez. Christine had lived in St. Tropez several years earlier for about one year, during her romance with Serge Bourgignon, and knew the town very well. She led us down many side streets, which to me were quite charming and romantic, to a quaint old restaurant off the beaten path. It too, was charming, emanating a feeling of deep warmth and welcome. I felt very indebted to my newfound friends for many things, among them being the fact that they spoke mostly in English, even to each other, rather than in their own language, so as not to make me feel uncomfortable or left out.

The dinner was delicious—at one point Armel called to me from the far end of the table where she sat. She was holding up a bit of parsley that we each had on our plates. She told me to eat my parsley because it was good for me and was a healthy food. This small gesture touched me at the time, and now I think of it and remember Armel's smiling admonition every time I see parsley on my plate, and I eat it with a silent salute to her.

While we were eating, a convention of young homosexuals came in and sat at a long table next to ours, becoming the subject of much amused conversation at our table, as they became involved in what seemed a frenzy of loudly affectionate bickering.

After dinner we went for a long walk, Christine strolling ahead slowly, by herself. Behind her were Nissan and Armel, and in the rear, Claudine and myself. Soon Christine was far ahead of us and looked quite lonely. I knew she had been in St. Tropez long ago with Serge and I assumed she was lost in her thoughts. I moved to join her, but Claudine held me back and said, "Leave her be."

"Memories?" I asked.

"Oh no," Claudine replied reassuringly. "She only wants to fart."

I laughed so hard at the sudden incongruity of this remark that I thought my head would burst, and the others wondered what was happening. When Claudine told them, Christine became quite upset, and for a while we all just walked on saying nothing—but I was bursting to laugh!

Finally we approached a remote, deserted part of the harbor, a small dark area far from the rest of town. There was a beautiful moon and it was really quite a glamorous setting, like a retouched post card.

Sensing my awe at this picturesque scene, which was obviously all quite new and different for me, the girls, who were now in giddy spirits, began talking in obscene four-letter English words—in the most casual and innocent manner. When they saw the look on my face they became hysterical and explained how easy it was for them to say these words, which, to them, had really no impact or meaning, other than the knowledge of what they would mean to one whose language was English.

On the ride back to Castellaras the girls sang French songs; and how I would have loved this week to go on forever!

The next morning I had breakfast with Sheila again, and took a closer look at the Picasso paintings, bathing myself in hero worship for this master who dwelled *so nearby*!

Afterward, in mid-morning, we all went to a little theater in Cannes to see a movie that was playing as part of the film festival, and starring Christine's little actress friend Anne Gabriel. It was a delightful little comedy and Anne was very cute, playing the role of a misunderstood bride.

In the afternoon we drove to Cap d'Antibes to visit more of Christine's friends. There we were met by two very tall blond girls, one of whom owned the home we were visiting. Her husband was a very jolly fellow, whom one could not help liking on sight. Sammi Frey was also there, as well as Gicky, the fellow we had seen the day before in St. Tropez. Gicky, as it turned out, was Brigitte Bardot's personal photographer.

We were all sitting outside on a hill by the house, overlooking the Mediterranean, and our blond hostess brought out some delicious delicatessen snacks to munch on. Suddenly a girl, brown from the sun, dashed by me, dripping wet and wearing a bikini. She was shivering and drying herself with a towel as she ran into the house. It was the girl I had seen in St. Tropez who turned out to be Gicky's wife. I smiled, and forgetting where I was, said, "She's better than a poke in the eye with a sharp stick!" All of a sudden Sammi Frey stood up and gave me a menacing look. I remembered that he had just received a six-month sentence in Rome for slugging a photographer of the notorious "Poparazzi." I laughed and explained to him that what I had said was an American

Jayne Mansfield at the 1964 Cannes Film Festival. (PHOTO BY THE AUTHOR)

expression, and that it was strictly a compliment for the lady. Smilingly, he bowed his apology and sat down, and inwardly I chided myself for my momentary lapse of good behavior.

Then the girl came out from the house, fully dried and dressed in a blouse and shorts. She joined Gicky, who was sitting on a doorstep near the table with the food. The rest of us were sitting on chairs or on the ground. She was introduced to us as Anne Dussart, and Gicky put his arms around her and playfully bit her ear. This made her eyes dance to an inner music that was brightening her shy face. I found that I could not look away from her, for this was the most animated face I had ever seen! It seemed always in motion, delighted in its own quiet secrets.

After lunch the group went in the back of the house to play a game of some kind, and since it required a knowledge of the French language I went in the living room to sit and relax. Then Claudine came in and lay down on the couch with a headache. We talked for a while, and then I got up to walk around a bit. I noticed Anne Dussart drying the dishes in the kitchen. She was wearing a long-sleeved blue velvet pantsuit, and in her hair she wore a matching bow. Her figure was petite and exquisite, and she seemed strangely yet contentedly apart from everything. She noticed me looking at her from down the hall and continued to dry the dishes, and I went back in the living room to talk some more with Claudine.

Soon Anne walked in carrying a tiny infant in her arms. She sat down in the arm chair next to me and smiled without speaking, then put a nursing bottle to the infant's lips. It was her son, Emmanuel. I took a pad of paper and a pencil and drew her picture, a profile, as she sat talking quietly in French to Claudine. It seemed to please her very much. Then she got up and left. A few minutes later she returned and sat down next to me again, this time without the child. She looked at me and smiled, still saying nothing. She spoke only a smattering of English, so I asked Claudine to tell Anne for me that she had the most animated face I had ever seen. Anne was flattered and began asking Claudine all sorts of questions about me, who I was, and so on, and in her shy way she responded as if fascinated by Claudine's information.

Then Anne posed for another drawing, this time full-faced. I noticed that her voice was very gentle and musical and I was wishing that I could somehow convey that in the drawing. In my fancy I even imagined someday doing an animated portrait of her on film, and was about to remark on this to Claudine, but then thought better of it when I realized that she was not bursting with joy over this whole scene.

I continued with my drawing, having totally surrendered myself to this marvelous face. None of us were talking now, and there was an overwhelming sweetness of silence that clothed this whole idyll.

It was as if the room itself hung somewhere off in space, and for that brief slice of time my model belonged to me, and me alone.

For the strangest reason this quiet little moment was to have the most powerful *aftereffect* on me that I can recall. Most singularly of all was the quietness of the way, bit by bit, the moment pieced itself together—and simply happened.

Visually, it was a sort of *interior pastorale*—and the delicate sensuality of it was probably the most deceiving aspect of its ultimate potency upon my pysche. Can you imagine, in my life long art studies, steeping myself in the odalisques and arabesques of Ingres and Delacroix and Matisse, wherein are portrayed the sensuous beauties of dreamworlds, painted with flawless beauty in settings of hypnotic color, conceived solely to intoxicate the senses—can you imagine the impact of such a scene in *reality* upon one who before had known them only in the fantasy of art books? To be sure, like anyone else, I had seen countless beauties of every variety in all conceivable situations, but I want desperately not to fail to convey the difference of this scene and its impression upon me.

It was a *moment musicale*—a delicious springtime idyll entirely unsolicited and unexpected, suddenly enacting itself before my eyes, and I was in the midst, in the *center* of it! First of all it was the face—that lyrically animated face of Anne Dussart. A small face; firm and delicate and musical—brown from the sun and dominated by large, dark brown, heavy-lidded eyes that danced with light and merriment, topped by thick brows that met at odd angles in the center, between which was the most fascinating, serious little frown-mark that seemed to scold her own amusement. Then the lips—full and sensuous, forming a mouth framed at both corners by two tiny lines that echoed the little frown-mark. Her small nose with the beauteous flaring nostrils echoed in turn the promises of her exquisite cheekbones. And all this was framed by the most tantalizing head of brown hair parted in the middle and combed slantwise down each side of her forehead, and set upward in the back in an array of large curls, topped with a blue velvet bow that matched her outfit. She was wearing a blue velvet two-piece with long sleeves that temptingly embraced her small, slender body. Emerging from it were white ruffled cuffs at the wrists and a small white collar about her long feminine neck. Her tanned hands were a sensuous contrast to those white cuffs that rounded her delicate wrists, and her meticulously manicured nails added a flavor of delightful edibility.

She sat in a large, ornately decorated armchair, resting her cheek slightly upon one hand, looking directly into me with a quizzically content stare of unspoken curiosity. And the effect was pure music! She was *the French face incarnate*—a direct spiritual descendant of all those incredible mesdemoiselles of Fragonard and Boucher and Watteau, the eighteenth-century painters of French femininity and elegance; and yet she emanated equally all the earthy sexuality of the modern woman of France, in some respects so like her close friend Brigitte Bardot, yet so much more delicate and superior in her quiet refinement.

Directly facing us was the dark and shapely Claudine, languishing on the couch like a succulent harem slave, watching sullenly the nonverbal communication between Anne Dussart and myself, and forming a languidly beautiful counterpoint to it.

Behind Anne and myself, and facing Claudine, was the large sliding glass window that looked out upon the bright blue day of Cap d'Antibes and the shimmering eternity of the Mediterranean, dotted here and there by small white sails, giving to the whole scene an all-encompassing rhythm of classic beauty, surpassing any ever composed by the great masters of such fantasies.

And, there I was—the surprised recipient of all of this, sketchpad in hand, recording this musical fact that explored my eyes with such earnest yet idle expectancy. It was beyond my powers to capture the essence;

perhaps Ingres himself would have been helpless before such magic. She was an étude from Debussy or a dance from Ravel materialized before me, waiting to be sketched, and I was not equal to it. She was the embodiment of an ancient French minuet, and I was mesmerized by it, secretly delirious.

Oddly, a couple of months later, upon hearing the exquisite little entr'act from the Suite #2 of Schubert's ballet *Rosamunde,* the strangely quaint femininity of this music was to re-create in my head, perfectly, this image of Anne Dussart; and to this day, and most probably ever after, whenever I hear it I can see Anne and this hauntingly lyrical scene in my mind so clearly that I find myself drifting nostalgically back to that mysterious little moment out of time that was Cap d'Antibes in the springtime.

Soon the game outside was over and all the guests came bursting in. Then our blonde hostess put on some classical records, and after listening and talking a while we decided that it was time to take our leave and head on back to Castellaras. As we left I caught a quick glance through the window at Anne, sitting with Gicky on the couch listening to the music. Our eyes met for one very brief instant as I walked by. It was a lightning flash.

On the way back Christine said that she had invited Anne Gabriel and her husband for dinner and hoped we would get back to Castellaras before they arrived. However, first we had to stop in Cannes to shop for food. Nissan and I waited in the car while the girls did the marketing, going from one shop to the other and to the large open market. Occasionally one of the girls would come up to the car to ask our opinion or advice of a certain food, as to what we would like for dinner, and so on. I was enjoying myself immensely, and all the agony and heartbreak that had launched the turn of events that originally brought me to Cannes seemed, at the moment, worlds away.

When we arrived at sunset in Castellaras, Christine found a note on her front door from Anne Gabriel and her husband, saying that they had waited for half an hour, and then left. We were all very disappointed, and Christine tried unsuccessfully to reach them on the phone. However, she made a couple of other phone calls, including one to Sheila, inviting her over for dinner.

When she hung up the phone after talking to Sheila, Nissan told her that he thought it sounded bad when she said "yeah" instead of "yes." He felt that it was not proper for someone speaking another language to use the slang of that language because it seemed too presumptuous, unless one spoke the language perfectly. Christine was slightly hurt by this, saying that everyone told her that she spoke English with an American accent and did so very naturally. I told Nissan that I understood his point but that I felt it was very proper and natural for Christine to say "yeah" if she felt like it, and that it was not at all presumptuous on her part. Christine felt better, and the matter was quickly forgotten.

When the table was being set I began to help Christine with heavy chairs she was bringing into the room. But Nissan admonished me with a reminder that I was not in America, but in Europe, where the women alone make the preparations for dinner, heavy chairs or not. So I gladly listened to my advisor and went into the kitchen to see how the food was coming along. It smelled awfully good, and two of the cooks, Armel and Claudine, were about to put me to work peeling potatoes when I remembered Nissan's admonishment and started to leave. However I got roped into peeling a few potatoes anyway.

Christine told me that Anne was coming, and I was glad that she had been able to get in touch with the Gabriels, as I wanted to tell Anne Gabriel how much I enjoyed her in the movie. Soon Sheila arrived and I told her how we spent the day, and then from the window I could see a whole group of people coming down the stairs to the house. It was the two blond girls, the jolly fellow, and behind them came Sammi Frey, and then Gicky and Anne Dussart! Anne had little Emmanuel in her arms, and I was so delighted to see this warm friendly group that I had enjoyed so much during the afternoon, now coming to spend the evening!

Anne and Christine were talking in one of the rooms, and I walked in and asked Christine why she had not told me Anne was coming, since she knew how captivated I had been by this little French face. She replied that she *did* tell me Anne was coming, and then I realized that I had misunderstood her to mean Anne Gabriel was coming, when actually she was talking about Anne Dussart. Anne looked back and forth from me to Christine, knowing the conversation was about her, and I wondered how much English she could really understand or speak.

Later, Gicky was alone with little Emmanuel in Christine's room where they had arranged a little place for the baby, and I went in to talk to him. He spoke excellent English, and with his great open face told me how difficult it was for him when looking at little Emmanuel to realize that this was actually *his* baby! I told him I knew the feeling very well. He said that he and Anne were living in Paris, in the fashionable suburb of Neuilly, and were now staying with their friends in Cap d'Antibes on a brief vacation. Just then Anne walked in and seemed surprised to see me there, and stood and listened to our conversation, looking with that bright gaze from one to the other. He told me that he was a painter, but for a living worked as the photographer for Brigitte Bardot who was a close friend of Anne's and his. He said Sammi Frey, recently Bardot's lover, was his closest friend, and was also staying on vacation in the home at Cap d'Antibes.

Then it came time for us to be seated at the table and I took a seat, and then somebody, I think the jolly fellow, suggested that we be seated "boy, girl, boy, girl," and Anne sat next to me, at my left, at the head of the table. To her left sat the jolly fellow, and to my right sat the tall blond girl who had been our hostess that afternoon. Christine sat at the opposite end of the long table, and near her right were Gicky and Sheila Duncan. Everyone seemed to be seated congenially, and a dozen conversations started at once.

The girls had prepared a special salad that was different and delicious, and the main course was Armel's special recipe, involving macaroni and a half dozen mixtures of other superbly tasty delicacies.

I poured some wine in Anne's glass saying "Pour vous, Madame," and she smiled and said "Anne." The blond girl was afraid that I would think I said the wrong thing, since it was the first French she heard me speak, and said, "No, that is correct, you said it very well." Anne was wearing a large pale-yellow kerchief on her head and looked quite regal. I could not help noticing, as she held the wine glass, how beautifully manicured her nails were, and then I suddenly realized I was noticing her too much and felt guilty. But Gicky and Sheila were having a very animated conversation at the far end of the table and I realized how silly I was to feel guilty; everyone was having such a good time, and being infatuated with this little face was part of the fun.

Christine looked good, too, dressed in a long-sleeved black velvet outfit with pants, with white collar and cuffs from the blouse underneath, similar to the way Anne was dressed; but they were completely different nevertheless. I could not help admiring Christine's great *style,* her innate sophistication and complete naturalness. And sexy as hell.

Soon, for no apparent reason (the wine had hardly been touched yet), Anne began to get giddy and hysterical, laughing uncontrollably, and was joined by her girlfriend, the second blond girl, who sat on the other side of the jolly fellow. He looked at me and shrugged and said something about the mystery of women, which only made them more hysterical.

Then later, everyone told stories and jokes in English, as sort of an English-speaking contest. Gicky had the hardest time, taking the longest to tell his joke, but did very well, and I thought what a nice fellow he seemed to be for Anne.

Then the tall blond on my right dished some more food into my plate, saying, "This is for being so good to my little friend Anne."

After dinner everyone milled about, striking up new conversations with new people. Claudine sat in a corner with Sammi Frey, taking advantage of this situation to interview him for her Paris newspaper. Anne sat alone in a big armchair, and I wanted so much to really talk to her, by herself, and yet somehow I still felt guilty about it. Finally I went over and knelt down by her chair. I told her, in English, that she was beautiful, and she blushed, then smiled and said, "I don't understand." I laughed and said, "Oh yes you do!" Then, after a little more confused conversation she said, "After you meet Picasso, you come to Paris?" I replied yes, I planned to. Then she said, "When you come to Paris, you call me?" I became flustered and when I tried to ask her number she motioned toward Christine and said I could

Armel, Claudine, and Christine having
breakfast on the patio of Christine's house in
Castellaras. (PHOTO BY THE AUTHOR)

get it from her.

Sheila told me that Gicky was quite a conversationalist and wondered
what kind of painter he was, Claudine having said that he was not a very
good one—but Claudine was very critical of everyone, and possibly a little
jealous. She told me that Gicky was also a lousy photographer and that
Anne was really not all that bright. But anyhow, I loved Claudine's biting
humor and we became buddies of a sort.

Later the tall blond girl told me to call when I got to Paris, as Cap
d'Antibes was only their summer home and that they lived in Paris the rest
of the year.

Gicky had told me earlier, before dinner, that he loved the drawings I
had done of Anne and was going to keep them, and thanked me profusely
for them. Now, as the evening was coming to an end, I almost wanted to ask
for them back.

After the guests left we decided to wait until morning to clear everything
away, and I walked Sheila home. When I got back everyone was already in
bed. I went downstairs to my room and noticed that Claudine's door was

open and her light still on. When she heard my footsteps she called me and I went into her room. She was in bed and asked me to stay a while and talk. I sat on the bed and was suddenly listening to Claudine's sad tale of woe. It seems that she was engaged to Maurice Jarre, the talented young French composer who had written the film score for *Lawrence of Arabia,* and later for *Doctor Zhivago* and others, and that during their engagement Jarre fell in love with the actress Dany Robins, and here the tale became very long and involved, and sad for Claudine. I offered her my sympathies and so forth, and then went upstairs to see if Christine was still awake. She was, so I turned on her light and sat on her bed. Then she, too, unfolded her tale of woe about Serge, even showing me an old newspaper clipping with a photo of the two of them on the beach, in happier times. Her love for him seemed almost to be an obsession. We spoke of many other things for quite a while, and when I came back to my room Claudine shouted for me to leave my door open, as the quiet and darkness frightened her.

The next day was the last of our happy little junket together. When I arose, Christine, Armel, and Claudine were sitting at a table on the outer patio overlooking the most beautifully colorful view of Castelleras. It was a breathtaking sight to encounter just after awakening. They were having a breakfast of coffee and rolls and a few other delicious-looking things and I joined them. They were all still in their robes, and Nissan was in his upstairs room, dressing. When he came down we took many pictures, and Nissan jokingly tried to persuade Christine to pose without her bra, but she would not.

Nissan told me to be sure to see a new French film called *Umbrellas of Cherbourg*, which was entirely music and written by a new composer of great talent named Michel Legrand. He told me it was filmed in beautiful color and had a delightful story that he then explained to me from beginning to end, in order that I might understand the plot if I go to see it.

Christine put her bare, golden "coppertone" legs across my lap for a final massage before we all dressed, got our things together, and drove sadly back into town.

When I walked into the Walsdorff-Victoria from the street entrance, after a final farewell and wave of goodbye to my good friends, I felt like a guilty teenager who had stayed out too late, and was half anticipating a reprimand from Monsieur Pierre, who in fact exclaimed that I was missed and that it was good to see me again. It was that time of afternoon when the sun was not shining into the lobby, and although the great old lounge seemed warm and friendly, albeit totally deserted, and the familiar smells of carpeting, vague cuisine preparations, and "European seaside hotel" in general bid me a happy welcome, still I felt slightly forlorn and very lonely as I walked through the gray light of the lobby and up the stairs to my room with several letters from home that Monsieur Pierre had handed me. I was greeted by the little room as if I had been living there half my life, though in fact it had been little more than a week since I had taken it.

And so began my wait for word from Peter Viertel, the first of a long series of waits.

Within a few days Peter called me, full of gusto, to say that Duncan had told him and Deborah of my visit. Peter said that he had never seen Duncan so wildly enthusiastic about anything before—so we were darned well going to have to get together. He said David was raving about the portfolio and the animation idea, and how eagerly he was looking forward to seeing the work himself. He said that he and Deborah would try, as soon as possible, to arrange a trip to Madrid and Dominguin, and then notify me when to join them.

On May 13 I received the following telegram from Madrid:

> BEST DAY TO SEE DOMINGUIN IS MONDAY 19
> OR TUESDAY 20 MAY REGARDS
>
> VIERTEL

So fast! Needless to say, I was elated and eager to meet the splendid company that awaited me in Madrid.

6

Madrid—and Dominguin

I ARRIVED IN MADRID BY LATE AFTERNOON TO FIND THE CITY CELEBRATING
one of its many holidays, overflowing with tourists and visitors who added
to the abundance of heat, dust, and traffic. I had made reservations at the
Hotel Palace, and my taxi driver circled the city before dropping me off
there, only a few blocks from where he had picked me up. No matter, the
fare was only a few pennies, but as I was soon to discover, time was
everything. My reservation had been pointless, every room of the hotel was
filled, and the desk clerk told me he doubted if I would find a room in the
entire city.

I was lugging one large valise, one small bag, and my huge portfolio case;
manipulating two with one hand and dragging one with the other,
sweating and cursing at this large disappointing city that to me seemed
only an overblown version of L.A.'s Pershing Square. I lugged my way to
the American Express office to see what help I could get, only to find that
they were closed for the holiday. Some helpful person somewhere
suggested I go to the bus station (from which I had just come), since one of
their services was to locate rooms for incoming tourists. I was told that
there was absolutely nothing left. I tried calling Peter Viertel at Dominguin's home, but the lines were not working—a circumstance with which I
was later to become all too familiar. I sat on a park bench (watching the sun
begin to set) wondering what sort of bed it would make for the night. Then
in the distance I saw the Madrid Hilton and figured that the lobby of this
elegant hotel would be a more comfortable and cooler place to meditate.

The man at the desk took great pity on me, and with a series of knowing
winks got on the phone and found me a room at a place called the Hotel
Rondo. Smiling wanly with a shrug of one shoulder and shaking his hand
back and forth from palm-up to palm-down, he apologized that it was not

the best place in town, but that I was lucky to get *any* place at all.

The cab had to park down the street from the entrance to the Rondo, because (shades of L.A.!) the street was being torn up and improved. I was approached simultaneously by a very serious-faced hotel porter of about age six years and a very jovial porter of about ninety, both in very proper maroon-colored bellhop uniforms, and my bags were transported in their good hands past the back stairwell at which sat three or four other child-bellhops in maroon uniforms, to the waiting area near the freight elevator, where they were to reside until reaching my room some two and one-half hours later. This was to be my prison for three days; for no sooner did I become settled in my room than I awoke from a short nap to the always surprising and unmistakable sound of a torrent of summer rain!

I blessed the roof over my head and briefly thought of the many alternatives from which I had so narrowly escaped; then I fell back into a deep and happy slumber. For all its pitfalls, I was here—I was in Madrid—step number two on my journey to Picasso.

Those three days in the Hotel Rondo were frustration itself. The dark gray sky outside was a continuous mass of endlessly downpouring rain, and I was confined either to my small dark room or the long narrow lobby, forever brightly lit to offset the stormy blackness of day seen through the large picture windows that looked onto the inactive street paralleling the front of the hotel. There was a third room, though, that also housed my imprisonment—the large, dignified dining room, very plain and yet somehow elegant, with crisp white cloths on every table and a wall-sized mural that was a fair, though overblown, copy of Goya's *Festival at San Isidro*, showing crowds of eighteenth-century Spanish picnickers under a yawning, clear blue sky, enjoying the vast panorama of the nearby city as seen from the hills on which they were relaxing; they were all exquisitely dressed. It was always very pleasant to see, my only respite from the rain. Besides, the hostess, a once-darkly-beautiful woman in her early fifties, was fond of me and I was always given preferential treatment by her, personally. And the food was excellent for such a third-rate hotel. However, third-rate hotels in Madrid are accustomed very often to housing those who would find such places unthinkable in another city, since very often finding a place to stay in Madrid is a herculean task, and reservations mean nothing.

The fellows at the service desk were also most kind, impressed as they were by the fact that I was in Madrid specifically to see Dominguin, and they were continually trying to reach him for me by phone, but the lines, even in clear weather, are abominable—the storm making communication virtually impossible, except once! They actually reached Dominguin and I was called to the phone in a flurry of excitement. I could barely hear him, nor could my friend at the service desk do any better. Finally Dominguin put Peter Viertel on the phone, and through crackles of static and roars of

66

empty sound I could faintly hear him asking me where I was staying so he could come and get me, but he could not hear my voice at all.

There were almost always great clusters of people in the lobby sitting at tables or on the sofas and chairs (very soft and comfortable) or at the small piano; for this long, narrow brightly lit lobby that overlooked the stormy day was also a combination lounge, writing room, and social gathering for the hotel tenants. These people were nice looking, young and old alike, restrained, including several pretty girls, *all* with families, all happy, active, but never loud, as the almost constant thunder and lightning precluded all other noises.

My room on the third floor was hot, and it was absolutely necessary to leave the window open, and even through the rain the stench of urine rose up from the street, through the rooms and into the hallway. I drank water directly from the tap without considering that it was an extremely foolish thing to do (Viertel and others told me that later, but I half knew it anyway), and yet nothing happened at all, not even a stomachache or a mild case of the runs.

Lying on my bed that first dark afternoon, I wrote three amateur poems in sonnet form, which pretty well showed my state of mind at the time, as the possibilities of meeting Picasso began accelerating at whirlwind speed and I was caught up in that sense of destiny which inevitably produces the most melodramatic of verse:

> My Canvas is a Screen
> How can these rhythms, not of sound, but form,
> This great variety of things unsaid
> That swing and swirl, that rage and storm
> Stay long contained here in this simple head?
> There is no canvas they will stay upon
> From any mural they would leap aloft
> Appearing now, and in a moment gone
> The loudest color soon transformed to soft,
> Then moves; as on a magic carpet flight
> To trace the lines of some remembered face
> Or blaze the light of day through dark of night;
> My canvas is a screen of endless space.

That was the third of the three. The second one, called "Night Thoughts," is no better:

> These thoughts, as I await the Master's nod,
> That crowd as excess colors on the spectrum wheel!
> As if, from worshipper to throne of God
> They fly in sparks by messengers unreal;

Where ends the sky through which they strangely soar?
There is no measure for Reality
But in that rule by which these night-thoughts pour
As if with some unknown legality.
I enter, blushing not, to regions odd,
That but in dreams before I dared traverse;
And now, as I await the Master's nod
These thoughts at night I have transcribed to verse.

On the afternoon of the third day the rain exhausted itself to a gray drizzle, and with enormous relief I left the hotel to take a walk (for the first time) up the street. Toward the end of the block a group of men and women were standing in the large, open, garagelike doorway of what appeared to be a bicycle shop. I approached with great curiosity to find that the object of their attention was a small television sitting on a tool shelf inside the dimly lit shop. There was a bullfight on the screen, which was (I was to find out soon enough!) being broadcast live from the Plaza del Toros. Two women in this small group were discussing the bullfighter, a new bold young showoff called El Cordobes; one of the women was speaking Spanish, and the other was speaking Italian, but they seemed to be having no trouble communicating. The Spanish lady was standing beside me, directly to my right, and the Italian lady, bright-eyed and pretty, was sitting on a bench looking away from the screen to talk to my neighbor. Suddenly I felt a searing pain in my bare right forearm, accompanied by a scream from the Spanish lady herself. Why was she digging her nails into my arm? Why were the others screaming as well? The answer was on the television screen, for El Cordobes was being dragged along the ground by the horn of a bull buried in his gut, and his face was contorted in the agony of a prolonged scream.

For weeks afterward the front pages of every newspaper in Europe were to proclaim in bold black headlines the latest in the condition of the new hero of the arena, and as he improved, coincidingly, so did the gashes on my arm where, as if by proxy, I too had been gored. The picture of Cordobes's being gutted, across the arena by the bull's horn, appeared soon after as a double-page spread in *Life* magazine, and similarly in most publications across the world, pointing once again to the drama and cruelty of the bullfight, at the precise moment in time when I was to meet the magnificent matador, Dominguin; and my bearing my own scars as privy to the goring itself, as though completing this bizarre ballet of criss-cross events, intertwining at neighboring points in time, to converge at last upon the central theme once and finally—*Dominguin!*

Once again enveloped by the sumptuous elegance of the Madrid Hilton lobby, but this time flooded with the unique friendliness of morning light, I watched as Peter Viertel strode toward me, grinning. I had never seen him before, nor he me, but we knew one another on sight. Tall, lean, with short-cropped gray hair brushed forward, he had a ruggedly sculpted face with a gentle, cultured genuineness and warmth.

"Wes, at last," he said, and I agreed, "At last," and we shook hands. "Anxious to see what you've got in there," he pointed at my large black portfolio case, and soon we were out in the bright sun of Madrid, both of us with much to say, flooding each other with words as we strolled to Peter's car. First, he had to pick up something at Dominguin's office (Dominguin was not there), and from there we would drive out to Dominguin's home, which overlooked the city. On our way to the car from Dominguin's office I noticed the pleasantness of the neighborhood in which the office was situated, for here was a rich, small avenue lined with leafy trees and small office buildings with little picket fences in front.

Suddenly, somebody yelled, "Hey, Compadre!" and we turned to see, sitting in the center of a sun-drenched side street, a long, black limousine, like a hearse on a holiday. A man was leaning out of the back seat, waving at Peter. We walked over to the limousine, and there, sitting by himself in the back seat, was Mel Ferrer. When Peter introduced us we exchanged an inexplicable glance of mutual dislike. It was not until Peter asked him if Audrey was with him that I remembered with a sharp pang of flushed excitement that he was the husband of my dream-woman, Audrey Hepburn. When Ferrer replied that she was not with him Peter then asked if she would be coming over to Miguel's that afternoon, and my hopes were suddenly soaring and then just as suddenly dashed as he replied that she would not be there.

Peter said goodbye, and as we walked off he touched my arm and said, "Say goodbye," and I turned and waved to Ferrer and told him that it was nice meeting him. Then I explained, jokingly, to Peter that the reason I had not said goodbye to Ferrer was that I felt guilty for being in love with his wife, to which Peter replied (half jokingly) not to let that stop me, as that sort of thing never seems to stand in the way of anyone around there.

Back on the road, he told me of the biography of Dominguin that he was writing called *Love Lies Bleeding*, and that he would send me one of the proofs as soon as they were off the press. He was enthusiastic, I was enthusiastic, and we were sharing a newborn fun.

I felt a tinge of excitement as we approached Dominguin's home, far above the dissonance of the great city that spread itself below in tints of blue beneath the hot Spanish sun.

We went through the magnificent house and out into the large expanse of backyard where there were several guests sitting by the pool, including Peter's wife, Deborah Kerr. Introductions were made all around, and among the smiling faces I met my hostess, Dominguin's wife, the former Italian movie star Lucia Bose. Her shy manner, coupled with the beauty of her dark and aristocratic face, drew one to her instantly, and I was sorry to find that she spoke no English.

69

I was directed to a little cottage that housed a group of dressing rooms at the far end of the yard, and given a selection of trunks; and after having made the change I joined the other guests at the pool, consisting, at the moment, of Deborah Kerr and her daughter, the others being scattered about in the house or yard, or nosing about in the kitchen, from which were drifting a variety of intoxicating aromas, and to which my empty stomach responded by performing several noisy somersaults.

Here was Deborah Kerr, pale and exquisite, sensual in her "ladyness," because she was real and full of humor, being hovered over at every turn in our conversation by Emilio the gigolo-looking sculptor, with long black sideburns and eyes that he himself probably thought were irresistibly sexy, whittling away at a small wooden head of Deborah. She was totally oblivious to it, and chatted away charmingly in her personal, instant-intimacy kind of magic way that made one like her and confide impulsively in her.

She spoke of Peter as though I had known him as well as she, and showed warm interest in every confidence I shared with her, never losing her humor or genuine concern over what was being said. She was not able to stay in the sun for long periods, so as we lay in our swim suits, she on her stomach and I on my back, we must have made an amusing study in black and white, since by now my tan was deepening to an almost charcoal like brown. Her fourteen-year-old daughter joined us occasionally and added moments of frivolity to the conversation by posing riddles without answers, and then plunging into the pool to splash about widly.

Finally Deborah brought the conversation around to my "mysterious portfolio."

"David Duncan was positively uproarious about it," she said. "Peter said he's never seen him so charged up like that. Your work must be fantastic—David said it will scare Picasso—that he'll be scared into working with you on this animation, But Peter says none of us are to look at it until Miguel gets here."

"Oh God," I said, "I'm starving. It's driving me crazy to see them over there on the patio running in and out of the house preparing the tables for dinner, knowing we can't even *think* about eating till long after he gets here."

"You poor dear!" Deborah laughed. "I'll get you some tea and a small snack, but just a small one, hear, so as not to spoil your appetite." And before I could stop her (and not wanting to) she was gone and back already and kneeling beside me, pouring tea and chatting musically and humorously, so that for a while I did not care if Miguel *ever* showed up.

Soon after, Peter sauntered toward us, wearing a robe over his trunks, his conversation with beautiful Lucia now ended. "Aren't you swimming, Wes?" he grinned. "Come on and join me—that water looks delicious, doesn't it?"

"Yes," I said, "but I think I'll just stay in the sun and be lazy."

"Oh," Deborah gasped, "won't you swim? Let's all take a dip!"

I can not swim, you see, but stupidly, I did not want to admit this to my water-loving new-found friends. So I took the long way around and tried to kid my way out of it. "I drowned once," I said. "So now I won't ever go in again."

"Oh no! How *terrible*!" Deborah put her hand to her face in a sympathetic gesture that made me feel ashamed that my kidding was taken seriously, and that Deborah assumed that what I meant was that I had *almost* drowned and now was afraid to go back in. "I don't blame you," she said. "You drink your tea and relax."

"Oh, nonsense," said Peter, bobbing his newly soaked head out of the water. "The thing for you to do is *get back in* ! C'mon, I'll be right in here with you—nothing can happen to you, and you'll get over your phobia!"

"He's right, Wes," Deborah smiled. "Go ahead in."

But you see, when you *can't swim*, and you've just told a lie that you *can* swim, all you want is that somehow somebody will *change the subject*; and it was just at that precise moment that, at the far end of this great expanse of green lawn, a slender, darkly handsome figure appeared, surrounded by merrily squealing children who danced about him and caused a broad smile to light his face. It was Dominguin.

He looked at me directly, I being the only stranger in a familiar group, and his eyes were instantly pleased, and there was no affectation in his warmth. I felt totally accepted before a word was spoken. There he was, Dominguin! Hemingway's Magnificent Matador—tall, lean, sensuously handsome—above all, elegant, and yet warmly relaxed, with fun shining from his dark eyes.

His voice was equal to his appearance of aristocratic ease as he greeted his guests and we were introduced.

It was with some surprise and confusion that I learned that several of the guests this afternoon were members of Franco's cabinet and their wives, and that in fact Miguel met with these men on a regular basis; since, due to the world-famous hostility of Picasso for Franco, which had been summed up in the immortal mural *Guernica*, and the close father-son friendship of Picasso and Miguel, one would have thought such a thing unthinkable. However, apparently, business being business, such was not the case, and I was to become increasingly aware of the great power and influence that Miguel wielded over the affairs of Spain.

Now everything came alive and, our pleasantly quiet idyll joyfully phased itself into a new merriment. I sat at a small poolside table with Dominguin, Peter, and Deborah, and the laughing conversation quickly turned to the purpose of my visit. "Come," said Dominguin in elegantly broken English, "to show me your work." He wished to see it with me first in private and Deborah jokingly shrugged her shoulders at me as I walked off with Dominguin.

"Ah!" Dominguin said, looking at one after another of my drawings. "Si!

71

Si! Si! Si, Duncan ees right! Bueno, Pablo must see this; I call him tonight. I will arrange everything." While I attempted to absorb these incredible words, Dominguin was speaking to Peter and Deborah at the other side of the lawn, and while he took a dip in the pool they came to look at the portfolio, and their reaction was equally incredulous and enthusiastic. Of course I was transported to artists' paradise, and my appetite for the great lunch that was being prepared on the inner patio became ravenous.

Dominguin's wife, Lucia, came over to ask me in Spanish if I preferred this or that as a portion of the menu, but not understanding her, and being so overwhelmed by the shy manner that bespoke her intensely magnetic dark beauty, I wavered, until a girl I had not seen before came to the rescue and intervened for me. Lucia nodded and walked back smilingly to her kitchen. The girl remained and introduced herself, and I tried to remember when I had ever encountered so much beauty before in one afternoon, save for that memorable day at Cap d'Antibes. She had black wavy hair, flirtatious black eyes, teasing red lips, and her name was Carla. Not knowing that she was there with her husband, one of the ministers of Franco's cabinet, I advanced myself in a manner I would not otherwise have done, and yet she reciprocated in like fashion, and sweetly questioned me as though she were doing an interview. So that when Lucia finally seated us all at our tables she seemed to take special care to seat us two tables apart; and when Deborah (who was at my table) noticed that we looked across at each other, she smilingly informed me who the girl was.

The dinner was almost shamefully delicious requiring the genius of a Dickens to adequately do it verbal justice, and I completely abandoned myself to it. Afterward, there was no time for conversation, for the hour of the bullfight was approaching and everyone made haste for the departure. Dominguin was beside himself, for the seats had been purchased in advance and I would have to sit separately, since I was not expected this afternoon. I hardly minded, but Deborah was especially put out by it, and was sorry also to hear that I was returning to Cannes the next morning; but I was most eager to get back to the Hotel Victoria where I could put in all my phone calls to the folks and to Walter to tell them of the great news, and to continue my wait there, with this newfound exhilaration. Peter told me that he would let me know the results of Dominguin's phone call to Picasso, and that if all went well Dominguin would come to Cannes to introduce us and oversee the whole affair. Deborah, in the meantime, told me that she was putting my "precious portfolio" under her bed for safekeeping, so that I would not have to lug it around at the bullfight, and had me accompany her to the bedroom where I could watch it safely ensconced with my own eyes. After the bullfight I would return to the Hotel Rondo, pack for my flight back to Cannes, say my farewells to my friends at the Rondo, have another look at Madrid by night, take a late dinner, then to bed where I would dream dreams bolder than the night before; and it had been arranged that early the next morning I would meet Peter and Deborah in the lobby of the Madrid Hilton where they would return my portfolio before my return to Cannes.

We all piled into the limousine, and Dominguin's chauffeur, Francisco, transported us in great style on the long ride back to Madrid for the magnificent event of this magnificent day—the Corrida!

I was left at the entrance of the imposing Plaza Del Toros to purchase my ticket, and the auto drove off with the others to a different side of the Plaza where the seating had been previously determined; but not before Deborah expressed her anguish that I would be seeing my first Corrida alone, and as the auto departed, she looked back at me from the rear window until the car was out of sight.

Here now is the black, red, and blinding yellow insanity of the bullfight: swarming masses of faces with the intensity of shooting flares, one of which I myself was slowly to become, not immune (*never* immune, I hope) to this magnificent kind of mystic madness (!), mystic in the truest sense. The best and most sensitive judges of such things, row on row, call it *art*. If certain concentrated portions of life can not qualify as art, portions of life with one foot in death, then art itself can claim no relationship to life.

"Tell me not in mournful numbers" of the cruelty involved. The bulls are born and bred *only* for the Corrida, without which they would not even exist. Their meat feeds orphanages, their courage is often rewarded with life spared, they are raised to *love* the fight, they are creatures of fury, and even more than the tiger of Blake's poem, they are framed in a fearful symmetry that thrills the eye. If you are indignant, stop first the death and maulings of football and boxing, or at least spare your horror instead for the brave toreros and matadors who face death daily for the fierce perpetuation of their national symbol, this stupendous ballet of courage, of Good over Evil, Man over Beast, Life over Death. And now:

If you hate it, are you right? A small nodding leper lodged in my bosom (with a faint tinkling of its bell) tells me that you *are* right, but then what a distinct joy it is to revel in my public criminality—I, a criminal, converging toward the arena with eight thousand other leering criminals to participate vicariously in this dazzling, inhuman choreography. *On with the crime!*

So, it begins as one approaches the plaza, like the entrance to any stadium, but with this difference: there is the feeling that one is part of a huge, slowly spinning windmill that is inevitably to pick up speed and whirl with a maddening force. And, like a murderer stalking his victim with the approval of the police, one passes through the dark tunnel, enters the swirl of bleachers under the bright afternoon sky, and, alive with anticipation, is seated.

Deborah's face in the departing auto lingered in my mind, but she need not have felt sorry that I was to see my first corrida alone—the strangeness of my neighbors only added to the welcome unfamiliarity of this new experience.

On the morning following the bullfight I was to meet Peter and Deborah

73

in the lobby of the Madrid Hilton where they were to return my portfolio, after which they were departing for Klosters, and I was returning to Cannes.

I arrived first, and when they entered and caught sight of me from clear across the vast expanse of lobby I was delighted beyond expectation as Deborah came toward me, arms extended, and embraced me warmly as Peter approached with my portfolio. Deborah then had to pick something up in one of the little hotel shops, and I kept Peter company while he waited for her. I was sitting on a couch, and he was pacing slowly back and forth while we talked. Then he came directly up to me and, after staring at me for some time, he said, with an emotional intensity that took me by surprise, "Wes—*God Bless!*"

7

Claude

THE DAY I RETURNED TO CANNES FROM MADRID IT WAS RAINING, THE FIRST rain I had seen there. I was exalted with my success in Madrid, and in my exultation I put on my rumpled white hat and walked the streets. It was late Saturday afternoon, and the shops were alive with people. You can never imagine how the world was smiling for me. I wended my way through every curving street and avenue; good God, everything sparkled!

Suddenly, it began to rain very heavily; I was then on the main thoroughfare, the Rue d'Antibes, and shoppers were ducking into the nearest shelters. My nearest shelter was (ah, sweet mystery of life!) an art gallery, Art de France, and I ducked inside, and my life changed once again, as it had changed the day before in Madrid.

Inside, a small group of people, a middle-aged American couple and a French woman, were discussing the purchase of a painting with the gallery owner, a beautiful girl in her early thirties, with blonde wavy hair, glowing red cheeks, and —bare feet! I began to look through a portfolio of large Picasso prints that were placed in file fashion in an open, bin. To my surprise, the girl immediately abandoned discussion of the purchase and walked over to me, beaming a smile of warmth and radiance that turned on all the lights inside me. She asked me in English if she could help me, obviously knowing me for an American despite my useless attempt at appearing native; I told her no, I was only looking at the Picassos, and she walked back to the small group to proceed with the bartering.

When they were finished the girl walked with them toward me, but then she stopped in front of me, as they continued on out the door with the

Claude's gallery, Art de France, on the Rue
d'Antibes in Cannes. (PHOTO BY THE AU-
THOR)

painting, covered for protection from the rain, which was now letting up a
bit. As the French woman reached over to close the door after her, she
looked over at us, and then smiling to herself she said, 'Huh! He says he
looks at the Picassos, *but he looks at the girl!*" Then she left.

This made the girl not only smile more than ever, but blush profusely, to
my great delight and amusement. We spoke briefly, and I realized that her
knowledge of English was limited, though she managed to communicate
with it quite adequately. Knowing I would return, I said goodbye and
continued my walk, The rain was now stopping and starting, drizzling and
pouring, and stopping again; and everything under the gray sky looked
more dazzling,more alive, than ever.

I shall never forget that day—casually perusing the side streets in the
intermittent rain—gray afternoon sky with that slight cast of diffused
purple, bright shop lights, magazine and book stores and fresh-fish shops

rubbing elbows with exclusive haute coiffure salons; multicolored umbrellas, shining wet streets—some cobblestoned and winding—all with that quality of timelessness mingled with the sensuality of the moment.

About half an hour or so later, still walking, I came upon her in the street! Her smile was beaming, that warm smile of good health, and again she blushed—and she tilted her head to one side as she approached. She wore no hat or scarf to protect her blond hair from the rain, but she now wore shoes, high-heeled, and she was with a young girl of fourteen or so. "Is my sister," she grinned, and the young girl smiled shyly. "Have dinner with me tonight," I said, and she quickly walked on with the girl, looking back and smiling more than ever, and with that tilt of her head she shouted, "Is eempossible!"

"Why?" I shouted, as the distance between us increased.

"Eempossible!" she cried, still with that same marvelous look.

"See you Monday morning," I said, under my breath.

I spent the next day, Sunday, in jubilant spirits; and first thing after breakfast on Monday morning I rushed down the Rue d'Antibes to the girl's gallery, Art de France. The bright sunlight that flooded her gallery was reflected in her smiling face. I learned that her name was Claude Aubry and that she and her husband Rogér were separated and on the brink of divorce, and that he was living in Paris where he ran another art gallery. When I told her why I was in Cannes and mentioned the help I had received from Dave Duncan, she beamed and blushed and told me that she and Duncan were great friends and that Picasso, before his seclusion, had paid daily visits to her gallery till Madame Picasso had to put a stop to it. When she saw my openly delighted reaction to her statement that she had the phone numbers and addresses of all the great living painters with whom her gallery had done business, she went to the back room and came out with a large file, setting it down on the front counter next to me. Then, in a fit of refreshing, near-adolescent blushing, she began reaching into the file and literally *tossing* to me the confidential addresses and phone numbers contained within. As I laughingly proceeded to catch them or pick them up from the floor I read them in amazement—Picasso, Miró, Chagall, Pignon, Buffet, on and on in dazzling confusion—why was she doing this?

Soon I realized that it was her naturally impulsive way of showing spontaneous trust, and I responded accordingly; it was the happy beginning of what we both knew would become more than friendship, and it blossomed quickly in the morning Mediterranean sunshine. I learned then that the young girl with whom I had seen her on Saturday in the rain was not her sister, but her stepdaughter Marie-France, and that she had a five-year-old son named André.

Claude. (PHOTO BY THE AUTHOR)

That evening I visited her once again in the gallery just before closing time; and sitting together in her back-room office, which faced out into the gallery, she asked me, in her heavily accented voice (and once again blushingly!) if I liked the "cinema." So, accompanied by her close friend Suzanne, we had dinner and attended a movie, after which we parted company with Suzanne. And so began a long friendship and cheerful love affair, in which, much to my great benefit (and sometimes slight chagrin) under these special circumstances, Claude assumed a sort of guardian-angel attitude toward me; and this consisted of a protective authority and responsibility for what I told her was my "mission" in Cannes regarding Picasso.

Suddenly, bewilderingly, I was no longer alone in this personal journey! Here now I had, as my constant companion and guide, loyal friend, very possessive lover, and more, a beautiful girl with the most charming and natural barefoot manner combined with an inborn sophistication and humor: Claude Aubry, around whom the art life of Cannes itself swirled, favorite of Picasso and Duncan, of Pignon, of art buyers and tourists everywhere—*mine!*

Now, after my success in Madrid with Dominguin, I felt doubly blessed; for I was surer now than ever before that there was some sort of predestined magic in all that was happening, step after step; that all would come to a dazzling climax in a meeting with Picasso; and that sun-brightened Cannes was the dream-stage upon which this play was to be performed, so intoxicating was the combination of my own self-confidence with that, now, of Claude's positive affirmation of my own beliefs.

There followed long auto trips each evening to different exotic restaurants to which Claude would introduce me; trips where I wondered, before reaching these restaurants over dark and mysterious roads, where in God's name we were going; punctuated by occasional weekends in the lush country estate of one of Claude's friends, with Marie-France and

Claude and her stepdaughter, Marie-France. (PHOTO BY THE AUTHOR)

little André, where inevitably Claude (with her exhausting sense of mischief) would play endless pranks upon me. Such as the afternoon I suddenly found myself completely alone for over an hour, until searching the foliage around the hills of the estate I heard the suppressed giggles of Claude and the children.

One night, in mid-week, Claude announced: "Tonight I show you St. Paul de Vence!" And I willingly acquiesced.

8

Enchanted Night

AS WE APPROACHED ST. PAUL DE VENCE I COULD SEE THAT MORE MAGIC WAS about to be done. Out of the vast stretch of highway and through the darkness of night the lights of this ancient walled village glimmered and flickered like a living fantasy waiting to unfold. Surrounded on all sides by acres of tree-covered farmland beneath the village itself, it was an apparition in the night; building upon building leaning and climbing in every direction, forming a fairylike hill that crossed and crisscrossed itself all the way to the top, all sealed together at the base by a large protective wall of ancient stone; a medieval oasis that laughed at Time.

In front, at ground level below the village, was a large elegant restaurant of obvious exclusiveness, with every wall inside adorned by breathtaking original paintings by Chagall, Miró, and Matisse, and a few by Picasso. One had to park there, Claude explained, in order to get into the village, for no cars would fit on the narrow, cobblestoned village streets.

We had a drink in this restaurant, and Claude took me on a tour through its many rooms, which were well occupied by mid-evening diners. The whole place had a quiet, red-carpeted plushness about it, with a rich golden glow that shone unobtrusively from the walls. Never had I seen such a gallery in such a setting, and the sophisticated elegance of the place was validated by these superb works of the local creators.

The village itself was another world: a safe, secure refuge from all other life and activity on this planet. It transported one immediately to the realm of the imagination, and one walked on the solid streets of a dreamworld. The ancient French architecture, with the shuttered windows in buildings that seemed to curve and fold and bend in upon each other over narrow, winding streets of cobblestone, was a delight beyond description. Each rooftop had its own individualized chimney, the combined effect of which was that of a mystically choreographed ballet of shapes and stonework. So clean was the ancient stone of the street that it reflected the lights in hues of deep blue and purple and red.

At the entrance itself, just inside the village, was a large fountain framed by a nearby set of quaint archways, seen in paintings and on post cards in the shops of Cannes. A slender, pure-white cat was balancing itself as it walked along the outer rim of the fountain's circular basin, its tail straight in the air. The most peculiar characteristic of this long feline beauty was that its ears were pinned flat down and forward against its very round little head. This, Claude told me, was the Village Cat.

As we walked up the winding street, one could not fail to notice the singular dramatic effect of the starry sky directly above and between the two sides of the street, because the rooftops appeared to be embracing the sky, just as the buildings themselves appeared to be embracing one another. One could well say, in fact, that St. Paul de Vence was itself an embrace, reaching out from the veil of a thousand and one Mediterranean nights.

Claude's beautiful smiling face with its healthy warm glow, her earthy naturalness combined with her sophisticated charm, her blonde hair softly reflecting the many lights and auras of sky and village, her white dress caressing her athletically sensuous body, seemed an apparition within an apparition. As we walked, Claude would point out the places of various shopkeepers or residents whom she knew, one or two of whom I had heard.

She chose well the old restaurant in which we were to dine. The doorway facing the narrow street upon which we were strolling was open, and only the two proprietors, a man and his wife, were present inside. The walls were of rough-textured stone, wherein one could discern many colors worn into the surface through centuries of exposure. The lighting was soft and golden; the tables were assembled pleasantly and covered with cross-striped tablecloths.

The man, just past middle age and heavyset, sat at a table by a phonograph machine, listening dreamily to the music of Mozart, and had a pleasant face. His wife, a tall, angular woman with brown hair parted in the middle and combed back in a bun, was equally pleasant. She wore an apron, and got up instantly with a smile when we walked in, and we all exchanged the usual musical-French greetings of the evening.

Behind the man, who remained seated and smiling, was a wall adorned with pots and pans of great character and a shelf of spices and seasonings of every variety, and a doorway that led to the kitchen. The *kitchen*!

God, I was hungry! Everything I had seen to this very moment whetted my appetite and teased all my senses to the point where it became imperative that I comsume, devour, and in some way eat it all, in total!

As we sipped our predinner wine, I noticed, at the man's table where he sat with the phonograph, a collection of records. I asked him if he had any Beethoven, and he said yes, and held up, right away, an album that read, "Beethoven—Concerto 4." What could have been more perfect than this piano concerto that I had already come to identify with the peaceful mystery and sunlight of the Mediterranean, ever since Nissan whistled its opening bars that unbelievable afternoon on the beach with Christine and Armel and Claudine.

With the first gentle hello of the beginning chords, as the phonograph played this mystical concerto of Beethoven, I was overwhelmed by a wave of strange nostalgia, not only for that afternoon on the beach but for the very moment I was then experiencing; and, even stranger, for those moments of beauty which I knew were soon to come.

The dinner itself was a magnificent, quiet feast. First, the bread, freshly baked, was so good that when I took the first bite of it, I fully expected a gendarme to appear in the doorway and place me under arrest. I had the Salade Nicoise, which I eventually nicknamed my "harmonious salad" because of the way the taste seemed to blend in so perfectly with the surroundings, and which has never failed me, least of all in this place with Claude. Certainly the joy in which we partook of the roast beef au jus must have made inroads in the appetites of the old couple, because they too began to eat what most probably was not their first meal of the evening.

Occasionally a fat boy with dark hair who looked in every other way like the older man would appear from the kitchen immersed in one chore or another; but what was really funny to Claude and me was that almost half an hour had passed before we noticed that the painting hanging on the wall facing us was a portrait of a man *identical* to our host, except for longer sideburns and clothing of an earlier era, and we recognized instantly that this was a portrait of the old man's father, who undoubtedly had been the proprietor of this place many years earlier; and his father before him, and his before him ad infinitum—Claude and I laughingly guessed—for a thousand years!

What made this perfect evening complete? The appearance, during dessert, of the pure-white cat with the flattened-down forward ears, purring and stretching and rubbing itself smilingly against our legs, and joining us as a companion for the completion of a most memorable and happy dinner.

It was as though by some strange enchantment or magic spell we had somehow spent the evening in a dreamscape by Marc Chagall; and so it was with no surprise that a few years later I was to read that Chagall had moved from Vence to the Village of St. Paul de Vence, which he has since made his permanent home.

9

Glad Day *and Sundays*

IN HIS BOOK ON RASPUTIN, COLIN WILSON MENTIONS THAT BOTH RASPUTIN and T. E. Lawrence (Lawrence of Arabia), stood *outside of history*, though both had a profound effect upon it. What he meant was that though they both played dramatic roles in the shaping of important events, they nonetheless take on mythological characteristics that place them more in the category of artistic than of political thought, not often to be found in the history books of schoolchildren, just as artists who shape the thought and development of mankind are not mentioned, per se, in *history* books.

Which is my roundabout way of mentioning that William Blake, the great painter, poet, and mystic of nineteenth-century England, was an artist who stood outside of *art* history. Though his influence on countless artists and poets is undeniable, and as a thundering champion of the power of the human imagination he inspired generations of creative thinkers, he nonetheless had no direct influence on the *course* of art, or on the direction in which it was already heading.

All of which, really, is to mention a picture by Blake called *Glad Day*, in which a naked figure of angelic innocence seems to be celebrating, by its joyful stance, the delights of a blue sky and all that goes with Nature at its purest and most refreshing. How, with such simplicity, Blake captured this truth!

And finally my point almost made, is this: have you felt this *Glad Day* feeling? Even if only for a few moments, when confronted by the colors of green and yellow and orange trees against a blue sky? I have; even driving through Beverly Glen Canyon of an early morning in Los Angeles after a rain or a good wind clears away the smog—Lord, what a sensuous, sensuous, sensuous delight! There is absolutely nothing like that fresh feeling of joy in nature, in *Earth*; despite all the horrors, heartbreaks, cruelties, ironies, wars, ugliness, the inevitablility of death—these fleeting moments of *Glad Day* are the lights that break through the dark, which tell of the thrilling reality of Creation that we are really too dumb, too crushed, and, in terms of evolution, too young to comprehend. Soon, to quote an old bromide, we journey to the stars, to thrills and new beauty beyond our richest imaginings, but what can match the serenity and gaiety of a bright day on Earth when all the elements of nature bear fruit and the songs of the birds rejoice in counterpoint? Absolutely nothing. Total fulfillment is in those fleeting glimpses of sure paradise.

But I tell you this because by some miracle of sustainment, this entire first period of almost three months in Provence was a continuous *Glad Day*, in my association with both nature and people.

My Sunday afternoons in Cannes, when I was not away in the country with Claude, stand out in my reveries like little round kaleidoscopes against a background of blazing rainbows, which is to say, they were not dull like my old Los Angeles Sundays. I did not actually do anything—nothing but stand back and let my vacuum-cleaner eyes suck in the entire swarming multitude of local French families and tourists promenading along the Croisette.

First, in the near background was that damnably soul-pacifying blue of the Mediterranean, peacefully dominating everything and linking it all together, so that chaos or disorder, visually, were impossible. And everything drenched in that transparent light from the yellow sun also gave that effect. Then, there was something so enigmatically timeless (what century is this?) about the strangely domestic sophistication of coastal French families together—one thinks of Manet, Suerat, Renoir, Monet; especially if one is an artist—these were the same Sunday afternoons in their paintings!

Then, sprinkled among the throng, the "bikini-clad" (as the newspapers always say) beauties of every conceivable variety and type. So—did one have to *do* anything to enjoy a Sunday afternoon in Cannes?

Once, when I was moving along in the center of one of these promenading throngs toward the far end near the statue, I saw the anxious-amiable face of dapper little Monsieur Borello, the hotel director, as he walked toward me. He was dressed more casually than when working in the hotel, and I was startled, so that when our eyes met, my glance must have imparted a bit of my own reaction to him; and so for an instant we were both terrified, the way acquaintances are when coming upon each other unexpectedly and (for what reason?) not wishing to say hello, so that we each quickly walked forward amid the crowd of strollers, on our separate ways. Here we saw each other every day and conversed jokingly, but *never* outside the hotel, so that coming upon one another in this way simply caught us unprepared. And yet the next day, in the hotel, we carried on as always, as if the little incident had never occurred.

One Sunday afternoon, however, stands out sharply against all the others.

It occurred at the height of my frustration over the seemingly endless waiting, when I sat upon the ledge (at sidewalk level) of a building along the Croisette, overlooking the bright Mediterranean, taking comfort in the swarms of strollers passing by me in both directions since I was lost in reading a fantasy from an American science fiction magazine I had just pruchased at my favorite corner magazine store. The story dealt with some artists of the past in their darkest moments, and how they were visited in these moments by angels in disguise, who gave them comfort and encouragement. Beethoven, upon the first realization of his impending deafness; Bizet, upon the ridicule and derision that greeted him after the initial failure of his opera *Carmen*. I, in turn, took the story itself to be a manifestation of my own angel in disguise, and felt great comfort and encouragement in the mere reading of it.

10

An Evening's Entertainment

ONE EVENING, IN THE MIDST OF WHAT SEEMED TO BE AN ENDLESS TWILIGHT, I was sitting with a woman who had recently arrived from Brussels—a beautiful blond countess. We were on the large outdoor terrace overlooking the hotel gardens, where we were having a cool drink to stave off the sultry heat of the darkening summer evening. Our table was just to the right of the doorway that led to the lounge and lobby, and from which issued a light, almost golden in contrast to the early blue glow of day's end. Scattered about us under this tropical sky were several other tables with guests; each, by now, so familiar to me, that they were as tenants of my imagination. The German couple: he with wide, billowy trousers and wide, billowy face, and she who seemed never to speak. The entire family from Paris: that seemed to thrive upon people taking notice of how beautifully they got along together. My American friend Jack Rude, his bright little son Richard, and his friendly, darkly sensuous Brazilian wife, Victoria: they were a chapter unto themselves. Then there was the delightfully possessive and warm middle-aged couple from England who promised me house and home if ever I should get to London.

Familiar surroundings and company, and so it was with great ease that I absorbed the regal presence and loveliness of my blond Belgian countess, (who had recently arrived at the hotel and whose room was just down the hall from mine) for she explained to me that never would she go to bed with a man (however convenient the arrangement) who had as his almost constant companion an unpredictable woman who was forever in and out of the hotel, sometimes even without shoes, who effortlessly flaunted an air of assumed authority, as if the ground beneath those bare feet was her own property, however charmingly she might dispense this authoritative air—this was the countess's summation of Claude, and it surprised me to hear with what fear, or rather awe, she spoke of it. However (she concluded her explanation), she was extending to me an invitation to visit her in Brussels, and to be her guest for as long as we both should see fit.

Just at that moment, there loomed above our table, or so it seemed *above,* a shadow blocking out that golden light from the hotel doorway that had been contrasting so pleasantly with that early blue glow of evening— *Claude!* I remember that I either smiled on the outside and felt sick on the inside, or feigned looking sick but was actually smiling somewhere inside myself; because Claude looked so formidable, so beautifully possessive as she stared down accusingly at us, accented doubly by being in semisilhouette against the door light, I had no choice but to adore her for what followed: putting her hands on her hips, she could not make up her mind fast enough whether to berate us in French or English, and instead sputtered "Huh! Ah!" and turned and stormed out. Just as the countess and I turned to each other, Claude stormed back in. "Deed you enjoying together?" She must have hated how badly that came out, and I thought that she must seem adorable even to the countess—but the countess was frozen in fear.

Before we could respond, Claude threw her head back in mock laughter, as much as to say, "they deserve each other," and then once again was gone.

"You're not going after her, are you?" asked the countess.

"Are you kidding?" I said. "She'll be calling in five minutes, as soon as she gets back to her place."

"What for?"

"I don't know," I replied. "But she'll call and then think of a reason. She won't just let it end by storming out—she has to know what happened after she took off, and can't possibly wait until morning!"

After a short passage of time (conceivably five minutes), during which I felt obliged to extoll to the countess all the many and lovable virtues of Claude, Phillipe came out to our table. Phillipe was the new night-clerk whose shift began when Monsieur Pierre, the impeccable concierge, went home to his family. He (Phillipe) was a handsome young university student who worked at the hotel during the summer, maintaining the all-night vigil until Monsieur Pierre took leave of his family in the morning, returning to that post for which he unquestionably was born. Phillipe was a likable fellow who charmed the ladies without a trace of effort, and to whom I owed a slight debt of gratitude for his handling of my dilemma concerning Rose Wang's unsolicited nocturnal visits.

"Madame Aubry is on the phone," he informed me with raised eyebrows, having observed the entire scene, as did everyone within sight. With a "there, you see" nod to the countess I excused myself and went into the telephone booth around the corner from the desk of the concierge.

Claude, unpredictable as ever, instead of chastising me for what, after all, could hardly be called a compromising rendezvous, was all honey. She chastised herself for her childishness, and insisted that on her behalf I invite the countess to have dinner with us that night, and that she would bring along her shy little stepdaughter Marie-France (as if to insure the peacefulness of an evening of total domesticity); and I could hardly refuse her this chance at regaining her dignity—not that she, in the slightest, had even for a moment lost it. Nor could the countess, bewildered as she was, refuse, and so it was that precisely at eight o'clock Claude pulled up to the hotel driveway with Marie-France, and the countess and I climbed into the back seat.

Claude had chosen for dinner another of her mysteriously located restaurants, which seemed to abound beyond number and never ceased to be a source of joyous surprise. Whether it was a dining place of extravagance or a little country place of earthly unpretentiousness, they seemed always to be isolated among the glories of the French countryside, and to unfold their culinary delights like the favorite uncle who used to surprise us as little children by pulling from his pocket a handful of jelly beans or other equally welcome favors for our eager eyes and anxious palates.

This night was no exception, for Claude was driving upward along a winding mountain road that slowly diminished the bright lights of Cannes until they were tiny stars spread out below us. She made no attempt to overcharm us in compensation for her earlier behavior, but was engaged with the countess in a level conversation that promised a friendly and quiet evening.

We were welcomed warmly by the proprietors of a medium-sized, rustic-style restaurant that smiled outward from its open door with a red-orange glow that only emphasized the total isolation of the place against the panorama of tiny lights and dark sea that languished so far beneath this lone oasis of quiet festivity.

The dinner was pleasant, and of course there was a slightly strained quality throughout the conversation that always just managed to hide itself, but all went very well. However, no matter what the temper or climate of the moment, when one was spending that moment in the company of Claude Aubry, the desire to be elsewhere could never show itself, and if the slightest trace of boredom or discomfort were to blink its eye, Claude had but to throw you a smile accompanied by a secret and unaccountable blush, and there would be no need to wish yourself elsewhere. It was always with this indiginous mixture of sure authority and womanly shyness that Claude would manage to accomplish these miracles of feminine persuasion, in such a way that it mattered not at all whether this was an artless charm or an artful trick. One and all, Duncan and Picasso included, succumbed.

89

And so it was that we succumbed to Claude's cheerful suggestion that we all have a healthy after-dinner walk and partake of the breathtaking view, the star-spangled sky, and the perfumed blossoms of the night! It was after some considerable walking, wherein I was quizzing the countess concerning the local popularity in Brussels of the Belgian painter James Ensor (the fantasist of delicious and delectable weirdness, whose bizarre visualizations had such a profound effect on my own artistic development and early explorations of the imaginary) when we noticed, almost imperceptibly at first, that Claude and Marie-France were no longer behind us. At first we assumed that they had merely fallen back to a slower pace, but soon enough everything fell into place, and we realized the full import of what was happening. Claude was *so sure* that the countess and I were having an affair that she devised this elaborate retribution and carried it out beautifully.

Angrily fuming, we began our way back toward the restaurant, a good fifteen minutes away. After a short while I turned in embarrassment to my companion and said, with what must have been a look of abject misery, "Countess, I'm sorry, but I'm afraid I have to go to the bathroom."

"Oh, thank God!" she cried, to my astonishment, "so do I!"

And without further ado, we split our separate ways, each to our own bush, as far from the other as possible, and relieved ourselves, beyond all humility, and to the accompaniment of distant and almost imperceptible *giggles!*

As we resumed our walk in dignity, surrounded by this celestial magnificence that we had both so unwillingly desecrated, the countess heard the faintest scraping of bushes somewhere beyond us and indicated to me her angry recognition of the source. I also acknowledged the obvious source, but refrained discreetly from mentioning the giggles I had heard during the course of our earlier delicate indisposition.

We finally reached the restaurant, only to find it—*closed!* Of course, when we had finished our dinner it was already closing time, our hosts had been ready to go, and it was a full half-hour since our walk had begun. And Claude's car was *gone!*

"At least," I smiled weakly to the countess, who smiled bravely in return, "we have one thing to be thankful for."

"We do?" she asked. "And what is that?"

"It's downhill all the way," I replied.

And so we began our long journey down the road.

Just as we were wondering how long it would take for the lights of Cannes to increase in size, we heard the wildly welcome sound of an automobile coming up the road from the opposite direction, and in one moment Claude had pulled up alongside of us, both she and Marie-France bursting with unmanageable grins. "Get in!" Claude commanded, albeit sympathetically. Before I knew what was happening the countess was *screaming* at Claude and kicking the car, and the smile dropped from Claude's face, and had I not quickly opened the door and shoved the countess inside, we would have been walking clear till noon of the next day.

No, it was not a pleasant ride back into town, though I blessed the automobile itself for its part in it—but the rest I have managed to block out entirely. Nor did it help matters that Claude had to drop the countess and me off at the same hotel—and that she knew that we each had a room on the same floor; so Claude waited icily for us to leave the car, and then sped off as fast as she could go.

I was so glad to be back in my room and looked forward in complete exhaustion to a good night's sleep, and was undressing myself in blissful anticipation of just that when there was a knock at my door and my stomach sank.

I opened the door and there was Claude, not standing on ceremony, but marching directly into my room. She looked quickly about and then her whole demeanor changed. "You mean—you mean," she stammered submissively, "there ees not the countess?"

I smiled.

11

Picasso!

IN THE DAYS THAT FOLLOWED I BEGAN TO FEEL A GROWING SENSE OF ANTICI-
pation. The environs of Cannes, which by the near-middle of June had
become those of such benign familiarity, with that bright blend of pleasant
history and exciting inevitability and promise, formed the ever-present
background by which my growing and swiftly deepening anxieties now
languished; and within the womb of which I now felt my entire surroundings to be flowing in the direction of my *rebirth*. Still, I was feasting
feverishly on that all-pervading placenta of southern sunshine, as my
expectations grew to an almost unbearable pitch. As if in preparation, one
brilliant afternoon when all about me quietly hummed, if not sang, in
anticipatory friendliness, I strolled absentmindedly through the park near
the beach absorbed in an account of "Lawrence of Arabia," buried within
the pages of the latest *Reader's Digest*.

Soon, before I was aware of it, I felt beneath my feet no longer the soft
down of park grass, but the solid and firm steadiness of sidewalk
pavement, and still absorbed in my reading, walked on. Suddenly a
familiar voice pulled me bewilderedly from the pages, and I found, upon
looking up, how far from the park I had come. For there standing in the
doorway of the gallery Art de France was the beautifully beaming face of
Claude, flushed and alive with that irresistibly disarming grin, and whom I
had just unknowingly passed! She was pointing frantically, squelching a
laugh, and confusedly I looked in every direction except the right one,
when finally to see, to my utter astonishment, that David Duncan was
standing only *inches behind me,* grinning from ear to ear, and shaking his

head from side to side. He was accompanied by little Lumpy, on the leash, and unwittingly I had almost passed, totally without notice, this great company of friends.

David commented jokingly on my "snobbery" with old friends, and then, his eyes glistening excitedly, told me that Picasso had been down the street only an hour or so earlier! Something inside of me dropped a mile as he explained that the Picasso limousine had pulled up outside the Madoura gallery (owned by Madame Picasso's aunt) three blocks down the street from Claude's gallery. The Madoura specialized in Picasso ceramics, and the Maestro had gone quickly inside to sign some of his works and to place his autograph in the gallery guest book, after which he briskly returned to the limousine, and away.

"I was right here at Claude's gallery," said David, "for the first time in ages, when word came to Claude and me that Picasso had been at the Madoura, only blocks away. I raced down there but he was gone. Missed him by only half an hour! If only I could have gotten to him in time—I could have arranged the meeting between you, I'm sure of it!"

Before I could complete the issuance of a long low moan, David interrupted. "Don't worry," he assured me. "It's the first time in a year he's been out, and it wasn't signing the work and the guest book that did it, believe me, those things have been there for ages. It means that he's ready—the time for your meeting is approaching, and unless I miss my guess, Dominguin will be here soon to engineer it. This is Picasso's way—I *know* him!"

Currents of electricity whirled tumultuously in my head as I stood looking at the large guest book lying open in the Madoura gallery. There, indeed, was the Wizard's name scrawled across a single page with a vigor unmatched by the signers of all the other pages: "Picasso 10.6.64"! And inscribed but an hour earlier! Tremulously at first, then boldly, I took my pen in hand and affixed to that open page my own signature, including the date as well, and stood there in disbelief at the very proximity of these incredible notations! Had Rembrandt himself signed the book within the hour, my disjointed sense of history and reality would not, *could* not, have been shaken more.

A new inner excitement took hold of me, and in the week that followed I found it difficult even to glance at the Picasso books in my room, much in the way a bride and groom consider it bad luck to see each other just prior to the wedding. More than that, I was beginning to feel an edginess I had heretofor managed to disallow; so that late in the afternoon of Saturday, June 20, in a fit of melodramatic childishness, I pounded on Claude's desk in the rear room of her gallery and told her that I had reached the peak of my anxiety, that too much time had gone by, and that I could no longer wait for Dominguin. Furthermore, I pounded, on Monday I would call Peter Viertel to see if he knew the status of Dominguin's schedule, and if it looked bad, I simply would go it alone, using Dominguin's previous conversations to Picasso about me as my calling card. When Claude saw that there was little to say that might dissuade me, she decided that the best thing to do would be to make my impulsive plan as workable as possible; for knowing Picasso's chauffeur and schedule as she did, she told me that the best time to go would be at 5:00 P.M. because Jacqueline Picasso is always in town to pick up her daughter Cathy at school, and, save for the servants, Picasso would be alone. Claude was to drive me to his home, where if necessary, I would climb over the gate, portfolio and all.

Of course I had my own apprehensions about this course of action, and when Monday came, being a great believer in signs, I was hoping to receive one, such as the time when Mrs. Stravinsky walked down the stairs to her house and drove off, at the precise moment at which I had pulled up in my car, across the street, clearing the way for me to make my entrance, resulting in the happy meeting with Stravinsky's close associate, Robert Craft. Therefore, it was with an odd feeling on this fateful Monday morning that I opened a letter from my parents to find, included in a delightful letter from my mother, this poem she remembered from Public School #6 in Brooklyn when she was six years old: "If a string is in a knot, Patience will untie it. Patience will do many things—Did you ever try it?" So that later, when Claude told me that she felt the following day, Tuesday the 23rd, would be the best day to go, I felt a great sense of relief, and in a short time convinced myself that tomorrow *would* be the day, for sure!

Early that evening Claude told me that David Duncan had stopped by the gallery, his first appearance since the day of the Madoura incident, a coincidence that astonished Claude because she knew that David had always been cautioning me about doing anything rash, and here I was, going to see Picasso the next day, on my own! Therefore, it was with a great sense of relief that Claude unburdened herself to David, and he told her to have me call him as soon as he returned home that evening.

"Jesus, Wes, that's the worst thing you could do!" David, in his gentle way, was letting me have it over the phone. He told me not to blow it after all this time, that no one had gotten this far in such a short time with so many good people pulling for him. He reminded me that when I called him after meeting Dominguin in Madrid, and after he had finished congratulating me joyfully on the great news, he then had told me to be prepared to wait a *long, long time,* as both Dominguin and Picasso were "up to their ears busy," and that he himself had to wait *two years* here in Cannes at the Walsdorff-Victoria before he got to see Picasso, and that in those days Picasso was *more* accessible than he is now! However, David laughed, he had a feeling that in spite of Dominguin's heavy business schedule, he would soon be arriving in Cannes to arrange the introduction. This was the calming influence I needed, and with all the "signs" that had been heaped on me I agreed entirely to wait until the proper time.

As fate would have it, my impulsive plan would never have seen daylight anyway. For at 8:00 A.M. the following morning my telephone awakened me—it was Claude, breathless and excited. "Wes," she cried, "ees so *strange*! Today I woke up early and thought: *today Wes sees Dominguin* and I went out to buy the paper—the *first time in years*, Wes, that I went out to buy a paper, and there on the front page of the *Nice-Matin* is beeg picture of Dominguin!" And, according to the accompanying article the picture had been taken the previous evening, Monday, at the Nice Airport, just after Dominguin's arrival from Madrid and prior to his jaunt from there into Cannes for what was to be, according to the aritcle, a surprise visit to Picasso!

I dressed hurriedly and rushed over, without breakfast, to Claude's gallery. Sure enough, there on the front page of the *Nice-Matin* was a photo of Dominguin strolling elegantly toward the camera, with a large heading that read, "Escale de l'amite pour Dominguin," and further into the article on a following page: ". . . Somme tout, Luis-Miguel a fait hier soir a ses amis Picasso la surprise de sa visite."

I tried to remain as calm as possible, for this was to be the climax of a two-month wait, and Claude, flushed and excited, sent her assistant, Monsieur Amureaux to bring me back some cafe noir and croissants. The coffee was welcome, but I had no desire for the rolls, and after a morning full of disjointed conversation I was a wreck. I had left word with pretty Maguy at the switchboard and with Monsieur Pierre, before leaving the hotel, to call me at Claude's gallery should anything come up, but there were no calls. Finally, shortly after eleven, I took leave of Claude and started anxiously back to the hotel.

I was no more than half a block from the gallery when Monsieur Amureaux ran after me, shouting "Telephone! Telephone!" and I turned back to see Claude standing in the gallery doorway, waving frantically, shouting "*Dominguin*! Hurry! Hurry!" I ran back and grabbed the receiver, to hear the voice of little Maguy, equally frantic, telling me that Dominguin and Madame Picasso were waiting for me at the hotel! "Maguy," I said, "tell them I'll be there in *one minute*!"

I must have covered the five blocks from Claude's gallery to the hotel in something like two minutes flat, leaving a trail of bewildered pedestrians along the Rue d'Antibes to marvel at the blurred figure who streaked by them with a transfixed expression of agonized ecstasy. Little Monsieur Pierre was waiting on the street by the doorway, waving me on hurriedly, and as I whizzed by him, through the hotel doorway, he cried, "In the back—in the garden!"

I was just in time to see Jacqueline Picasso and her daughter Cathy backing out of the hotel driveway, while Dominguin stood by giving directions. My stomach sank as I watched that familiar profile, framed by a pink scarf, that magnificent profile made so famous by scores of Picasso

95

paintings and drawings, vanish from view—after having come to see *me*! My disappointment, however, was soon dissolved by the warmly beaming face of Dominguin as he joyously greeted me with open arms, and came forward to embrace me. "Don't worry," he assured me, "you weel see her again very soon—she waited, but they had to go to pick up Cathy's girl friend."

We sat in the garden for a while and Miguel laughingly told me that when he arrived last night in Cannes he called Picasso, pretending that he was calling from Madrid, and asked would it be all right if he came to see him. Picasso, of course, was delighted—and ten minutes later when Miguel walked through the door, Picasso was bowled over with shock and laughter.

Miguel then asked me to accompany him to the Carlton Hotel where he could deposit his return-trip airline ticket and passport for safekeeping, explaining that when Picasso discovered that Miguel had been planning to return to Madrid today at 2:40 in the afternoon, he hid Miguel's passport and ticket under his bed, so that Miguel would have to stay an extra day. This forced Miguel to call Madrid to change all his business appointments, which was a great break for me; for Miguel explained that this visit was primarily to break the ice in broaching the subject of my film to Picasso, having found a brief hole in his busy schedule, which enabled him to make this hurried visit to Cannes on my behalf. He told me that he had almost made it several weeks ago as well, but before leaving he learned that Picasso was out of town for four days at one of his other homes, probably Vauvenargue. So now he was leaving his passport and airline ticket at the desk of the Carlton for "safekeeping."

As we walked slowly along, Miguel told me that he and Picasso had stayed up all night, till after four in the morning, discussing my idea. He said that it was the first time Picasso had ever been so excited about any idea other than his own, and that he wanted very much to meet me. Furthermore, Miguel told me that Picasso seemed to have a total rapport with my idea of a *new* kind of movement in animation, the continuous, progressively evolving flow of rhythmic form. This was the best news of all, like a key fitting into its proper lock and opening the door to a cosmic wonderland of a new art, long overdue.

After depositing his passport and ticket, Miguel suggested we have a drink, and we sat at a table outside the hotel, on the veranda overlooking the Croisette and the blue Mediterranean. At the table next to us was Roger Vadim, Brigitte Bardot's Svengali.

Miguel told me how Picasso had done a large book of marvelous drawings on the bullfight, called *Toros y Toreros*, and then called Miguel, asking him to write a text or a preface to the book. Miguel said that Picasso told him that it would be *Miguel's* book, and that he wanted Miguel to have all the profits that might come from it.! This overwhelming act of

Dominguin with the author. (COURTESY OF
BRUCE CAMPBELL)

generosity, said Miguel, was typical of Picasso toward those for whom he
held affection. They had met for the first time ten years earlier, in 1954,
when Picasso was attending a corrida in which Dominguin was fighting,
and had dedicated a bull to him. In return, Picasso offered to paint a
life-size portrait of Miguel, but Miguel suggested that he wait ten years, till
the two Spaniards knew each other well enough so that Picasso's painting
would be a true portrait of Dominguin. This pleased and flattered Picasso
greatly, and thus began a father-and-son type of friendship that grew in
admiration and respect through the years.

"Now, ten years later," smiled Miguel, "perhaps I weel presently remind the old genie of thees painting."

Our conversation soon went entirely to painting, notably to the great Spaniard, Goya. Dominguin confessed that although he knew really little about painting, he felt a strong affinity toward the work of Goya, especially his later, so-called "black" paintings. Of course this struck a deep chord in me, having all my life felt this same affinity for these large, mysterious works of such dark power, which seemed to embody all the mysticism of what for me had always been the *far-off* land of Spain—with its strange shadows and sensuous rhythms, which seemed always to emanate from the bowels of the land itself.

Dominguin laughed, and replied that for me to have sensed this made me more Spanish than a great many Spaniards he knew. He told me that the Spaniards had a word for this feeling, that it was called a *duende*. A *duende*, he said, is that mysterious experience of feeling, which, although one could not really define it, was probably the source of all true art. It was, he said, through intuition that one was aware of a confrontation with a person or thing that had this rare quality. And, in its most Spanish aspect, the *duende* revealed itself most fully in the works of Goya and Picasso, in the music of de Falla, and in the forbidding cries and haughty steps of the Flamenco—and, most fatally, in the arena of the bullfight itself.

To me, this conversation was a wildly happy verification of feelings I had always known, but had thought both to be rather peculiar to myself, and, indeed, to be rather peculiar *in themselves*, inasmuch as I found it impossible to apply them to anything in my life in relation to the direction I wished it to take. That is, until that bleak day in early April when a new world opened to me like a rainbow-colored bombshell over my head.

"These are the theengs," said Miguel, "that I discuss een Pablo's book, *Toros y Toreros*, and wheech Pablo and I have also discussed together."

When we parted, Miguel told me that there was a good chance that Picasso might wish to see me that night, perhaps for dinner; but since the old man was very changeable, Miguel said that he could promise nothing this trip, and that I should not get my hopes too high. But I was already too high to be brought down even an inch, especially after the events of this day, and I flew with the news to the Art de France gallery, where Claude was anxiously awaiting word. She flushed with excitement when I told her, and, touchingly, I thought I detected a look of pride as she smiled her warm smile right through me.

I called Duncan from the gallery, to let him know what was happening, and he, too, was excited and happy, and told me that he would be keeping his fingers crossed for me.

That evening, preferring not to wait in the confines of my small room (which would have become as a prison) for Dominguin's call, the call that for me could mean the beginning or the end of my impassioned dream, I instead sat in the lobby and informed Monsieur Pierre of my expectations and that I would take the call, when it came, in the booth around the corner from his desk.

The activity, the intoxicating sea air that enveloped the lobby from the open doors of the terrace, the dreamlike early evening sky—all these gave me a much needed sense of calm. The waiters and porters busied themselves back and forth through the open doors of the vast, elegant dining room, where even the earliest of the diners had not yet come to take their usual places.

I sat in a half-stupor and harldy recognized the countess as she took a seat beside me on the couch. I told her of the day's events, and to my surprise she responded with an irony I had never before seen in her. She assured me with a certainty, which she had no authority to assume, that Picasso would definitely not see me, and that she had heard so many things about his antisocial attitude to strangers, his habit of seclusion, and stubborn insistence on privacy, that in no way would he condescend to my bizarre reasons and personal ambitions to see him.

My mood was almost a trancelike state, and I found nothing within me with which to argue against her remarks, save for a quiet remonstrative assurance of my own confidence, especially when she informed me that she was leaving within the half-hour for Brussels.

"Anyway," she smiled, "I hope you get to meet him."

"I know that I will," I said.

"You mean you *hope* you will," she cried in dismay at my self-assurance.

"No," I replied. "I *know* I will."

"Knock on wood!"

"No!"

She repeated her demand, knocking on wood herself.

"No, of course not!" I remained adamant.

"But," she cried, "that's terrible, to be that way! I'm an optimist also, but in life, one must always be a *little* cautious!"

I stood by the window and watched as she got into her cab, with a sweet wave to me that, strangely, saddened me; and then, as the porter put the last of her luggage aboard and the cab disappeared down the street, it seemed to me the end of a segment of my life, however short.

Less than fifteen minutes had passed since the countess's departure when, at eight o'clock, Monsieur Pierre informed me that I was wanted on the phone! I ran breathlessly to the booth and picked up the phone. However, instead of Dominguin's voice, it was a familiar-sounding female voice that greeted me with a happy "Bonjour!"

"Bonjour, darling," I replied, almost relieved to hear the safety of Claude's voice, rather than to confront just yet the verdict on my whole future. There was a slight, gentle laugh, and then the voice said, "This is Madame Picasso." I felt as though the floor had given way beneath me!

"Monsieur Dominguin," she continued, "and Monsieur Picasso and myself would like you to join us for dinner tonight."

After my thanks and acceptance, accompanied by a wild pounding inside my head, which I was almost certain must have drowned out my words to her, she told me to call back at 9:00 o'clock and Miguel would tell me where to meet them. Then she gave me the phone number, which, on that first Monday morning in the Art de France gallery, Claude had already given me, along with that of Miró and Chagall and all the others.

Even through the burst of intoxication that overtook me with this sudden release of tension, I was well aware of the marvelous gesture and great courtesy in that it was Madame Picasso herself, rather than Dominguin, who had called me with this unbelievable invitation; and I felt already an affection for the company I was soon—deliriously soon—to share.

Prepared to call at nine o'clock as instructed, I was surprised and delighted when at five minutes to nine Miguel called *me* and happily asked me to meet them at the Felix Restaurant, near the Carlton.

While I dressed in my room, paying attention to every detail of my appearance on this, the most strategic, if not the most important single night of my life, I was informed, via the telephone, that Claude was waiting for me in the lobby to share my moment of delirium, and hopefully, to advance some last-minute instructions. As I descended the slight, winding, carpeted stairway, the final step of which took one within a few feet of Maguy's little switchboard, and turning left, past the phone booth, the desk of the concierge, and finally into the lobby proper, I came into view of Claude, who sat anxiously awaiting me on the sofa. I was so set upon inducing within myself a state of semitrance, a self-hypnosis in order that I should be equal to the importance of this evening wherein I was actually to be *judged* by a life-long idol, that I failed even to be jarred (just as I had refused to allow the countess's pessimism to stir me from the direction to which I had firmly affixed myself) by Claude's slight look of dismay upon my appearance. "Oh, stupid boy," she smiled tolerantly, "you cannot meet Picasso dressed like that!" "Dressed like that" was my dark suit and tie, my best clothes, for how else should I have expected to be received by the Picassos and company at the Felix Restaurant on this night of nights?

Claude slumped back on the sofa, and with a delicious pout, heard my explanation that I would see Picasso dressed no other way than with the respect due both himself and the occasion. "Picasso," she said, "does not care for ties and suits; he himself will be dressed simply in shirt and trousers; you will see, it will be very bad for you." I decided, nevertheless, to stay as I was, for fear that even if Picasso were to be dressed casually, which I was now assured he would be, the possibility of Dominguin in suit and tie, and even the remote possibility of Picasso himself in something more formal than usual, would have made my appearance in sport shirt and slacks unthinkable.

"Anyway," said Claude, with that disarming grin, "I am 'appy for you, and is good not only for you, is good also for Picasso. Is good for everyone tonight—and for me too." She was like a proud but concerned mother hovering over her little child prior to his venturing forth on his first day at school, and our dialogue was attracting the attention of those usual guests who milled about the lobby in search of whatever activity would attract their unsolicited attention.

Phillipe, who was now at the desk of the concierge, expressed his best wishes to me, feeling as he did, more inclined to be informal with Claude and myself than with the other guests, due to the tone of genuineness that radiated from Claude in such abundance. Monsieur Pierre wished me his best also, before retiring for home, as did darling little Maguy and Monsieur Borello, who, with his dapper little forcefulness, had pressed my hand proudly before leaving. Agnes shot me anxious little looks of empathy as she flitted about her work from the dining room, through the lobby, out to the terrace and garden diners, wishing not to approach me in the presence of Claude.

It was a short walk from the Hotel Victoria to the Felix Restaurant, but I left early, reveling in the powerful atmosphere of this totally magic night of June 23, 1964, in Cannes. To my right, across the Croisette, was the long stretch of beach—and beyond, the hypnotic expanse of the Mediterranean, black under the deep blue summer sky. In the water were the usual American ships decorated with strings of electric lights, which so appropriately reflected the festive gaiety of the restaurants, shops, and hotels that for several miles lined the street to my left. And above—not ordinary stars, but swirling, blazing, joyous Van Gogh stars. Though the air was warm, it stirred with a musical transparency that blended everything into a single unit of color and cheerfulness, topped like an ice cream cake by the Epicurean twin domes of the golden Carlton.

I truly felt a sense not so much of *unreality*, but of *timelessness*. After all, was not Picasso's career a monumental chapter out of art history, no less glorious a chapter than Rembrandt's, or even Michelangelo's? Therefore, was it any less logical to suppose that it was Rembrandt himself or Michelangelo himself with whom I had made this engagement? But what staggered me most was the knowledge that Picasso was coming out of a year-long seclusion for the sole purpose of meeting *me*! And further, that Luis Miguel Dominguin, the "magnificent matador," who had felt both the affection and sting of Hemingway's pen, had journeyed here from Madrid only for the purpose of introducing us! And further still, that Peter Viertel and Deborah Kerr had gone to Madrid to introduce Miguel and myself at the enthusiastic request of the great David Douglas Duncan! No, I correct myself—there was every bit as much a sense of unreality as there was of timelessness. I was seeing the whole universe as a network of doors, all open.

101

It made no difference to me that those I passed in the street, or who crowded the thoroughfare in clusters and small groups at the sidewalk cafes and still-open shops and confectioners, were tourists, or shopkeepers, residents, or sightseers or film people here for the festival—to me they were participants in this celestially choreographed event against the backdrop of magnificent stage setting that was Cannes-on-the-Mediterranean; and had a mythological being of any description—satyr, centaur, bacchante, or nymph—approached or overtaken me on my way to this magical rendezvous, I should have been no more surprised or astonished than the level at which my powers of astonishment were already firmly set. The girls who passed my way, dark-eyed or cream-skinned, blonde or brunette, shapely and bronzed, all with that delicious and sensuous rhythm of movement, were dreamily unaware that I, unanimously and simultaneously, possessed them; and just as surely as the strings of brightly lit electric bulbs on the American ships were glowing in celebration of this moment, because I possessed the moment, possessed also each of its components.

Further, I felt duty bound to joyfully acknowledge that even in such a thoroughly "Picassoid" setting I could not preclude the possibility that a vision of Chagallian lovers might suddenly appear in tender floating embrace, filling the sky above the sea in a firework of color in the deepest hues of blue and purple, red and green, to vanish in a spray of sparkling particles, as do those silent fireworks of summer nights such as this.

When I arrived at the Felix and informed the headwaiter, who was standing beside one of the outdoor tables, that I was with the party of Picasso and Dominguin, he ushered me inside to a long table, all prepared and waiting for the occasion. I sat in a chair next to it to begin a short period of waiting, when I became aware that all eyes were upon me, and the names *Picasso* and *Dominguin* were upon all lips. To be sure, in Europe, Dominguin was, in his way, as much a celebrity as Picasso himself, and the knowledge among the diners that *both* men were due presently to appear, set off sparks of electricity that shot from table to table like the quick crackle of a short circuit.

I felt, as I sat waiting, like an actor who sits in the wings in full view of the audience as he studies his part before the arrival on stage of the great actor himself. I rehearsed in my mind what Miguel had discussed with me earlier that day—that, first, the form of address I should use upon meeting the master was simply, "Bonjour, Maestro," and that, further, in the social atmosphere of the dinner, no business was to be discussed. If the Maestro decided, at evening's end, that he should like to partake further of my acquaintance, then I would be invited on the following day to his home; if, on the other hand, this dinner should be the sum total of Picasso's curiosity or interest in me, then I should hear no more, save for Miguel's own regrets and condolences the morning after.

Then, as though the curtain swung open upon a stage in which the members of the audience were players as well, and who had sat, before the curtain's opening, in full view of the set, the door opened and a group of people, at first dominated by Miguel's smiling face, began their entrance. I was looking anxiously for Picasso but did not see him. There was the handsome profile of the quietly magnetic Jacqueline Picasso, there were two attractive young girls who turned out to be Jacqueline's seventeen-year-old daughter Cathy with her girl friend, and there was a strange man with a long turned-up nose and decidedly French look of disdain—but no Picasso! Then, suddenly, I saw him, in front of the whole group, but so very short that he had been outside of my line of vision. He was shaking hands with the equally short, white-haired, and bespectacled Monsieur Felix.

I got up and walked over, as one crosses a stage, with all eyes riveted upon me, and Picasso, as if knowing me in advance, held out his hand and smiled his crooked, wrinkled, impish smile. I took it and said, "Maestro," as if, almost involuntarily, I were uttering a holy prayer. Then came all the other hellos and introductions, and at last I met the elusive Jacqueline Picasso, who it seemed I had been half-meeting in stages, and who looked directly into my eyes with a magnificent warmth, her own dark eyes twinkling gently with a sort of inner knowledge. Cathy was pretty and wholesome, and both she and her girl friend exhibited a maturity of manner that made one feel quite at ease in their attractive company. The strange man was Pierre Daix, who was just finishing a biography on Picasso, and Miguel whispered to me that he is a very jealous man and always bored, a fact that could be quickly observed even if one's powers of observation were impaired.

During these introductions a very singular, strange thing was happening. Miguel had warned me earlier that Picasso had a way of burning his eyes through you, stripping your soul naked, in some kind of almost mystical evaluation process of his own, when the occasion arose. And while I was busy shaking hands I suddenly turned and saw Picasso standing right beside me, looking up at me with those intense coal-black eyes, so questioning, so searching, so burning, as if he were taking some sort of mental photograph—and then suddenly relaxing as if the shutter had snapped, as if the picture was taken, developed, and processed. It was an eery sensation! And though throughout most of the evening Picasso seemed essentially shy, he had performed this one act of visual contact with distracting boldness.

The first thing he asked me was, "Do you paint?" I answered yes, and he said, "So do I—a little !" He spoke in Spanish (in deference, I suppose, to the presence of his compatriot Miguel), and Miguel did all the translating between Picasso and myself; so that the reason for the laughter that followed Picasso's remark reached me by delayed action through Miguel's

103

translation, followed by my own delighted reaction. Jacqueline spoke beautiful English and was also most solicitous and helpful in assuring a conversational flow with regard to any translating. On an occasion of this importance I dared not rely for communication on what skimpy Spanish or French I might have had at my command, and I had no desire to turn the evening into a test of language or linguistic examination of any kind; and since Picasso spoke no English whatsoever, I was honored to have translators of such elegance.

Picasso sat across the table from me, with Cathy on his right, Cathy's girl friend on his left (directly across from me), and Pierre Daix on the girl friend's left. Miguel sat to my left with Jacqueline Picasso at his other side. It was with a silent salute to Claude that I observed, laughingly to myself, that everyone *was* dressed very casually, Picasso himself in a simple sport shirt and pants with a pale orange cartigan sweater. I saw before me Claude's beautiful face, pouting and shaking from side to side.

The evening, then, began in an atmosphere of benign pleasantness and expectation amid the color and brilliance of friendly and intelligent company and surroundings that were as if designed and constructed by the most astute and ingenious of stage directors.

I soon became aware that I was, for a brief period, the recipient of a most childlike and subtle game; for whenever I was looking somewhere else Picasso would ask me a question in Spanish, of which I, being otherwise occupied, would be totally unaware until Miguel would nudge me with the translation of it—and when I would look at Picasso to answer he would be looking elsewhere, as if no question had been asked. This amusing but distracting and thoroughly "Picassoid" game lasted, fortunately, no further than the playful point he wished to make; perhaps it was another test I had unknowingly passed.

He asked me dozens of questions, finally turning serious, and looking at me directly, with a mixture of warmth and genuine curiosity: Do you like Madrid? What is California like? *What do you paint?* This last was the most complicated to answer and I replied "People, mostly," to which he nodded with an approving, "Ah, *si!*" and which I answered further by explaining that I preferred to "paint" in *motion*—in *animation*.

"Pablo," said Miguel, catching my ball and running with it, "that's one thing you can't do!" Picasso, in response, laughed with a gentle chuckle and his face lit up with new interest. Touchdown!

At this point the restaurant photographer approached the table with a polaroid camera, and asked, respectfully but hopefully, if any pictures were desired, and after a general polite but negative shaking of heads in response, Dominguin said something to Picasso, who nodded in return, and then told the photographer to take a couple of pictures, which he happily did; and after handing Dominguin two color polaroids complete with mats, Dominguin paid the man and then whispered to me, "For you,

104

Wes—souvenirs." This was touching enough, but Miguel then asked me which of the two I liked best, and after making my choice he handed the picture across the table to Picasso and told him to sign it for me. "Write 'to my good friend Wes,' " he told Picasso, and just as Picasso was smilingly about to do so, the waiter suddenly appeared, out of nowhere as it were, and placed before Picasso the dish of eggs and macaroni he had ordered earlier; so that Picasso, in the sudden confusion, upon returning to the autograph, signed merely (upon the mat beneath the photo) his name and the date: "Picasso—23.6.64." Although I had momentarily cursed the sudden appearance of the waiter for exorcising what was to be an intimate, albeit slightly colored, inscription, I was nonetheless thrilled by the honored signature; and these two photographs, showing the entire company and immortalizing this joyful evening for all to see, were to become precious treasures that I would prize all of my life. I thanked Miguel warmly for his thoughtfulness, which, most appreciatively, I was growing almost to expect from him.

So, dinner had arrived, and although the Maestro had ordered modestly, the rest of us ate lavishly, partaking of delicious steak dinners and the usual embellishments. "Is it not strange, Picasso said, cutting with his fork into the macaroni, "that we are *both* from California?" He looked at me sharply. At first I was confused as to his meaning, being taken, once again, by surprise, but as his face began to wrinkle into that great impish grin I laughed and said, "Of course! *La Californie!*" His pun had been a reference to the mansion of that name he had occupied in Cannes several

Dinner with Picasso! Notice the Master's signature and handwritten date at the bottom. (PHOTO BY RESTAURANT PHOTOGRAPHER)

Clockwise, from lower left: Jacqueline Picasso's daughter Cathy, Picasso, Cathy's girl friend, biographer Pierre Daix, the author, Dominguin, and Picasso's wife, Jacqueline. (PHOTO BY RESTAURANT PHOTOGRAPHER)

years earlier. He thought this was a great joke and laughed good-naturedly, raising his eyebrows and looking from one of us to the other.

There were moments when, with delirious reflection, and however briefly I allowed these moments to linger, it seemed almost beyond comprehension that I should be sitting across table from, and as a *guest* of, the man who would be remembered, most indisputably, as the greatest painter of the twentieth century and one of the handfuls of artistic immortals of *all* time—assuredly, the illogic, the almost irrationality of what was indeed the reality of the moment, as fleeting as that present might be, dazzled my preconceptions of life to the certainty that what we call life is actually, without question, a *dream* with the consistency of a soft clay that we can mold to any desired shape merely by the *persistence of will.* This must be so, and yet, when we allow ourselves to wander in the passage ways of this sort of meditation, we become aware, invariably, of another, more all-pervading presence that is, of course, the Ultimate Dreamer, of which *we* are the soft clay to be molded.

It was during one of these brief moments of, I think, understandable reflection when I was aroused from my fleeting revery by a question directed to me from Jacqueline Picasso. She was leaning behind Miguel, who sat between us, to ask me, in her gentle, tiny voice, exactly what I do in

106

California; and when I leaned back to answer, I broke the arm off my chair and it fell to the floor with a bang that stopped all conversation in the restaurant. In answer to Jacqueline's question I said, "I break chairs," and Miguel threw his head back with laughter. Picasso, with raised eyebrows, laughingly told Miguel that I was very strong, and I handed the arm of the chair, which was beautifully shaped and curved, and intricately carved, to Picasso—for its sculptural possibilities, I thought—but I neglected to verbalize it. Jacqueline caught on immediately and translated my thought to Picasso and he looked (rather blankly, it seemed) while the dapper little Monsieur Felix—his black coat tails flying in his own wind, and looking like a Toulouse-Lautrec poster that I dimly recalled—ran up with a new chair with two arms.

Picasso's eyes darted continuously from table to table commenting in a low voice either to Cathy, who sat at his right, or to Cathy's girl friend, who sat at his left, on one or another of the customers. For all the interest his arrival had provoked, he was in an overall way more continuously interested in the various diners than they seemed to be in him. At one point he became lost in himself and sketched a bull on the tablecloth. At another time he was reminded of what sounded like a nursery rhyme or limerick with lecherous overtones as he secretly recited it into the ear of Cathy's girl friend, who laughed in a half amused, half respectful way. And Pierre Daix, all through dinner, was in a state of complete boredom, half awake and saying nothing.

Claude's pouting face flashed before me again when Picasso suggested I take off my tie and jacket, which I did willingly for it really was quite hot. I wanted so much to talk to him then about the animation, the new idea, the "new kind of movement," Picasso seeming then to be so open to me; but, of course, out of deference to Miguel's wisdom that the dinner conversation should be only casual, with the assurance that should Picasso "approve" of me he would invite me to his home the next day, where he would then see my work and we would really talk, I held in check my eagerness to discuss it then and there at the dinner table.

Finally Picasso asked me to say something to him in Spanish and with Miguel's assistance I said, "Usted esta mi idolo!" ("You are my idol") which made him blush tremendously. Ordinarily I would have jokingly sung, instead, a chorus of "Alla en el Rancho Grande" or something, but I was so thoroughly imbued with my sense of mission that everything I did and said was related almost exclusively to that.

Then I said something for which Claude all but demolished me, for what she considered a boldness and impropriety on my part, when I told her about it afterward. It was simply that I had asked Picasso, in return, to say something to me in English. He pondered, stammered, and then finally said, in Spanish, "I can't think of anything at the moment—I'm too nervous."

107

When we all got up to leave there was a loud patter of feet and flashing of bulbs as we were surrounded by seven or eight photographers who had been waiting respectfully for dinner to be completed before pouncing hungrily upon us—or rather, upon Picasso and Dominguin. Suddenly Picasso looked over at me and pointed back toward the table. Before I could analyze what he was trying to convey, Jacqueline said, "Your jacket and tie—you forgot them!" Picasso smiled warmly and a flashbulb immortalized the instant.

Outside we posed for many pictures. As we stood by Picasso's long black limousine to say our goodbyes for the evening, Jacqueline winked at me and said, "We'll see you *soon*," and Picasso was grinning from ear to ear. Miguel told me that he would call first thing next morning. "It went beautifully," he smiled.

Like that vision of Chagallian lovers I had fancied might appear on my walk to the restaurant earlier in the evening, I myself seemed to be floating back to my hotel like a Chagallian acrobat. I remembered briefly drifting in front of the brightly lit display of live lobsters in the large, horizontally rectangular tanks at the corner sidewalk exhibit of the Hotel Martinez—an advertisement of their irresistible cuisine—before swimming on home through the intoxicating air of that unbelievable summer night! David Duncan's friendly and well-meaning first words to me rung deliciously in my head: "Save your time and money, Wes—your chances of meeting Picasso aren't even one in a million—they're minus zero!" And yet, it was Duncan's hand that had extended itself warmly to me across the chaos of my then-collapsing world to bring me to this night; a fact that I saluted silently and gratefully as I opened the door to the warm smells and colors of the Hotel Walsdorff-Victoria and made my way once more to the quiet welcome of my small room. And although that night I would sleep the sweet sleep of fulfillment, relief, and happiness, I could hardly wait for the morrow, for the moment of *real* truth—the presentation to Picasso of my idea.

I arose early the next morning, expecting at any moment the possibility of that fateful phone call, failing to take into consideration the clear likelihood that Picasso and Dominguin would almost certainly have repeated the conversational marathon in which they had indulged until 4:00 A.M. on the night of Miguel's arrival, and consequently would be asleep well into the late hour of morning. And so, after informing Claude by telephone of the previous night's exciting events, and of the even more exciting prospects of the day that had just now begun, and with the promise of seeing her that evening for dinner, I took my post on a chair in the sun-drenched lobby of the hotel, under the watchful and sympathetic eye of Monsieur Pierre, who was almost as anxious as I for the phone call to come. And although I was still wrapped in the cocoon of recent events and triumphs, I began to withhold from myself any feelings of self-congratulations, which feelings, in fact, were being speedily replaced by an awful sense of such terrible and agonizing anxiety that every minute seemed like an hour, almost beyond bearing.

I took my usual breakfast of café noir and croissants with butter and jelly at a small table in the lobby, and though this was ordinarily pleasurable to me, on this morning of mornings I hardly had the stomach for it. The morning, after an eternity of plodding, soon turned to noon; and the day being particularly sunny and warm, most of the guests were taking their lunch in the garden area at the tables, which were in abundance beneath the leafy trellises, bounded on one side by a high wall that overlooked a most attractively scenic and narrow side street and on the other by the hotel grounds, and offered a cozy and shady luxury to the diners, who lunched in splendid comfort. It was a luxury for which I felt no attraction, however, in my dismal and intense anxiety, despite Monsieur Pierre's urgings that I should relax and eat, mingled with his assurances that should the call come he would dash out to the garden to fetch me. It was not until one o'clock that I submitted to the necessity of lunch, and at precisely the moment at which I raised the first forkfull of food to my mouth, Monsieur Pierre ran breathlessly to my table to inform me that Dominguin was on the phone, and I abandoned completely a stunning variety of dishes that Henri had placed so lovingly and with such pride upon my table, to my unappreciative eye, and raced like a madman, Monsieur Pierre panting anxiously behind me, across the grounds, into the lobby, and, finally, to the phone booth.

Dominguin informed me that Picasso's chauffeur, Janot, would be at my hotel within the half-hour to take me to Picasso's home, and to be sure to bring with me the portfolio of my work! Bombshells of joy exploded overhead in this second great release of tension and expectation, and I was more than ready when Janot made his appearance. I knew him instantly, of course: the same large, big-shouldered man in the dark suit who had been standing quietly beside Picasso's limousine the night before when we were saying our goodbyes amid the lightning of flashbulbs, and who seemed to generate a quiet self-assurance in the importance of his particular station in life and his singular access, on a continual basis, to one who was being constantly yet unsuccessfully sought after; so that he had the bearing of one who had learned to content himself with the envy of others, as a mantle he must wear, noticeable to anyone of sensitivity who saw him. His manner was simultaneously reserved and friendly, though more of the latter, and I would as soon have welcomed him with a riotous embrace; and when he informed me that he had first to go to the Carlton to pick up Dominguin's airline ticket I smiled in recollection of the reason for its being there in the first place.

Of all the events in my life that I could recall with a sense of true satisfaction in terms of the materialization of time-worn dreams, only one could match the event of that miraculous meeting of the previous night; and that was the exhilarating drive in Picasso's limousine up the winding road that led to the Picasso mansion, Notre Dame de Vie, at the top of the great hill; a limousine driven by the chauffeur of Picasso himself, at the Maestro's own request. The exhilaration was enhanced by the fact that only days earlier I was preparing to leap, unannounced, over the Picasso gate, and now I was arriving in response to his summons, in his own car.

Cathy came out to greet me as I was walking toward the front doorway, and behind her, a moment later, her girl friend appeared, smiling. "They're inside," Cathy motioned, and through the open passageway I could see the shining faces of Dominguin and Jacqueline Picasso smiling out at me as they stood beside a table in one of the rooms toward the rear. I almost dared not look about me, but sensed, instead, the treasures that surrounded my every step, though a large, colored work of wood sculpture, which stood on the floor in the hallway near the room I was about to enter, caught my eye. Still, even before entering the room, though through the open doorway I could see very little, I was aware that Miguel and Jacqueline were its only occupants, and upon entering I saw that Picasso was not present. As if in response to my unspoken query, Jacqueline motioned toward another room and said, "Pablo is not well, he's very, very tired, and is in his bed."

"I'm afraid," said Miguel, "that last night was a bit too much for the old man, and I kept heem up again till morning."

I was aware that Jacqueline herself showed genuine signs of disappointment that Picasso could not be with us. "Won't you be seated?" she smiled gently, motioning toward a fragile looking chair nearby. As I lowered myself into the seat she suddenly smiled, and with a mischievous glint in her eye said, "*Attencion!*" referring jokingly to my chair-breaking incident of the previous evening. I laughed and stood back up, then kneeling down I said, "I'd better sit on the floor."

"I would like to see your work," she said, suggesting that I lay it out upon the table. When she got to the large board with a continuing sequence of paintings representing a bullfight in simulated animation, culminating in a repainted version, in the final square, of a work by Picasso (all the previous squares being visually fluid examples of a metamorphosis directed toward this final picture) her face became flushed, and with a trace of astonishment in her voice she looked at me and said, "Has Pablo seen this?" When I replied (with surprise to the question) that he had not seen it, she turned quickly to Dominquin and said, "Miguel, *Pablo must see this!*"

"No," Miguel replied, "not now."

Jacqueline responded with a look of slight bewilderment, and then turning once again to me with a look of urgency, asked me if I was going to Madrid with Miguel that afternoon or was staying in Cannes. When I told her that I would be staying on, she grinned broadly, and with visible relief,

110

she said, "Then can you please leave your work here so I can show Pablo this afternoon, and I'll have the chauffeur drop it off at your hotel this evening."

Dominguin, this time more firmly, said, *"No, not now!"*

Jacqueline, who then appeared to be squelching her own feelings of confusion, smiled weakly and shrugged her shoulders, and with a look of resignation said, "Miguel knows best."

"I know my man!" Miguel replied; and then, turning to me with an expression of complete assurance, said "If you accompany me to the airport I weel explain all to you."

And, indeed, the drive to the airport was a revelation. Miguel explained that the thought of such a project as my film had stimulated Picasso to the point of trauma. He said the old man, in so many ways a little boy, was so changeable and yet so *dedicated* to whatever he should decide to undertake, that the herculean task of learning and then mastering this new and exciting medium of animation both fascinated and frightened him. Miguel said further that this would be the first thing in many years that Picasso would become involved in other than through his own initiative, and that above all, he did not want to be obligated to anything or anybody, for which one could hardly blame him at this stage of his fantastic career. "One theeng of which you can be sure," Miguel emphasized, "Pablo *wants* to do the feelm!"

Dominguin continued that Picasso had told him that morning that he was afraid the film might be too difficult, and Dominguin had replied (per my previous instructions) that it was not necessary for him to do much, only the "key" drawings, which I myself would then proceed to animate, or if he wished, and hopefully he *would* wish, he could learn and participate in the animation process itself; to which Picasso cried, "But I *want* to do it myself!" This was a complete turnabout in thirty seconds, to which Dominguin had assured him that he could do anything he liked. Miguel then told me that Pablo would probably end up doing thousands of drawings once he became involved because he could not work any other way. And yet, said Miguel, to sell Picasso on an idea is like courting a woman; that timing, discretion, and tact were everything. This, then, explained Miguel's psychology in not showing Picasso my work on this particular day, after that morning's exhausting conversation in which, Miguel said, Picasso stood naked before his window, looking out over the horizon, with an excitement he had never before seen in him. This beginning, Miguel felt, was sufficient for the time being, and that he would try to return to Cannes sometime within the next two weeks. Meanwhile, he said, Jacqueline *wanted Picasso to do this film very much,* and was in complete accord with us on everything, and would continually be discussing it with Picasso at home.

At the airport Miguel showed me a copy of his *Toros y Toreros,* which he had brought with him from Madrid for Picasso to inscribe, and the inscription covered the entire front page of the book, a matter of obvious pride to Miguel. I accompanied him to various windows where he had need to inquire about this and that, bits of information or messages to be sent or received, and invariably we would be distracted by the sight or the passage of a beautiful girl, to the point that, having fifteen or so minutes of leisure before flight time, we decided to walk about and partake of those sights. "Why," cried Dominguin, "always at the airport one sees such beautiful women?"

"Especially," I said, "when one has so little time to do much about it."

"Perhaps," he replied, "eet ees one of life's leetle ironies."

I returned first to my hotel room to call my parents and tell them of the unbelievable events I had just experienced, and their excited jubilation stirred my happiness to a new pitch of intensity and joy, so grateful for their example and encouragement and love. Next I called Walter Bien, and his reaction was also one of volcanic elation, expressing a great pride in me. He thanked me for the justification of his patience and faith in me, for which he, also, had put himself on the line.

Then I went to Claude's gallery, where I received the embrace of embraces, and after some excited conversation I went into her office with her and called David Duncan.

Duncan was wild with happiness, and greatly excited for me. He told me that now that I'd met Picasso and Jacqueline, been to the house, and so on, I could contact Jacqueline *myself* without going through anyone else; in fact, he advised that I do this, in order to discuss the film myself with Jacqueline, making the whole thing *entirely* clear to her. First, he said, she must realize that millions of people who otherwise would never care for or understand Picasso would see this film and have their eyes opened in a way that would be otherwise impossible; and second (to me most important), that animation could just possibly be the greatest medium for visual art in the history of art itself, and that, though as a *medium* it was over half a century old, not one truly major artist had used it as his own; that Picasso *must* be the first to do so, certainly the most natural to introduce an innovation of the sort that I now offered to him.

I told David that Miguel had informed me that Jacqueline was well aware of the potential of such a film, and wanted very much for Picasso to do it, to which David replied that he felt Dominguin had made a big mistake in not allowing Jacqueline to show Picasso my work that afternoon, or whenever she felt it proper, for certainly no one knew the old man's changeable moods and climates as well as she herself! But now, David said, since I had committed myself to await the next word from Dominguin, I had best do it, of course; but to give it no longer than two weeks, at the end of which, should I have heard nothing from Dominguin, to go back to the Picasso home myself, and without disturbing the Maestro, to leave my portfolio with the servant at the gate, accompanied by a note addressed to Picasso and Jacqueline. Then, after allowing the proper period of time for him to have seen the work and digested it, to call Jacqueline to discuss the results. This, I agreed, was exactly what I would do, for by now I had come to see Duncan as a sort of mentor, and my respect for him was infinite. "Damn!" he said, "if only I was back on the old terms with Picasso, I'd have your film for you! Believe me, outside of Jacqueline, no one knows that man like I do; but bless it, anyway, Wes, it looks damn sure now, and to have come this far so fast is purely unbelievable! Sheila will be so happy when I tell her—and I'll bet even little Lump will bark for joy!"

Several days later I received the following letter from Chuck Jones (co-signed by his assistant, Les Goldman), containing the most eloquent and articulate praise I had received for seeing my dream through to this end. He referred to a letter I had sent to SIB Productions regarding my dinner with Picasso, and writes of his own vicarious "participation":

tower 12 inc.
Chuck Jones

6290 Sunset Boulevard,
Hollywood 28, California   A Subsidiary of SIB Productions
HO. 6-3393

June 30, 1964

Mr. Wes Herschenson
c/o Hotel Walsdorff-Astoria
100 Rue d'Antibes
Cannes, (A.M.)
France

Dear Wes:

Splendid news! (and I seldom use exclamation points—things usually either speak for themselves and provide their own emphasis—or they don't and if not, all the punctuational pyrotechnics will not abet their importance) but in this case! I'm not a great hand for vicarious experience, preferring to go abed with my own, but I was damned thrilled to have dinner with you and that truly fabulous group—I enjoyed it and my admiration for your conduct and determination in this whole matter is unbounded. No one can say for himself what others should say for him — so I will say it; you have done what few people ever have the courage or imagination to do; grasped a supreme piece of folly of a truly grand kind, taken it firmly by the tail, swirled it, handled it with the gentle diplomacy needed to handle the wild and the impossible and triumphed beyond all expectation. I'm proud of you and I want you to know that I would continue to be so if the whole thing collapsed at this moment. The day of the grand gesture is proved not to be ended by your action and all of us here who are privy to the matter are exalted by it. The love of any idea is always pretty much the same, I guess: the unwillingness to accredit the impossible; the bravery and strength to implement a dream into reality; the gentleness and subtlety to cut the gem to your own shape when you have it in your hands.

Well, I am only here to help you; timing, cutting and cinematic staging and the unique qualities of animation itself are at the service of this wonderful project, I am certain that this is the break-through that the art of animation has been waiting for for over twenty years, *these* will not be pictures of pictures but movement itself telling a new kind of calligraphy and story. It is not only a great thing for Picasso but is potentially the birth of a new art form.

Thank you for sharing it.

Signed/ Chuck Jones
&
Les too

If I was to follow Duncan's suggestion to wait no longer than two weeks to hear from Dominquin before bringing my work back to Picasso's villa, I decided that these were to be two weeks I would really enjoy, free of the anxiety and tension that had been my constant companions till my meeting with Picasso.

But Fate had other plans for me, and after several days spent in dream like exhilaration, I came down with a bad case of influenza. It seemed to hang on and on, and although I was taking antibiotic medication, which I had brought along with me from Los Angeles, I was confined pretty much to bed in my Walsdorff-Victoria quarters.

One night Claude, who had been checking on me regularly, came into my room to find me burning with fever. It was very late, about twelve-thirty or one o'clock in the morning, and when Claude observed my weak condition, coupled with the fact that I had eaten virtually nothing for a couple of days, she decided that it was time that I had a good bowl of hot soup. The fact that the kitchen was long since closed, and that no one was on duty but Philippe, at the desk, meant nothing to her. About fifteen or twenty minutes after Claude had left my room the door burst open and I saw her, silhouetted against the light from the hall, carrying a tray with a steaming hot bowl of soup! Behind her was Philippe, inquiring as to my condition, and following Claude into my room. As Claude sat on my bed and began spoon-feeding me until I took the bowl from her to continue on my own, Philippe laughingly told me how she insisted he let her into the kitchen before she turned the hotel upside down, and how the two of them practically did turn the kitchen upside down in their attempt to find all the necessary paraphernalia and ingredients to make me the soup.

I had been developing small, white sores in my mouth, and this condition was becoming increasingly painful, for every time I swallowed, it felt like a million sharp pin pricks tearing apart the lining of my mouth and throat, as if I were swallowing a glassful of needles, which account for much of the reason I had not been eating for two days.

My fever broke that night, thanks to Claude, who sat vigil the whole time; and the next day I felt that the flu bug had left me—but the needles and mouth sores remained! So that afternoon I went to see a kindly old doctor whose office was in one of the neighboring hotels on the Croisette, Doctor Levy; and I found to my relief that the sores were merely a reaction to the antibiotics I had been taking. I had either taken them for too long a period or the capsules themselves were too old, Dr. Levy told me. He gave me something to bathe the sores with but said that they could last another week, or longer. I was determined not to let the excruciating pain of swallowing spoil my inner celebration, and it did not—but my diet was restricted to malts and soups and whatever liquids I could manage for the sake of variety.

Finally, two weeks having passed since my dinner with Picasso and subsequent visit to his villa, Dominguin called. He told me that he had been hoping to return to Cannes to accompany me back to Picasso's home, but would be unable to make it. But no matter; I was simply (as Duncan suggested) to leave my portfolio at the gate with Lucienne the house-keeper, then wait for word from Madame Picasso. This I did.

I knew that nothing could or would go wrong now, but was nonetheless exhuberant with joy to learn from Madame Picasso that the Maestro was as enthused about my work as she had been. He wanted, indeed, to embark on that great adventure of animation, to learn it, embrace it, and master it—but first, he had to know exactly how much work was actually involved; and he requested that I return to Los Angeles, make a one-minute sample animated film (using that "new" type of visual movement I had been talking so much about), and then return to Cannes with the film and *all the drawings* that had gone into the making of it. In this way he could determine exactly how many drawings and how much work went into the one minute of animated film. It was a task I would undertake with enough relish to embellish all the world's hot dogs!

Arrangements were made for me to leave for Los Angeles (via a brief

Paris stopover) on July 17, and I still had a few days left in Cannes. My sores and the accompanying pain had still not abated one iota, but my thoughts were easily kept on a level above it all, considering the substance of those thoughts.

Cannes, like all of France, was preparing joyously for its great national celebration, Bastille Day, July 14, and in my fantasy I could not help noting the great proximity of it all to my own equally joyous and festive *inner* celebration. Let the fireworks begin!

I found a good leaning-spot on the beach near small clusters of people, just across the street from the Festival Building where throngs of onlookers were lined behind the ropes, seen only in silhouette against the colorful glare of the building, and waiting for the Great Show, as they were doing all up and down the Croisette and along the beach.

I was still in agony from the virus sores that spotted the inner walls of my mouth, but the fever was gone, and there were moments when I could ignore it all, and this was becoming one of them.

The three ships sat side by side, close to the shore but a respectable distance back, waiting to vie for the favor of the crowd. It was to be the annual competition between ships, held each Bastille Day night in the Bay of Cannes, sometimes with two, sometimes with three ships, which sent up alternating blasts of fireworks, each with the intent of outdoing the others, which is to say, "out-glorying" and "out-blazing" the others.

In spite of the pain in my mouth I was still swimming in the exultation of my meeting with Picasso and my exhilarating success in communicating to him my ideas; and since in three days I would be going home, finally, now wanting badly to go *home*, I took this entire affair as a personal celebration of my staggering and newfound glory—a celebration not by the citizens of Cannes, no, what did they know?, but by the gods who knew, and who could substitute the meaning of a national, historic celebration with that of a more personal, more immediate, and, praised be art, a more important one!

Well, the fireworks began! Do not expect words like *beautiful* and *glorious* or descriptions of what transpired, because the sky simply opened up, directly above; and the lights and the colors and the patterns and the crackles and the explosions came pouring out over us all, like the French Marseilles being sung by a million angels.

Don't laugh, reader—it was for me.

12

Paris—and Home

THE THRILL OF MY FIRST TRIP TO PARIS, AFTER MY FANTASTIC encounter in Cannes with the artist of the century—oh, what a *dream!* What a dream to be *savored!* Even the aggravating pain in my mouth could in no way dampen the joy I felt during these three brief but eternal days in paradise.

The immensity of the sprawling city took me by surprise as the plane flew overhead on this bright, immortal morning. I watched as the patchworks of trees and houses, so strange in their familiarity, whipped by the window as we neared Orly Airport, flying so low you could taste, smell, and hear all that the eyes embraced.

Everywhere was history, as new as it was old: the magnificent buildings, the most insignificant of them a landmark in the eye of this young artist-idealist-dreamer-reader of art history, worshipper of the masters; floating now within this dreamscape oblivious to all cynicism, incredulous at all he saw and smelled and heard and knew to be unreal and real simultaneously; the sky itself, not the sky as it ever was before, but part of the city, continued on high—there was no one thing separate from the other, but all of a whole, itself rejoicing in a pride born of the authority of beauty!

I risk ridicule whenever I reveal how I spent part of my first afternoon in Paris—in a movie theater! But how could I not? There, in a theater on the Champs-Elysées near my hotel, was *An American in Paris!* This film, which had changed my life when I first saw it as a soldier during the Korean War,

117

promising a life as it should and could be lived; this much I owed, and I paid my respects with the sentiment of a lover upon his return. To watch Gene Kelly, Leslie Caron, and Oscar Levant inhabiting on screen the very city that awaited me outside—instead of an army camp—can you blame me? And Gershwin! He was the first American to create Paris in sound, infusing the American ideal into the French reality, to create this new real-ideal Paris-of-the-mind, which I had every intention of celebrating, still fresh from the actual touch and sight of Picasso himself—Master of Paris in our own century. Could anything ever again be as perfect?

All I could eat were malts and soups, and even these were a source of great pain; and so for food I dined on the sights of the city until my mind got fat and full and gained a thousand pounds. The Place de la Concorde, Notre Dame, the Arc de Triomphe—it would serve little if any purpose to attempt to describe that which has already been described by masters and by enthusiastic scrawlers of postcards covered with exclamation points, as well as seen and lived by countless millions. Therefore, any further attempt to add to this overload of romanticizing would amount to nothing less than criminal assault. But—can a description of Paris-of-the-mind qualify as such contemptible presumption?

I allowed myself everything, mentally and spiritually; and I felt myself not merely a visitor or tourist, but a soldier of Art, having done battle and won, decorated with medals pinned on me by the great General of Art himself, and planning a new campaign with victory a certainty, with the greatest of new secret weapons—animation! I could hardly wait to rush to Montmarte where the old soldiers, now long gone, used to congregate and fight all their legendary battles of life and love and creation; and it was with an air of unbearable elation that I began my dream-walk in the afternoon sunlight and shadows through Paris, to the streets of Montmarte to visit these pleasantly haunting ghosts, not needing to ask for directions, but heading by sheer instinct through the crooked streets as if walking along the passageways of my own mind. The windmills of the Moulin de la Galette and the famous Moulin Rouge whirled in my head more as memories than as sights.

And one by one the ghosts appeared, walked through me, and were gone; only to reappear on another street or to be seen seated at the table of an outdoor café. In the time machine of my mind I could see them all, as with one of those cameras used by scientists to photograph the auras of people who have recently left a scene, leaving behind the colorfully burning vibrations in the shape of their bodies to be recorded by the ultrasensitive lens of the camera. In just this way I could see them all:

The darkly sensuous, aristocratic handsomeness of Amadeo Modigliani, the Italian Jew who splattered the wine of his tormented spirit across the face of Paris in the early days of our century. I saw him everywhere and anywhere, strolling adventurously along in his shabby brown corduroy suit and heavy shoes, drawing pad under his arm, filled with sheet after sheet of sensitively drawn beatuies, each page for sale for the price of a drink. He searches, in the pathos of his unquenchable thirst, for that refined ideal of feminine sensuality, and the shimmering heat waves of his departed spirit are so easily detected by the eager lens of my mental time camera.

He asks me if I have seen his friend Picasso, who is always good for a free glass of absinthe, and I tell him yes . . . yes! I have seen Picasso!—only two short weeks ago, but he lives now in Mougins near Cannes, too far a journey for poor Amadeo; and besides, Picasso has aged much since he last wandered the Paris streets with his wild friends of old!

And at No. 54 Rue Lepic I glimpse Vincent Van Gogh passing quickly through the door of his house; Lautrec, Gauguin, Renoir, Braque, Matisse—all of them, I see everywhere as ghosts—all of them, save one—the one not yet a ghost—he, the king of them all—he, with whom I dined two short weeks ago, flesh and blood; yet a ghost of history even as he lives; with nine more years of work to be done and battles to be fought in his war with "reality"—destroying it in order to re-create it in his own image—Picasso, the prototype of the artist, in imitation of his God.

That night I left my hotel to walk to the Eiffel Tower and oddly enough had an impossible time locating it: for it was not visible on any horizon within my view; and I did not really understand any directions that were given me by passing Parisians responding to my inquiries. Almost by accident it suddenly and magnificently appeared from behind a large cluster of trees—still distant enough so that even as I hurried toward it, another ten minutes passed before I stood close to it. It was late now, and very quiet here, and the tower looked down upon me like some great and silent friend—very powerful, very patient, and very old. But its age was undiminished by time; in its wisdom and silence it out-dazzled and out-symbolized everything. My view of the tower, actually, was separated by a low wall of three or four feet in height, and I was higher than the ground level of the tower, which reached into the sky above me. I sat on a bench surrounded by trees, and watched the stillness of this spectacle in contented silence.

It was then that I fancied, there beneath the Eiffel Tower, a midnight apparition of George Gershwin. It began (in my fancy) as a figure standing in the shadow of a nearby tree, from which emerged, in intermittent puffs, the unmistakeable aroma of cigar smoke. Then, the figure itself emerged, and adjusting the cigar to a corner of his mouth, George Gershwin walked toward me, hands in pockets, head forward, eyes downward. Softly, without looking up, he spoke to me as he passed my bench:

"Congratulations, boy," he said.

"Thanks, Mr. Gershwin," I replied.

"Georgie."

"Georgie."

"Gotta hurry, boy," he said, disappearing into the night. "Gotta hurry!"

Five minutes or so later, to my great surprise, the tower went dark. I had no idea that the lights went out at a certain time, though I had not really thought about it; and had I arrived twenty minutes later than I did I would have been greeted by a sight considerably less spectacular than the one to which I had just been witness. Nevertheless, I remained sitting where I was for a long time, puffing my pipe and thinking.

I spent all of the following day at the Louvre, in an ecstacy of unspeakable exhilaration. All those masterpieces, so familiar to me in such a personal way through their reproductions, now loomed before me in the oddness of their reality; *odd* because of my own inability to focus all of my life-long thoughts of these works (existing till now only in my mind) into the framework of actual space that they now occupied before my eyes. It had been the same with my Picasso confrontation: the necessity of having to gather the nebulous dream-thoughts of a world myth, and focus them down and into the confines of a given area of space, which this myth, in actual fact, occupies! The *Mona Lisa*, a legend in the minds of men, women, and children for centuries, spanning time and space without boundary was *there, on that wall*—filling dimensional space.

Many of my favorites, however, were unfortunately out on a loan to a big exposition then being held elsewhere. But the gigantic, wall-sized *Death of Sardanapoulis* by Delacroix was there, as was his considerably smaller but equally legendary *Women of Algiers*, whose magic had enthralled me through reproductions since my adolescence; this magic was enhanced by the fact that Picasso had himself painted fifteen large variations of this work, in the manner of a musician composing variations on a theme—or an animated film in still form.

No need to recount in detail my tour of the Louvre, except to say that my dreamlike awe of it all was compounded by the immensity and vastness with which this aristocratic old building spoke to me through the sharp echo of my own footsteps.

It was—all of this—as though I were receiving a reward for having received a reward, or being blessed for having been blessed; and I was well advised (by myself) to cherish these moments—for shortly after my return home I was to see all my dreams begin to crumble, one by one.

Upon my return to Los Angeles I was welcomed at SIB Productions as a truimphant hero, or at the least, by a "ticker tape parade of the mind" consisting of wide grins, furious handshakes, pats on the back, and ambivalent looks. Within one day I was summoned to an executive meeting at the "Round Table" with Walter Bien, Chuck Jones, Les Goldman, Sonny Klein, and others, at which I informed everyone of Picasso's request that I do a one-minute sample film in this new kind of "movement," then return to France with the reel of film, as well as all the drawings I made to compose the animation, in order for Picasso to weigh the two and see for himself exactly how much work was involved, that is, how much actual drawing was required per one minute of animation.

Walter was elated, and bursting with enthusiasm he suggested that I set to work immediately, with a budget of $10,000 if needed, which I said was not necessary, since I would be doing all the animation myself. Walter nodded approvingly, but to my great surprise Chuck Jones took exception. Here was the man who had written me the most articulate, beautiful, and flattering letter of praise, if not sheer adulation, after my meeting with Picasso, now suddenly crying, "We can get the best animators in town to do this! It must be done right!"

So incredulous were these words to me after all I had gone through and all that had been discussed both prior to and during my odyssey, that I could compare it only to a woman, who after nine loving months of a difficult pregnancy and a painfully agonizing labor, finally gives birth to her child, only to hear those in attendance say "We must take this infant and see to it that it has the best mother possible."

I reminded Chuck, therefore, that this was my creation and that the best animators in town would have no idea of what I intended to do. "You mean," Chuck said sarcastically, "that only you and Picasso understand this 'new kind of movement'?"

"Yes," I replied, with emphatic deliberation.

With that, Chuck stood up and walked over to the large window overlooking Hollywood far below. All eyes were upon him as he stood looking out. Then he turned to us, with actual tears of frustration pouring down his cheeks. With one look it was apparent to him that the others were in agreement with whatever I wanted. "All right," he said, shrugging his shoulders, "go ahead. Looks as though I'm out-voted. It's all yours."

The weeks that followed found me intense with a fierce joy, even as I floundered about in search of the correct approach, to get at that *something* I had been dreaming of for so long. Soon enough, I found the path—and drawing followed drawing as the visual rhythms seemed to unfold themselves before me. I felt that at long last I was doing what I was born to do, and that nothing could ever stop me now.

13

Depression—and Search

WELL, ALMOST NOTHING COULD STOP ME. AS THE WEEKS WENT BY, WALTER became harder and harder to contact, and the upshot of it was that, through some financial disasters, SIB Productions was on the rocks—finished! I was left without a backer, without money; for MGM was forced to close its books on all dealings concerning SIB until certain matters were cleared. I was still owed three thousand dollars in expense money and had to give it up for lost. Walter was heartsick, but there was nothing he could do. And so began a most painful and agonizing period of my life.

I was compelled to continue work on my animation, without recompense, and I was determined to find support elsewhere. Over the course of the long period in which I resolved myself to completing this task, I eventually reached the point where my drawings (done in pencil) had to be transferred, by tracing in ink, to transparent celluloid sheets, called *cels*; followed by the painting process, wherein these inked cels are turned to the reverse side and painted, using the inked drawings as guidelines. The individual colors, or paints that I desired were identified by numbers, which I would indicate on the specific areas of the corresponding pencil drawing. Traditonally this work is done, in the animation field, by what are known as "ink-and-paint girls"; it is basically a mechanical craft wherein the pencil drawings of the animator are carefully traced onto the cels, and painted, per instruction, according to the designated paint number, on the reverse side of the cel.

For this arduous task I was fortunate enough to have as my friends two of the best and most painstaking ink-and-paint girls in the business, Kim

Kelley and Vonnie Batson. They worked nights for me at their apartments, usually into the small hours of the morning, and then went to their regular jobs during the day. They did this without any thought of payment, having faith enough in the project to know that it would eventually succeed, and willing to gamble on it.

In the meantime I continued my search for a backer, never quite able to adjust to the irony inherent in the disbelief with which my story was constantly being received. I had gone to the William Morris Agency for help, armed with all the backing necessary to prove my story: photographs, letters, telegrams, articles, and so on, and I was given an interview by one of the Morris agents, Marty Dubow. Without even looking at my material, he told me simply that "Picasso and Stravinsky would never be interested in such a project," and turned me down flat! You can imagine, therefore, my intense satisfaction when, a few years later, the William Morris Agency, through Marty Dubow, became my representatives—enthusiastically and aggressively carrying out a most lucrative deal on my behalf.

But before this was to take place I experienced what seemed an endless procession of terribly dark and frustrating days—days of dread and desperation in the wake of having come *so close* to the total achievement of my goal, before the collapse of the MGM backing under the auspices of SIB Productions.

The question now was, who could I turn to? Surely, I thought, in this great city of art benefactors and patrons, this motion picture capital of the world, *surely* there would be someone who would be interested in the fact that I had Picasso and Stravinsky waiting in the wings to make my film a reality—the greatest artist of the twentieth century and the greatest composer of the twentieth century. What tragic irony it would be if now, after coming this far, I were unable to convince a soul!

After discussing this absurd dilemma with family and friends, my mother suggested the possibility of Vincent Price, the famous actor who was renowned for his interest in and patronage of the arts, and who at this time was associated in this capacity with Sears. At first rejecting the idea on the grounds that it seemed too unlikely a shot, too intangible in any case to consider seriously, I decided eventually to give it a try.

After obtaining Price's home address in Beverly Glen Canyon, I drove one afternoon in early October to the estate, armed with my large portfolio of drawings and paintings, which I had designed to illustrate the general "feel" of my intended film, similar to the portfolio I had left with Picasso. I had no doubt whatsoever that I would not only get in to see Vincent Price, but that he would be enthusiastically receptive to my ideas.

To my surprise and relief the large gate to his estate was opened, and straightaway I drove inside up the winding driveway. I came to a stop in front of a small cottage that was located a short distance from the massive house. A woman emerged waving her arms, and inquired as to the purpose of my visit. She was apparently some sort of secretary, and I introduced myself and told her briefly why I had come, and then asked if Mr. Price was at home. With a sharp look toward the house (which told me he was at home) she said that he was out, and that furthermore, if I wished to discuss any business with him it would have to be through his agent, whereupon she gave me the agent's phone number and bid me goodbye.

Burning with that all-too-familiar fire of frustration, I drove to the nearest phone booth and dutifully called the agent, only to learn from his secretary that he was out of town and would not return for two weeks. *Two weeks!* And then, surely, only to be turned down by the *agent* of the man who was this moment unquestionably at home only a short distance away! What did these agents and secretaries know or care? I was inflamed with an anger that has never yet let me down, and I knew that within the half-hour I would be discussing my film face-to-face with Vincent Price himself.

I returned to the estate, this time parking on the street out of sight and slipping in through the gate unseen, portfolio in hand. Walking briskly yet cautiously toward the large house I came to a long outer stairway and climbed it arbitrarily, only to find, upon reaching the top, that it had led to nowhere, and I was facing an empty wall! However, far below at some distance on the grounds, I saw a gardener who seemed to have taken notice of me, and I realized that if I was to be at all successful in locating the doorway that led to Vincent Price, I had best expedite matters considerably. I approached next a large side door at ground level, behind which I heard the sound of a vacuum cleaner. I knocked loudly and heard a voice shouting over the noise of the cleaner, and then suddenly the door swung open and there, standing before me, was the tall and thoroughly benevolent figure of Vincent Price himself! He was dressed in casual jeans and greeted me with a sort of surprised and friendly "Hi!" I introduced myself and asked him if I might speak to him for a moment, and without hesitation he warmly invited me inside, ushered me to his study and asked me to sit down and tell him what it was I wished to discuss!

Never have I received such a cordial audience, considering the audacity of my unannounced and uninvited visit, and Price listened with unswerving interest and enthusiasm to my every word, giving his undivided attention to every detail of the illustrations I took from my portfolio as I spoke. He knew and understood immediately the breathtaking potential of such a project, and was instantly committed to its realization.

After exchanging phone numbers he promised to get in touch with me as soon as he had thought over which approach would be the best, and it was with great elation that I returned to my car on the street, after walking with great deliberaton past the small cottage of my recent rejection.

The following excerpts from several exchanges of letters should serve as narrative for what followed, with a brief note to say that Price pursued several courses; first, through the introduction of Ralph Altman who had a direct channel to Morton D. May, the president of the May Company Department Stores (whom Price considered a more likely candidate for financing than Sears); and second, through his associate Harry G. Sundheim, Jr., of Vincent Price Enterprises in Chicago, as the most direct link to a possible Sears backing. The excerpts:

THE MAY DEPARTMENT STORES COMPANY
Office of The President

October 22, 1964

Dear Mr. Herschensohn:

I read your letter with interest, but unfortunately I can't think of any suggestions for you. I think that if Picasso would animate a film on the bullfight, it would be an extremely worthwhile project. . .

You seem to have as good connections as anybody in the film industry and the only hope I can see for the project is to get one of the major film companies to make this substantial investment in the project. Certainly our Company is not large enough and does not have wide enough distribution to support a project of anywhere near this magnitude. Sears might be large enough to do so, but no doubt you have discussed this possibility with Vincent.

I am sorry I can't be of more help to you.

Sincerely,
Morton D. May

MDM: bm

Vincent Price Enterprises
20 East Cedar Street
Chicago 11, Illinois

Harry G. Sundheim, Jr.

November 6, 1964

Mr. Wesley S. Herschensohn
Los Angeles, California

Dear Mr. Herschensohn,

Thanks so much for your very interesting letter of November 1 as regards your project with Picasso.

It might well be, as Mr. Price suggested to you, that Sears might be interested in financing such a project; although, as I am sure, as Mr. Price told you, I have no authority to speak for Sears.

Would you, therefore, be kind enough to let me know approximately what would be involved, cost-wise. . .

November 12, 1964

I have given a great deal of thought to your very nice letter of November 8. . .

I have also discussed this matter with certain of the Sears people, and I must tell you, frankly, that they do not feel that it is a project that they would want to enter at this time.

Even though it sounds most exciting I think you better forget the possibility of Sears financing this project.

Thank you, nevertheless, for your interest, and for submitting it to us.

Sincerely yours,

Harry G. Sundheim, Jr.
HGS:rl

While the efforts of the Vincent Price associates were taking their ultimately unsuccessful course, I continued to pursue every other avenue that even hinted of a possible likelihood of eventual fruition.

Considering the chance that an already thriving animation studio might be interested in joining forces with me, I took that route and visited Bill Melendez, producer of the popular "Peanuts" television cartoons. Bill was very impressed with my venture but said that he was unable to expand his forces beyond what he was presently handling.

"But, jeez," he said. "Here you went off and did the kind of thing everyone else just talks or dreams about doing—took off like a hairy eagle for France and Picasso—and *got* him! Wish I could join with you on this thing, but it's impossible for me. Good luck, Wes!"

Next I paid a visit to the aging Max Fleischer, who maintained offices on the lot at Universal Studios. Fleischer, with his brother Dave, was the creator of the brilliant Betty Boop, Popeye, and early Superman series of animated cartoons of the thirties and forties, as well as some superb full-length feature films—he was one of the great old masters of the industry. I was surprised and delighted by the audience he gave me, and we spoke for hours. Though he was no longer really active in the business, he extended a fatherly affection to me and praised my project as something extraordinary that must be done, and insisted on driving me to my parked car before leaving for home.

I also spoke to Herb Klein, who produced art films for the great financier Bart Lytton, ex-Hollywood screenwriter, whose large Savings and Loan Association was constructed on the site of the old Hollywood landmark The Garden of Allah, on the Sunset Strip, and which devoted itself in part to Hollywood memorabilia. I also spoke to Saul Bass, another old master whose work I greatly admired—all to much praise, but no action. It was hard to fight back the despair, the awakening awareness of the actual possibility of defeat; but I so believed in the rightness of my idea, that I dragged myself onward, swearing to persevere.

Next, and most promising, was a brilliant professor of archaeology named Ted Carpenter, whom I had met through my brother and who was involved with him in some minor business affair. Ted was co-author of the McLuhan books and theories that swept the nation for a while (*The Medium Is the Message*, e.g.). Ted worked hard to interest a multimillionaire associate of his in Canada, Sam Zacks, in the project; and Zacks, in turn, promised to speak about it to his close friend Taft Schreiber, the head of Universal Studios. In the meantime Ted continued to supply me with invaluable moral support.

In the middle of October 1964 I received from Ted a copy of a rather cryptic telegram that Sam Zacks had sent to him regarding Schreiber, dated October 14; at the bottom of the telegram Carpenter had typed the following message for me:

Wes—Have spoken to Sam Zacks at length and written to him at even greater length, describing your project. He will be both talking & writing to Schreiber.

Ted

Ultimately, I did meet with Schreiber, and the Picassos that I saw hanging in his office at first gave me great hope, but this hope was extremely short-lived. For Schreiber, after listening patiently to my story (with an *expression* of patience on his face), proceeded to tell me how unrealistic my project was in a *commercial* sense; and with an idea as totally uncommercial as mine was, he told me that there was *no way* he or any other producer who was in the business of making money would *invest* that money in a venture so doomed to commercial failure, noble as it might be.

After a heated exchange of words, fired by my anger at his verdict, I turned to storm out of his office; but as I reached the door he called me back, in a gentler tone. Explaining that he had consented to see me out of respect for his friend Sam Zacks, he went on to say, half-smilingly, that when he was a young man he was as strong-minded as I was, and that I had much to learn. How right he was.

One day I got a frantic call from a man who identified himself as Mike Shore. He had heard about my project with Picasso and wanted to meet me. He, too, had been involved with a Picasso animation project—not through Picasso himself, but through an old war time friend of the Maestro's named Joseph Foster. Furthermore, it was not intended to involve any animation on Picasso's part, but merely for Picasso to design the "look" of the picture, which was to be a film on *Don Quixote*.

Shore asked me to meet him for breakfast and said that I would recognize him if I looked for "a dissipated version of Francis Lederer." I assured him that our projects were of a different nature, and declined his offer to combine them into one; however, he left satisfied that there was no conflict. A year later I was to learn, from a most unexpected source, that this Foster project did not succeed, and for a most unexpected reason.

Next, I headed for the Venice offices of Charles Eames, having recently read that the great Eames, inventor and designer of much of our modern furniture, was now into film making—and he seemed a likely candidate. Although he was out of town, I hit it lucky in the person of Pamela Hedley, a delightful and attractive English lady, secretary and assistant to Eames. She was totally fascinated with my project and instantaneously became a great champion of "the cause." Eames himself was away in Europe on an extended stay, and Pamela worked diligently to set the works in motion for me, trying various approaches, but to no avail.

Finally, she suggested I see her friend Jean Renoir, the renowned French film director, acknowledged genius of the cinema, and son of the great impressionist painter Pierre Auguste Renoir. I was pleased and delighted at the prospect. A meeting was arranged, and it was with great pleasure that I headed, one bright afternoon, for the Renoir home on Leona Drive in Beverly Hills.

There was a pleasant aura about the house as I approached, and my warm anticipation as I rang the bell was matched by the warmth of a large pair of dark bright eyes that looked up into mine with a friendliness that was so disarming I had to remind myself I had never met Mrs. Renoir before this moment. The wise and knowing look of her eyes was flattering, inasmuch as it gave one the impression that this look was a reflection of what she was seeing. It was one of those nonverbal communications that seemed to say "We *know*, we two—don't we?" She was a small, energetic, almost wiry looking woman with black hair combed straight back, and she bore herself with a mixture of great inner beauty and humor.

After introducing ourselves I stepped inside, and she told me to wait in the living room while she fetched her husband. I was enveloped in an atmosphere of sumptuous serenity! As is my wont, in my observations of a new surrounding, I dwelled on nothing in particular but on the total impact, which in this case was one of a sunny friendliness pervading everything. Paintings and sculptures by Renoir the father dominated the general elegance, all of which was bathed in the soft afternoon sunlight that seemed to emanate from the room itself.

As if to complete this happy picture, like the final piece of a jigsaw, Jean Renoir himself entered the room—a large hulk of a man in his seventies, with a bald head and pink complexion and a gentle, noble face all the more kindly for its almost homely demeanor. Homely, that is, were it not so beautiful! Limping from a wound in the leg he received during the First World War, he walked over to me, hand extended, and smilingly introduced himself, looking into me with those kind, sad eyes that had seen everything, but never enough.

"Pamela tells me you have a most interesting mission in life," he said in a rather heavily accented voice after we had seated ourselves. "She speaks very highly of you and thought that we two should meet!"

"I'm glad you were able to see me," I said, "and honored to meet you." After which I disclosed to him the details of my story from the conception of my idea, through my meeting with Picasso, and on up to the present deplorable and frustrating state in which I now found myself.

"It would seem" Renoir said, "that you have reached almost a dead end, and yet I have faith that it indeed is not so. First, let me commend you, young man, on your great artistic courage. I am happy to see that such dreams as yours are still being undertaken in this tired old world. Secondly, I would do everything in my power to give to you the aid you require in the accomplishment of this great dream; but the film you propose consists entirely of animation, and I—I am a director of live films, what is there for a director of live films to direct in an animated movie?"

I smiled in acquiescence at this plaintive query, explaining that I had not come to him in expectation that he would direct my film, but only that Pamela had thought we should meet and that possibly he would have some ideas that might help me to find a way out of my dilemma.

"Primarily though," I said, "I wanted only to meet you, and Pamela's initiative in bringing it about only served as an excuse on my part to do so."

"Well," said Renoir, smiling in acknowledgment, "you see—if you had some live-action story to accompany this animation, *then*! Then I would, in effect, be able to direct your film, so to speak, and I could collaborate with you in this way on your project. But first, we must get a story, eh?"

Something flashed through my mind, like a single frame from a movie, but was gone before I could grasp it.

"You have something?" asked Renoir, observedly. "Something occurs to you?"

"For an instant, I seemed to remember something," I replied, "but I've lost it."

"It will come," he said. "Sooner or later we will find it."

Our goodbyes were even more cordial than our introductions, and both Renoir and his wife, whose name was Dido, insisted that I call or drop by any time I should desire, and that their home was open to me any time I wished. I had no idea then under what happy circumstances I would be making my return to the Renoir household.

14

Ray Bradbury

So the shore-line stage was set, and in a few minutes the two men would meet. And once again Fate fixed the scales for shocks and surprises, arrivals and departures. And all the while these two solitary strollers did not for a moment think on coincidence, that unswum stream which lingers at man's elbow with every crowd in every town.

—Ray Bradbury, "In a Season of Calm Weather"

A MONTH OR SO LATER, IN EARLY DECEMBER 1964, I WENT TO THE CORONET Theatre on La Cienega Boulevard to see an evening of three plays by Ray Bradbury, featuring *The Man in the Ice Cream Suit*. I went full of anticipation, for the great Bradbury had long been an idol of mine.

This adulation had begun many years earlier when, as teenagers, my brother Bruce and I used to spend every Sunday afternoon at the Tivoli movie theater in West Los Angeles. As part of our regular routine, we would go next door to the little magazine stand when the movie let out, and look through the magazines while waiting for Dad to pick us up. I was a particular devotee of the science-fiction and fantasy pulp magazines, and I was always especially delighted to see a new issue of *Amazing Stories* or *Weird Tales*, both of which have long since become classics of the publishing industry.

One particular Sunday afternoon I took down from the rack a new issue of *Weird Tales* and was flipping excitedly through its pages, when my eye was caught by the opening paragraph of a story by Ray Bradbury, whose name was new to me. I was then about sixteen, and I guess Bradbury was about twenty-three. What caught my eye was the unusual wording of this opening paragraph, which somehow struck a chord deep within me. I can in no way recall the precise phrasing, but it was a description of someone on a beach who was discussing the goose bumps on his arm, and the sand of the beach; but no matter—it was the *way* it was written, something so magical and musical about the arrangement of the words, something so evocative about the sea, the sand, the sky, the goose bumps on the flesh, that I found myself totally enchanted, and read the little tale to its conclusion. From that moment on, the name Ray Bradbury had for me a special meaning, and with each successive issue of *Weird Tales* I looked for it with wild anticipation, always delirious with heart-thumping joy if it was there, and crushingly disappointed if it was not. His stories, though fitting into the categories of "weird," "fantasy," or "science-fiction," seemed to me far beyond such labels, and opened within me endless new possibilities for creative magic.

As it turned out, of course, my taste was shared by many others, to the point where, ultimately, Bradbury was to become known as the greatest writer of science fiction of the twentieth century. I think, however, that the science-fiction label is somewhat of a misnomer, and that to restrict the Bradbury creativity to this particular genre is, at best, misleading.

So, many years having come and gone, it was with unabated enthusiasm that I anticipated this evening of the three Bradbury plays, nor was I in any way disappointed. After the performance the entire audience was invited to partake of refreshments in the outer patio, where Ray conversed heartily with his fans. My date suggested that we go over and talk to him, but I was not of a mind to buck the crowd that surrounded him, and we left without making the attempt.

Two evenings later, however, I walked into Martindale's Book Store in Beverly Hills, to see Bradbury browsing at one of the book stands! My first inclination was to walk over to him to express my enjoyment of his plays, when I realized that he was in the middle of a jovial shouting conversation with one of the salesmen across the room; and being in an introspective mood, I balked, not wishing to call any undue attention to myself. Later that evening, at my parents' house, I mentioned the incident to them—the odd coincidence of my seeing Bradbury so soon after attending the performance of his plays—and they remarked that I should have introduced myself, after having been an admirer of such long standing, among his very first, in fact.

As fate would have it, the following evening I went once again to Martindale's, and there again was Bradbury! However, it was an exact repetition of the previous evening; the loud, jovial, long-distance conversation with the salesman, and my ridiculously stubborn mood of introspection. And again I left without approaching him.

Fate, however, is not to be denied, introspection notwithstanding. The following Sunday afternoon I was driving with my friend Donna when she asked me if I would mind stopping off at the big Rexall drug store at the corner of Beverly and La Cienega so she could buy some makeup she needed. While I was browsing through the store, I saw—need I say it? Yes, Ray Bradbury stood once again in my path. I decided then that I would put Fate's little game to an end, though I saw no purpose in it, not being a celebrity hunter nor wishing to embarrass Bradbury or myself. I remembered then a line from one of the three plays, *In the Chicago Abyss*, where the leading character, one of the few survivors of an atomic holocaust, is recalling all the trivial little things that went to make up his world, things he hardly noticed, things he took so much for granted before the Bomb obliterated all of it. "Remember," the character says, after recalling all the Campbell Soup labels, and looking dreamily off into the distance, "remember the little Clark candy bar with its bright orange wrapper?" He then proceeds to exult in the memory. Noticing that I was standing but a few feet from the candy section, I bought a Clark bar and walked with it straight for Bradbury.

"Ray Bradbury?" I shouted, louder even than those jovial, long-distance tones I had avoided earlier in the week. Bradbury turned quickly around, surprised. His face lit up when I continued my pronouncement. "Ray Bradbury, I would like to present you with this Clark bar with the bright orange wrapper, in appreciation of a pleasant evening at the Coronet!"

He roared with laughter, head thrown back, and taking the candy bar, with flushed face, he said, "For me? Really?"

"Yes, for you!" I laughed. "Really!"

We conversed pleasantly for a while, then he asked me about myself and I told him about my project with Picasso. To my surprise he turned beet red, and I thought that he was going to explode with the expression of wonder and amazement that all but burst through his face. It seems that Bradbury had been trying to meet Picasso for seven years, through correspondence, with the aid of some close art-dealer friends of Picasso in Paris—but to no avail.

"A bad shot," I said. "Picasso doesn't correspond."

"And my God," cried Bradbury. "You actually *met* Picasso? And *know* him?"

He then asked, almost pleaded, for some part in the project, and when I told him it was to be an animated film with no "live" story he said, "Why not a 'live' story to be integrated with the animation?"

He went on to tell me about a short story he had written for *Playboy* magazine in 1957 about a young American couple who go to France, on a whim, to meet the great Picasso, and that it was to some degree similar to my own experience. I told him that I had read the story when it came out, and that it possibly had some subliminal effect on my own decision to see the master. "It was *me* you were writing about!" I told him, and he laughingly agreed that it must have been. It suddenly occurred to me that the one-frame instant of thought that had flashed on and off in my mind when Renoir and I were discussing the possibility of a live-action story was no less than a lightning recollection of the very Bradbury story Ray and I were now discussing! I mentioned this to Ray, saying that now, possibly, there could be a live-action story for Renoir to direct. Bradbury went insane. "You know Renoir too?" he screamed. This was another long-time idol of Bradbury's whom he wanted to meet.

"I'll get to work on a production synopsis immediately, based on the short story from *Playboy*," Ray enthused. "By the way, it was titled 'In a Season of Calm Weather.' Here, I'll write down my office address and phone number, and if you can stop by tomorrow afternoon I'll have something ready to show you!"

Sure enough, that very next afternoon, Monday, December 11 (my father's birthday), Ray had typed up a one-page synopsis titled "Note on the Production of: *In a Season of Calm Weather.*" His office was a small, one-room nook in an office building on Wilshire Boulevard, in the heart of Beverly Hills. It was cluttered with delicious memorabilia of all sorts, in the center of which stood a small desk with an electric typewriter. It was not long before we discovered the incredible similarity of our tastes from early childhood: the lustful appetite for the old comics, pulps, and movies; the great, aesthetic "junk" that was so crucial to the development of our imaginations; all that marvelously innocent outpouring of naive genius that was the product of our times in America, and that contributed so magnificently to the seemingly undiscriminating joy and discovery of the happy creations of the early cartoonists, animators, writers, and moviemakers who allowed their brain-children to be born without those confining barriers of "reality," "intellectualism," and "good taste."

We yelped and laughed like a couple of schoolboys playing hooky, so wild was our elation over the whole thing. The entire meeting, in fact, was punctuated with an awful lot of loud and unsophisticated giggling, hardly the hallmark of two grown men on the eve of a profitable business transaction. This was the beginning, however, of what was to become a life-long friendship of mutual respect and good cheer.

I told him of my many adventures with David Douglas Duncan and Dominguin in my search for Picasso, and he expressed a great admiration and awareness of Duncan and his work.

"I'll send you a copy of the short story," said Bradbury, "which is included in an anthology called *The Day It Rained Forever*, which you can send on to Mr. Duncan when you tell him about our meeting. He sounds like he'd get a great kick out of the whole thing, and I hope one day for the opportunity of meeting him also!"

15

The Triumvirate—Renoir, Bradbury, and I

A DAY OR SO LATER, AT RAY'S REQUEST, I PHONED RENOIR AND TOLD HIM OF Ray's great desire to meet him, and how the story from *Playboy* magazine would serve as a superb foundation for a live-action supplement to my Picasso animation. Renoir could not have been more delighted, and expressed his own desire to meet Bradbury, whom he had long admired. An appointment was made for the following Saturday afternoon at the Renoir home.

I had been working on a series of colored drawings that I was inserting into a notebook of transparent plastic pages with a dark-green leather cover to make a compact presentation of illustrations to show any prospective financial backer. I had begun this work after my first meeting with Renoir, who had suggested that an animated film of such scope should embrace the entire history of mankind, both mythological and actual. After my meeting with Ray I enlarged the book to include a Xerox duplicate of Ray's production note as well as a duplicate of the six-page story itself, which I inserted at various portions of the book, between appropriate pages of drawings. I added also a title page announcing "In a Season of Calm Weather," with the subtitle (my own) "An Homage to Picasso by Ray Bradbury," all of which served as wording upon a full-page water-color illustration of Picasso drawing his mythological creatures in the sand of the seashore. Standing behind Picasso, unobserved, was a man witnessing with awe the creation of this Sistine-like sand mural. This man, of course, bore a more than slightly discernible resemblance to myself; this whole scene was illustrative of one of the closing moments of the story.

It would be appropriate, at this point, to give a brief summary of "In a

Season of Calm Weather" as a necessity in illuminating practically all of what is to follow.

George and Alice Smith, American tourists, are on vacation in Biarritz, France. To Alice's dismay, George can think of nothing but the possibility of meeting Picasso—whom, rumor has it, is in the area. George would give anything to own an original Picasso.

One afternoon George strolls alone along the beach. It is totally deserted, save for one other figure, who upon spying an ice-cream stick picks it up and begins to draw incredible figures along the sand. George approaches, and standing behind him unnoticed, watches as the man works away furiously, gradually covering the entire stretch of beach with a miraculous frieze of dancing, prancing creatures of Greek and Mediterranean mythology; satyrs and goats, centaurs and maidens, dryads and unicorns, all in joyous whirl of life and wild gaiety.

George trembles as he begins to realize what is taking place. Finally the old man is finished, and stands up, tossing away the ice-cream stick. He turns, surprised to see George; he smiles and shrugs as if to say, "Look what I've done—forgive an old man this, eh?" George manages to say the man's name once, in a whisper, to himself, before going absolutely panicky as to how he can preserve this masterpiece in the sand! Find a repair man, race him back here with plaster-of-Paris to cast a mould of some small portion? Run back to his hotel for his camera? No time for any of that, the sun was already setting, so George did the only thing left to do—to walk along this miraculous sand-mural and look; and walk and look till the sun was down and there was no more light by which to see.

Back at his hotel, at dinner, George is too overcome with emotion to share this incredible experience with his unappreciative wife, telling her (in reply to her mundane questioning) that nothing interesting had happened to him that day. But yes, he did swim out too far.

Suddenly George picks up his head as if to listen for some distant sound. His wife asks him what it is he hears, and he tells her to listen. She still hears nothing and asks him again what it is he hears.

"Just the tide," he says after a while, eyes shut tight. "Just the tide, coming in."

On the appointed Saturday afternoon I picked up Bradbury, and we drove to the Renoir home in Beverly Hills. Ray has a dread of all machines, including the automobile, and consequently has never driven one. The irony of this phobia has, of course, been observed on many occasions with no small measure of wry amusement. On the way I showed him my book of drawings, and he reacted with such glee and roared with such pleasure that one would have thought that each page was the eighth marvel of the world. I was, in fact, proud of the little green book, which was a pictorial embellishment of the concept Renoir and I had discussed on my first visit—that of the history of mankind—and I utilized the foldout technique on several of the drawings, including a Picasso-Michelangelo-Sistine-Ceiling effect on one of the biblical sections. The final illustration, also a foldout, was a bird's-eye view of the first drawing—that of Picasso drawing in the sand with the observer standing behind him—only now one sees the entire beach covered with Picasso's mythological creatures prancing and playing "along and along" for as far as the eye can see.

Dido Renoir met us at the door and was as warm and as gracious as she was that first meeting. She left us in the living room while she went to call Renoir. While we waited, Ray absorbed the luxurious surroundings like a small boy standing in line to see Santa Claus, then looked quickly once again through my book of drawings, closed it, held it tightly to his chest with both arms and cried, "What a treasure! What a rare treasure! It expresses exactly what I was trying to say about Picasso in my story!"

When Renoir entered the room the air became instantly permeated with the mutual enthusiasm and warmth of the two men, who had both been long-time admirers of one another for many years, and now, at last, were finally meeting. Renoir pointed to several Ray Bradbury books on his shelf and remarked at Ray's great popularity in France, at which Ray beamed more joyously than ever.

After we were seated the conversation continued in its lively exchanges of mutual admiration, and eventually we came to the exciting subject at hand, at which time Ray recounted to the older man the odd and hilarious circumstances of our meeting scarcely more than a week earlier, briefly summarizing his short story and subsequent production idea. Then he invited me to show my book to Renoir, and it was accepted with a smile of eager curiosity.

Ray huddled nearby to look over Renoir's shoulder as the book was opened, and I was overjoyed by Renoir's rapturous exclamation of approval.

So this gentle hulk of a man called Renoir and this widely smiling voltage of a man called Bradbury together pored over my green book of drawings and devoured each and every page. Bradbury looked up at me occasionally to repeat his "What a treasure!" exclamation, and Renoir would nod in enthusiastic agreement. To have reached the imaginations of such vastly different temperaments and to have penetrated, even momentarily, to so profound a level of their own creative furnaces, gave me a satisfaction beyond which I had no need to travel—at least for the moment. The bright sunlight that flooded this happily sumptuous room immortalized this scene upon my brain.

"Yes," said Renoir, "the entire history of the world!"

"The events of history entwined with mankind's mythology," exuded Bradbury. "All of a piece—moving from the dawn of life, the creatures rising from the sea, mythological as you present them here, through the beginnings of civilization right on up to our own mythology of space—'the eighth day of Creation,' the continuance of the Bible and all the wonderful mythologies of ancient Greece and Rome as Picasso has imagined them for us—one long march, one great parade, from the first day of Creation on through to beyond the future itself!"

"The story of Mankind as Picasso would see it," said Renoir. "Such a film would be a most stupendous undertaking—a landmark not only in the history of films but in the history of art itself!"

"Yes!" I said, for how well these two men grasped the meaning of the pictures. "And the animation should carry the flow of it along like a great river, without pause!"

"Like an *ocean*!" cried Bradbury. "Never mind a river!" We laughed. This was a most marvelous occasion for laughter.

"We must form a partnership of three," said Renoir. "We must each of us, together and separately, vow to do everything in our power to see to it that this film is made. Each with our own contacts must spare nothing to see to it that whatever 'powers-that-be' who can get this film financed for us are convinced of its important potential. It's *essential* that this film be made, and I for one will do everything in my power toward that end."

"And I!" cheered Bradbury.

"And I," was my echo. "But I'm afraid I've pretty well exhausted my resources! I can't tell you how thrilled I am with the new possibilities that have arisen here this afternoon!"

"I must not let you get your hopes up on my account," smiled Renoir benignly, if not without a trace of tiredness. "Many is the dream I have presented to the Hollywood moguls with the greatest of hopes, men who themselves approached me with films *they* wanted me to do for them—but when faced with the dreams of my imagination they were quick to back off, crying that my ideas were not *commercial*!"

Bradbury and I shook our heads in knowing stupefaction.

"Mind you," smiled Renoir, raising his finger expressively, "my films all made money, but the acclaim was always predominantly more of a critical than a 'popular' nature."

"Damn!" cried Bradbury. "Your films are immortal works of art! How much money did Rembrandt make, for God's sake, or van Gogh? If we artists only created to please the money moguls, the whole history of the world would be without one damn work of art!"

We laughed again, quietly painful grunts of sad acknowledgment.

"Then we are partners? said Renoir, extending his hand.

"Partners!" Bradbury and I exclaimed, joining our hands with his.

"Between us," reiterated Renoir, "I am sure that somehow we will come up with the money and backing to make this film!"

Renoir had read Bradbury's short story "In a Season of Calm Weather," but now refreshed his memory by quickly rereading it, as well as his one-page synopsis for the film treatment, both of which, as I mentioned

138

earlier, I had inserted among the pages of my drawing book. As he did so, Ray and I feasted our eyes upon the treasures within this beautiful room.

"God!" said Ray, "what a living museum this place is! Can't you just feel the presence of the old painter himself? Huh? Look at these sculptures, too—the tenderness just seems to melt the very bronze they were cast in—you can smell the sap of life bursting through, huh?"

Ray had a way of absorbing beauty that made the object observed seem as his own unique discovery, and whatever one's own feeling before this revelation, it seemed to recede swiftly in deference to the boundless Bradbury enthusiasm, as if one happened to be present at the very moment some dreamy-eyed miner, who had been tenaciously panning for gold, had suddenly hit upon a gigantic, dazzling nugget. Ray's electric enthusiasm, as he came upon each treasure in the room, like some fever-maddened explorer who had just found himself witness to Atlantis rising from the sea, made me feel as though I had not really seen any of it on my own.

I could not help but feel the tremendous bond between father and son—Renoir the great impressionist painter, and Renoir the great filmmaker who expelled, in his personal aura, the sum total of all those years that from childhood he so carefully embraced, like a great coat of gold he spun about himself as he grew; so that now he wore it with a quiet pride that needed no accounting for its being; one sensed the kindly spell it cast upon all who might pass within the presence of its beauty. I really saw these paintings, these sculptures, these soft, voluptuous, sensuous women in their floppy hats, puckering lips at happy children, the old man sitting there rereading Ray's story—all of this I saw not fragmented, but as *one*, and the Beverly Hills sunlight that streamed through the windows unified it, gave to it a cohesiveness exactly as the Paris sun must have done well over seventy years earlier when the now bald head was covered with golden curls and the child Jean sat "making his camel's coat," had begun spinning his coat of gold, exactly as his father had painted him then. What a marvelous, timeless air of simplicity pervaded this bond between father and son!

Ray felt it and was respectfully treasuring every drop, his face reflecting an inner glow full of the adulation he had so long felt for this noble elder statesman of the arts. He and I were both, I suppose, like gleeful children allowed to spend a short time in the clubhouse of their favorite baseball team, providing they behaved themsevles and did not stay too long! But our hero gave no indication that we were overstaying our welcome and, to the contrary, bid us sit down to partake of the refreshments Dido had just brought into the room, and to discuss now the handling of the live-action portion of the film.

First we reviewed the story itself, which in terms of "plot" was rather sketchy, inasmuch as it was written primarily as a sort of poetic vingette, and in what ways the story could be expanded to encompass the breadth of a film (animation not withstanding) without losing any of that sense of pure Bradbury poetry. This, of course, would be up to Bradbury himself, at some later date, and then we began to play the game of casting the characters we would like to see in the roles of George and Alice Smith. Renoir mentioned his fondness for Leslie Caron, for whom he had written the play *Orvet* in 1953. Ray and I both expressed our enthusiasm for this pixie, whom I said was a real "artists' woman"—but, of course, being French she could hardly play the prosaic American role of Alice Smith. Not that she need remain "prosaic," said Bradbury, but the strong role in any case should go to the man George Smith. I suggested that were we to get Audrey Hepburn, for example, the role of Alice could be expanded, thereby expanding in turn the role of George, with a Gregory Peck or someone of similar stature. "Ahhh!" sighed Bradbury and Renoir. "Audrey Hepburn!" It was a game, but we were having fun, and the game would eventually have to assume the dimensions of a real and earnest pursuit.

At any rate, here at last I had found the support that I knew was to carry me through. And what prestigious and high-born support! Needless to say, I was delirious with a joy that at this moment was immeasurable.

Bradbury had brought with him a copy of Renoir's book *Renoir, My Father*, which he then asked Renoir to inscribe for him. Renoir, in turn, pulled down from his shelf one of Bradbury's books—I believe it was *Fahrenheit 451*—and had Ray write an inscription for him. At that moment I regretted my long-standing attitude of never imposing upon those of stature with whom I might come in contact, and watched enviously as the two wrote absorbedly in each others' books! Renoir's inscription in Ray's copy of *Renoir, My Father* was a lenghty one, and written in French. Renoir translated it verbally for Ray, and it said something to the effect that Renoir's father would have admired Ray and would also have been honored to have met him this day; and I could not help but agonize about how much such an inscription would have meant to me in my own copy of Renoir's book, which I had not brought—but I said nothing.

Thus, after shaking hands all around and repeating our vow to make this film a reality, Ray and I took our leave of the Renoirs and drove off with an optimism far more glowing than even that with which we had arrived.

16

Follow-Up

FINALLY, IN JUNE OF 1965 A CRACK APPEARED IN THE BLACKNESS OVERHEAD and a beam of light burst through in the form of interest from MGM, and Jean Renoir and I were given an appointment with the studio's story editor, Lewis Morton. Just how abiding was this light, we were soon to discover; and one bright afternoon I called for Renoir at his home and we headed, with high hopes, for the sprawling studio in Culver City.

As we got into the elevator, a couple of young fellows with unusually long hair got off, and before the door slid closed I noticed Renoir scrutinizing them in an especially concentrated manner. This was at the time when the style was just beginning to appear, so that such a sight was unusual, rather than the order of the day, as we know it now. Hardly unable to avoid noticing Renoir's attentive look I smilingly commented on the extraordinary length of the young men's hair, noting that it might take a while to get used to this new fashion. To my amused surprise, Renoir took wide-eyed exception to my remark, stating that long hair was the style he had grown up with, and that short hair for men was actually the peculiarity of this century alone; and he expressed a nostalgic delight at the return to "normal" hair length.

The elevator door opened and we stepped out into a long hallway that seemed to stretch endlessly in both directions. Renoir looked at me expectantly, assuming that I knew whether to turn left or right; and not knowing, I arbitrarily (though hesitantly) turned to the right, and Renoir followed my lead. It was not until we were halfway down the corridor that it became obvious we were going in the wrong direction and turned to retrace our footsteps in the opposite direction. I felt terrible about this, because with Renoir's lame leg and advanced years, it was with some difficulty that he made the walk, and consequently our pace was very slow. Having passed the elevator, our point of departure, toward the opposite end of the corridor, we got halfway down the other end when I stuck my head in the nearest office and inquired as to the whereabouts of Lewis Morton. We were on the wrong floor! With great pangs of guilt I escorted Renoir, at our snail's pace, back to the elevator; and, as he was such a great sport about acting completely oblivious to his infirmity, I (following his lead) pretended to do likewise.

When we got off the elevator on the correct floor, however, we were confronted once more by the endless corridor yawning from left to right, and standing ground, I looked determinedly in both directions and told him to wait by the elevator while I looked for the office.

Finally, we were seated in Lewis Morton's plush office and made immediately to feel at home by this most pleasant man, who expressed great interest in our project. First he told Renoir of the great esteem he had so long held for him, and of the high regard and respect he had for both Renoir and Bradbury. Then, looking at me with a warm grin, he told me that though he had never before heard of me he held me in equal regard and respect, simply due to the fact that two such men as Renoir and Bradbury saw fit to associate themsevles with me in such a grand project. He felt sure that the powers-that-be at MGM would be as excited about this venture as he was himself, and after a lenghty discussion about how we all wished to go with this film and the directions it could take, Renoir and I left the studio with a soaring optimism. And since, initially, it was MGM, through their now-defunct subsudiary of SIB Productions, which had overseen my first journey to Picasso, I had especially good feelings about the rightness of a positive outcome; a feeling concurred by Lewis Morton, who was aware of my project's history and who was delighted by the pictures in my green presentation book, which he kept for use in pushing the project.

And, as our hopes soared, plummeted, and soared again as interest within the studio brightened and darkened alternately, the final plunge came in the following letter that, accompanied by my green presentation book, was delivered to me by a messenger from MGM:

June 14, 1965

Mr. Wes Herschensohn
7168 Melrose Avenue
Los Angeles, California (46)

Dear Wes:

Per our conversation, we were unfortunately, unable to get the green light on IN A SEASON OF CALM WEATHER, the project you presented to us involving Messrs. Renoir, Ray Bradbury and Picasso.

As you know, we did everything possible to put this over and I'm extremely sorry that it didn't work out for MGM.

However, we do appreciate your courtesy in giving us a crack at it, and here's wishing you all the best with it elsewhere.

Kindest personal regards,

Sincerely,
Lew Morton
Story Editor

LM:t
Enclosure
(Delivered to Mr. Herschensohn by hand)

There were many letters exchanged during this bright period of new friendships, and the following ones exemplify their tone:

Dear Wes:
    Here is a copy of THE DAY IT RAINED FOREVER, with the story IN A SEASON OF CALM WEATHER clipped with a paper-clip, to send to Mr. Duncan.
    I also enclose, on a separate sheet of paper, my brief description of how I feel the short-subject would enclose Picasso, yet give him freedom to create the animated mythologies. This, too, you may send to Mr. Duncan.
    I look forward to meeting with you and Jean Renoir, soon.
    Thanks for a stimulating hour.
    Best from yours,

signed/ Ray B.

Ray Bradbury   December 11th, 1964

P.S.
I've signed the book on the title page for Mr. Duncan!

DAVID DOUGLAS DUNCAN

CASTELLARAS 53
MOUANS-SARTOUX
A.M. FRANCE
Phone: Cannes 902453
15 January, '65

Dear Wes:

Have been working around the clock since returning from New York december 1. Struck out in my efforts to sell the deluxe picture version of YANKEE NOMAD, so now am writing it, flat out. Hit something like 50,000 words last night, so tomorrow am packing Sheila, Lump, Guffy the owl and all my writing gear into her red Austin and heading for Gstaad, switzerland, so that she can ski this winter instead of gazing at the near mountaintops, wistfully. We will be there a month: c/o Les Caprices Apts, Gstaad . . . that name *must* be an error! Shall check.

We got Ray Bradbury's book, with pleasure. Maybe he has forgotten, but he once came to my home in Rome and read the story about the dream re Picasso on the beach. I see this version as something even stronger than the bullfight film. I hope it works out. But don't count on the Maestro for any kind of cooperation. Not that he's not interested; he just gets submerged in his own projects—as you have now seen. I still have no contact: how I wish that I did, for maybe I could really help you get it on the front burner. Anyway, we all must cherish dreams as we go along—maybe this is yours. Mine? . . . am now starting a new one!

We wish you were here to head north. Sheila and Lump would cut you in on their hot chocolate—I'd con you into writing a couple chapters while I went out on the lifts to oggle the scenery. This is no letter. Just a note to tell you how we are rooting for you, and awaiting your return.

Saludos,

signed/ Dave

Please thank Bradbury for his book, for me. I'll catch up one day.

TIME AND LIFE BUILDING
Rockefeller Center
New York 20

JUdson 6-1212

March 10, 1965

Mr. Ray Bradbury
10265 Cheviot Drive
Los Angeles 64,
California

Dear Ray:

  I've forwarded the Picasso/Herschensohn/Bradbury package to Don
Congdon, as you requested. Perhaps you've forgotten, but you had told
me about this project when I was on the Coast in December. I still find it
an exciting concept, but nothing has happened to change a basic fact of
LIFE: the brass just ain't about to finance a film. But when you're set up
and ready to shoot, flash the word: all kinds of mutually rewarding LIFE
treatments might become possible.

  Keep me posted.

                                          Bests,
                                          signed/ Dave

                                          David Maness
                                          Articles Editor

DM:bs
airmail

                                          Dear Wes—
                                          Onward and upward!
                                          More next week!
                                               Best
                                                 Ray
                                                 3/17/65

17

Madrid and Dominguin—Again

ONE DAY, A SHORT TIME LATER—THIS WAS IN AUGUST 1965—I RECEIVED A call from Tom Tannenbaum, head of the West Coast television office of the now-defunct Seven Arts Productions. He told me that for years they had been trying to seduce Ray Bradbury into doing something with them for television, but to no avail. Now, Tom said, Ray had suddenly said *yes*, but that the only thing he would consider doing was the Picasso film of Wes Herschensohn, and he gave Tom my number.

The following morning I met Tannenbaum in his office, and liked him instantly. He was a tall, pleasant-looking man with a look in his eye full of ironic humor, and a mischievous air coupled with a sort of ambivalent mercurial quality that was simultaneously direct and evasive, a charm that made one immediately wish to know him better. He was married at that time to a famous and very beautiful model named Barbara Darrow, and was proud of his brother-in-law, Pancho Gonzalez, the great tennis champion. Tom's late father, David Tannenbaum, had been mayor of Beverly Hills, a man most highly respected by the entire community. (Tom himself has since become senior vice-president of television production for Paramount Studios, and later senior vice-president executive for television at Universal MCA Studios.) A most talented and amusing man—especially amusing when he let me know, in his honest and direct way, that he had his doubts about my story, finding it very hard to believe; and that a simple phone call to Dominguin, in his presence, would dispel all those doubts.

So it was with great gusto that I placed the call to Madrid from the Seven Arts office, knowing that Tannenbaum would not for long be a doubting

Thomas; and when I explained the purpose of my call to Dominguin, he was both amused and elated that the project was at last beginning to move again. Tom was literally wild with joy, and spoke at great length with the delighted Dominguin.

"Jesus!" cried Tom, after hanging up the phone. "I can't believe this! I was actually talking to the great Dominguin! When Bradbury told me about your project I thought he had fallen for some kind of snow job; I mean, Picasso, Stravinsky, Dominguin, those men actually interested in working on a film of this kind!" Tom laughed uproariously. "I said to Bradbury, 'Wes Herschensohn? Who the hell is Wes Herschensohn?' "

Preparations for a trip to Madrid were soon under way, following subsequent conversations with Dominguin, who would be acting as Picasso's authorized power-of-attorney in the signing of any contracts, since Picasso himself would never attach his signature to any document of a legal nature. (This became only too evident in the now-famous legal battle over his estate that ensued after his death in April 1973.) For myself, I was not all that enthused on the idea of doing the film for television as opposed to the large motion picture screen, but it was certainly better than no film at all, and to that extent I was indeed relieved and, soon enough, appropriately enthused.

Tom and I began the first step of our journey to Madrid by stopping off at the Seven Arts head office in New York, where we were to pick up Tom's boss, Robert Rich, the executive vice-president of Seven Arts, who was to make the trip with us. I was to present my portfolio to Rich and all the executives of Seven Arts and explain the entire concept of my film at this meeting before the three of us went on to Madrid. The very businesslike New York atmosphere of the office was at first a little disconcerting as I approached the conference table of suit-and-tie executives, but there was something so likable about the solicitous courtesy of Bob Rich, something so "square" and open, that I was put quickly at ease; and as Bob Rich went, so went the executives. My portfolio was an instant smash, and Tom was as delighted as I at the smoothness and cordiality of the meeting.

The three of us sat together in the first-class compartment on the flight to Madrid, the most unlikely trio imaginable and yet entirely compatible and good-humored. This was the first trip to Europe for both of these men, and neither could conceal their almost childlike joy. Nor could I conceal my amusement at the relationship of Rich and Tannenbaum. Bob Rich, so square and proper, hair combed back so flatly in place, speaking almost in platitudes, already missing his wife from whom he had never before been away; and Tom Tannenbaum, the debonair swinger with the knowing look who would glance at me with amusement and raise his eyes to heaven at each of Rich's platitudes—but with an affection for his middle-aged boss that I most certainly shared.

It was late in the evening when we landed exhausted at the Madrid airport, to the familiar applause of raindrops and confusion. After submitting to the routines of retrieving baggage and customs inspection, we waited at the designated spot for the arrival of Dominguin's limousine, which was to take us to the matador's home, where we were to be guests during our brief stay in Madrid. After half an hour we began to realize that there was obviously a mix-up, for no limousine or familiar face was in sight, nor did we hear what would have subsequently been the welcome sound of our names being paged over the loudspeaker system. After placing a call to Dominguin's home I was, with great language-barrier difficulty, informed by a servant that Dominguin was in *Paris* and was to return on the following day!

Tom and Bob greeted this news with enthusiasm equal to my own, and, disgruntled, tired, and hungry, we took a taxi to the Madrid Hilton. Our troubles, however, had only begun! Before we arrived at the Hilton I had already warned my companions of the difficulty of obtaining a room in Madrid, even *with* reservations, and related to them the experiences of my first trip to this fair city. Tom, however, assured me that we would have no problems, and I somehow felt comforted by the unseen backing and authority of the powerful Seven Arts Corporation, which I had not at my disposal on my first lonely visit to Madrid, and I was content to put my trust in these powerful hands. When the hotel concierge informed Tom that there were no rooms available, he unflinchingly explained to the concierge that the attorney Greg Bautzer was one of his closest friends, and that Greg Bautzer was the attorney for Conrad Hilton himself; for everyone knows that there are *always* rooms available in hotels of this kind for the right parties, and it simply is up to those right parties to make themselves known, as Tom was correctly doing.

"I don't care," responded the concierge, "if you are Conrad Hilton himself, sir! We do not have a single room left in the entire hotel!"

Remembering my identical plight one year earlier, after being informed now, as then, that there were no rooms whatsoever left in town, I suggested to Tom that he ask the concierge to check with the Hotel Rondo, where I had found the only available shelter in the city. Predictably, that shelter was still available, but there were only two rooms left, and we told the concierge to reserve them for us.

"Is there room for us in your dining room?" Tom asked facetiously. " "We're dying of hunger."

"Oh, of course, senor," replied the concierge. "You may leave your bags here at the desk and enjoy a fine dinner. They are holding your rooms at the Hotel Rondo, so you may relax and dine at your leisure, senors. At your leisure."

And we did; compliments of Seven Arts we ate a hearty meal, during which I attempted to raise the spirits of my companions by explaining to them that neither the city of Madrid nor Dominguin were discriminating against them, and related my devastatingly identical experience on my first trip here; even to the extent of extolling the virtues of the simple but charming Hotel Rondo, which was to house us for the night.

"And as for Luis Miguel," I explained, "he just got his wires crossed, but once we get to him you'll see that he'll go out of his way to make it all up to us. Really. The most gracious guy you'll ever meet."

And with that I was greeted by a look in Tom's weary eye that set me to laughing almost uncontrollably.

After retrieving our bags at the desk and being assured by the concierge that a taxi would be available within minutes, we waited outside expectantly, the rain having temporarily subsided. After ten or fifteen minutes without a cab in sight, we decided to walk, baggage and all, to a more densely populated area of the city where finding a taxi would be a simple matter, expecting that one would certainly come along as we walked. It was not long until we discovered that there *was* no densely populated area—in the small hours of the morning; and finding ourselves in the middle of a sprawling, completely deserted intersection, we decided to split up and stand at opposite ends of the intersection, hoping thereby to increase our chances of attracting a taxi. It then began to rain once again.

We were three miserable men, incredulous at our own plight, unable to believe that such a ridiculous thing was actually taking place; when suddenly, from his post on a far corner of the intersection, Bob let out a yelp, and within seconds the three of us were converging maniacally on a lone taxi that had ventured miraculously into our lair; and like wild beasts attacking a long-awaited prey, we pounced upon the vehicle and burst inside, shouting "Hotel Rondo! Hotel Rondo!" at the startled driver, who must have thought that all hell had broken loose.

Predictably, the street in front of the hotel was still in a state of upheaval, or "repair," exactly as I had left it over a year earlier, and Tom and Bob were aghast at the dismal appearance of the building itself; so it was with a mixture of relief and apprehension that we approached the hotel desk. After the clerk acknowledged our reservations, Tom asked him what kind of rooms he had for us, inquiring, that is, as to their condition, those being the only two rooms left in the place.

"Sheet," replied the desk clerk, in broken English, shaking his head sadly.

"You mean," asked Tom confusedly, "we have no sheets?"

"No," said the clerk. *"Sheet!"*

And how right he was! Tom and I agreed to let Bob Rich take the single room down the hall while we accepted the dingy room with two narrow beds that directly adjoined the only toilet on the floor.

The decision that Tom and I were soon forced to make was whether to open our window and freeze to death or leave it closed and die of the smell of urine. Compounding this circumstance was the fact that one of the tenants on our floor deemed it necessary to enter the toilet every fifteen minutes, to add insult to injury with a supply that staggered the imagination; and had we been able to sleep this would have rendered such a blissful state impossible at any rate. Before actually settling into bed, however, we decided to check down the hall to see if Bob was faring any better, only to meet him halfway, on his way to our room to express his agonized dismay; whereupon both men turned on me with a look of incredulous disbelief— that I could actually have spent three days here and come away extolling the charms of the place as I had done at dinner. I explained that I had forgotten the smell, that I had been staying in a nicer room, and that at least the hotel dining room would be a welcome surprise. I related the pleasantness of the attractive hostess I had befriended during my stay, as well as the delicious cuisine.

Morning could not have come soon enough, and the three of us were the first to enter the dining room for breakfast. To my dismay the friendly hostess was not there, and the only familiar sight to greet my eyes was the wall-sized mural copy of Goya's painting of the picnickers in the countryside, and even this now looked very different to me, for in my imagination I saw it through the bloodshot eyes of my weary friends.

After some difficulty in conveying our selection to the waiter, we settled for the safe thing—eggs. With a twinge of pain, I prefer to pass over Tom's reaction to the eggs, except to say that he thought they were the worst he had ever tasted.

"Well Tom," I smiled brightly. "How do you like Madrid so far?"

Dominguin was all apologies as we drove away in his limousine while Tom turned for one last look of disbelief through the rear window, as the charming little Hotel Rondo grew smaller as Francisco, Dominguin's chauffeur, drove away.

"You see," explained Miguel, "I thought you were to arrive *today*, and when you called me thees morning just as I was returneeng from Paris, I felt as though I had been gored by a bool!"

We all laughed, relieved that the nightmare was over, and it was clear that my companions had already fallen under the spell of elegance and charm that constituted the personality of the legendary matador who was to be our host for the next couple of days.

Dominguin, noticing our bleary-eyed and disjointed condition, suggested that we postpone all talk of business and spend the day relaxing at his home on the outskirts of Madrid, and he instructed Francisco accordingly.

I must pause here to note in passing a minor distraction regarding Spanish pronunciation as opposed to the Mexican pronunciation of the same words, which was to become a source of great private hilarity between Tom and myself; who, both being raised in California and used to the Mexican version of the Spanish language, found it difficult to adjust to the

150

Statue of Dominguin at his ranch. (PHOTO BY
THE AUTHOR)

difference in these particular pronunciations. For example, the *s* sound in the Mexican dialect was in these cases the *th* sound in true Spanish, causing the familiar *gracias* (or *gra-sious*) of our Mexican neighbors to become *gra-thious* in the language's homeland, and ad infinitum. Therefore, *gracias, Francisco* became *grathias, Franthisco* and so on; and to our tired ears and almost complete exhaustion, these sounds became for Tom and myself a signal, each time they were uttered, for a suppressed hysteria almost beyond bearing. So that, to us, *Grathias, Franthisco* in turn became *Grathiath, Franthithco* and there followed a nightmare of will power in our attempt to prevent the tearful laughter in our eyes from overflowing into a raucous guffaw that could only offend our gracious host.

Once settled poolside at Dominguin's lush residence, the four of us enjoyed the afternoon sun with grateful relish, and relaxation was the order of the day. Tom, who was concerned about the condition of his clothes, decided, as was sometimes his custom on trips, to hang them in the bathroom and turn on the hot water in the shower till the accumulating steam vaporized the wrinkles out of the clothing. For this purpose he used the little building near the pool, which served as dressing room and guest house with a large bathroom and shower adjoining the bedroom.

After an hour or so, Dominguin commented on the fact that our friend "Tomás" had been gone for an unusually long time, suggesting that such a process should not require the entire afternoon, and he decided to see if Tom was having any problems. I watched as he walked over to the guest house and opened the door, then got up to join him. The entire room was filled with a curious haze, through which one could discern the limp figure of Tom Tannenbaum sprawled across the bed.

"Tomás?" Dominguin inquired. Then louder, *"Tomás?"*

Upon which the limp figure began to stir, as Tom lifted his head sleepily and looked at Dominguin standing in the doorway, through the haze. "Huh?" said Tom, "wuzzat?" Then, sitting bolt upright he cried out in bewilderment. "Omigod! I must have fallen asleep! The bathroom! The steam! My clothes!"

When the bathroom door was opened the two men were almost overpowered by the steam, and shielding his face with his arms, Tom rushed over to the shower to turn off the water. When the air was somewhat cleared, a scene of total disaster began to come into focus before the dismayed eyes of the two men. For the bathroom walls were not the usual tile walls Tom had been used to, in the hotels in which he had on previous occasions used this steaming process for his clothes; instead, what once had been four beautifully papered bathroom walls was now a nightmare of decomposition. Each individual row of wallpaper was curling forward and downward at a different rate of surrender, and with a cry of despair and guilt, Tom rushed in and frantically attempted to push each row of paper back into place, individually and simultaneously. Dominguin, who had by now come out of shock, began to laugh in disbelief, and as he watched Tom, in his guilt, so uproariously attempting the impossible, he fell down laughing at the sight.

"Well," I asked Tom shortly afterward, "how do you like Madrid so far?"

"Muy thenthasional," he replied.

That night the four of us were sitting on the outer patio sipping our after-dinner drinks when Dominguin leaned over to switch on the television set. He turned to us, grinning broadly. "The Saint!" he announced. I never mees eet!"

"The Saint?" Tom asked. "You mean the one with Roger Moore? I didn't know it was seen here in Madrid."

"Oh, si!" replied Dominguin. "Dubbed een Spanish, but I explain to you as eet goes along, anyhow ees mostly action."

Suddenly, after ten minutes into "The Saint," a vision of loveliness appeared, but not on the television screen. It was Miguel's wife, Lucia Dominguin, dressed in a ravishing blue evening gown. With a shy smile of acknowledgment to Tom, Bob, and myself, she flashed an unmistakable look of anger at Miguel, who seemed unaffected, and she quietly said something to him in Spanish. Turning to us, he explained that Lucia had just reminded him that they were supposed to attend an important party this evening, but he explained to us, and then to Lucia, in Spanish, that he would not leave his guests. We, of course, implored him to go on ahead with his wife, assuring him that we would be perfectly all right, and would feel terrible if he stayed home on our account.

"But, señors," said Dominguin, "eet ees not entirely on your account! You see, I never mees "The Saint," I look forward to eet each week, and theese party—eet ees not important that I attend—Lucia can go by herself!"

There followed a quiet but heated exchange of words between husband and wife, after which a furious Lucia stormed off to attend the party alone.

"So much," smiled Dominguin weakly, "for the married life."

After "The Saint" was over, the three of us spent the remainder of the evening, before retiring, in lively conversation, with Dominguin doing most of the talking. He told us about his relationship with Ernest Hemingway, who had for a long time been a great admirer of Dominguin's until, after some sort of falling out, had switched his allegiance to Dominguin's cousin, the great matador Ordoñez. Subsequently, Hemingway wrote an expansive article on bullfighting for *Life* magazine in which his intention was to pan Dominguin (his former hero) in favor of Ordoñez. Dominguin, however, informed Hemingway that if this article was printed as written he would "own" Hemingway, and when the article finally appeared in the magazine, the references to Dominguin had been toned down considerably.

Next we were treated to a firsthand view of some of Miguel's most

The author at Dominguin's ranch home—
and wearing his hat! (PHOTO BY LOIS
SEGERMAN)

impressive scars, which he proudly revealed to us from under his pulled-up shirt. Then he brought out a stack of his corrida photographs showing himself in action, saving his favorite, and by far the most startling, till last. In this photo, Dominguin was pinned to a wooden wall at the far end of the arena, by one horn of the bull which was implanted into the wall between Dominguin's legs and *directly under his testicles;* and in this way the bull had lifted him several feet off the ground and thrust him against the wall. Dominguin laughingly recalled the horrified screams of the women as the entire multitude rose, horrified, to its feet. And yet Dominguin survived this ordeal without a scratch, for the bull's horn had missed that sacred portion of the anatomy by an infinitesimal fraction of an inch, serving only to lift him off the ground and pinning him to the wall. It was a photograph Dominguin understandably prizes above all others, as a constant reminder of his great good fortune!

Another time, however, he was not so lucky. For once, he laughingly recalled, a bull had actually succeeded in partially severing one of his testicles. Rushed on a stretcher to the official corrida physician, Dominguin took one look at this doctor and decided that he would not let him touch him, certain that this man would amputate without hesitation. Upon which, holding his own testicle in place, Dominguin ordered his brother, who was among those in attendance, to take him immediately to his own physician. So, unbelievably (but true), Dominguin, leaning for support on his brother's shoulder, and still holding himself together, left the arena and got into the first taxi they saw. The taxi, however, was occupied by a staid and very proper English lady who expressed horrified shock at the intrusion. The taxi driver instantly recognized the famous matador and saw the situation, racing like a demon for Dominguin's doctor. For almost the entire duration of the trip the proper English lady never ceased her admonishment of her intruders' bad manners and Dominguin's incessant spilling of blood. She was silenced, finally, by Dominguin's assurance that he was not about to sacrifice one of the family jewels for her!

While on the subject of bullfighting, Tom asked Dominguin for his opinion of the young matador who at that time was all the rage, and known internationally as the new hero of the arena, whereupon Dominguin smilingly dismissed him as a "butcher." Afterward, before turning in for the night, he called us over to a table in the living room to show us his real "pride and joy." It was a small cutout, a statue of flat wood with a picture pasted on either side, given to him by Picasso. Looking at the front, we saw Picasso himself, grinning mischievously in his famous striped shirt and baggy pants. On the other side of the cutout, however, was Picasso again—another front view, but this time stark naked, and grinning even more mischievously than before!

That marvelous set of ceramic dishes by Picasso upon which he had painted (in silhouette) his impression of an entire bullfight in sequence form, and which Dominguin had on display on the wall above his mantelpiece, was a source of amazement and delight to Tom and Bob and most certainly to myself, who had seen it on my first visit to this wonderful home.

When we were shown to our rooms, Tom and I could hardly hide our amusement when Dominguin took us quietly aside to apologize for giving the best room to the "old man" whom Dominguin admired and felt should be shown the proper respect.

The following day, at Dominguin's office, the talk of business was finally under way. Dominguin told me that Picasso had wondered what had happened to me after one whole year; that out of loyalty of his promise to me he had refused his old wartime friend Foster's request to design the characters and settings for an animated film of *Don Quixote*. This, of course, was in no way similar to my project, wherein Picasso was to actually *do* the animation with me. Dominguin said that Picasso wondered why he had never heard from me throughout the whole past year, and I replied, "But how could I tell Picasso that no one was interested enough to finance it?"

We had been introduced to Dominguin's representative, Señor Vicuna, who was going to work with us on the business arrangements, and it was agreed that in the following month, September, we would all meet for further negotiations at the Seven Arts office in New York; hopefully, to finalize the deal and ensure a speedy and agreeable shift into actual production and the ultimate participation of Picasso himself.

18

New York—and the Nadir

WHEN DOMINGUIN ARRIVED IN NEW YORK (THIS WAS SEPTEMBER 1965), IT was with a big splash; he appeared on all the talk shows, including Johnny Carson's, and had many newspaper and magazine interviews as well.

Tom and I made the trip to New York together, and, as fate would have it, we once again had reservation trouble at the hotel and were stuck together in one room. Actually, it was a suite with a large living room, but the bedroom contained only one bed. We stared at the bed disconsolately and bemoaned the fact that we would have to share it! Upon pulling back the spread, however, we discovered happily that the *one* bed became *two*—twin beds joined together as one. Even though they were connected at the heads, we made the best of the situation and got some sleep before the big day.

On the morrow, at the Seven Arts office of Bob Rich, we met with Dominguin and a bevy of Seven Arts executives. Señor Vicuna had been replaced by Dominguin's new partner, Pedro Rodriguez, a handsome, blond-haired, blue-eyed man with refined, chiseled features, who spoke English fluently.

To my surprise I suddenly received the highest compliment of my artistic career when Dominguin announced to me, in front of this crowd of executives, that Picasso treasured those drawings and paintings that I had left with him on my visit in 1964; that, in fact, he kept them stacked against the wall of his bedroom among his favorite things—and that once, to illustrate to Dominguin an artistic point he was trying to make, he pulled

157

out a certain board on which I had painted a series of bullfight pictures in sequential order and said, "Ah! This is what I mean! This is *magnifico!*"

In regard to the business transactions and agreements and dis-agreements themselves, of which this meeting was only the beginning, and which ultimately spanned a period of three months or so, it can be summarized in this way. Elliot Hyman, the head of Seven Arts, was by no means pleased with the fact that Picasso himself would be signing no agreement; and he wanted Dominguin to guarantee that Seven Arts would receive all of Picasso's animation drawings at the completion of the film—this as *collateral*—an amount that of course, would have surpassed the cost necessary to finance half a dozen films! Also, Hyman wanted a European director named Costa-Gavras, of whom neither Tom nor myself had ever heard; while we, of course, along with Ray Bradbury, could conceive of no one but Jean Renoir—and refused to give in on this point. Though, privately, we were beginning to doubt whether Renoir would be able to perform this function, due to failing health.

One point that was agreed upon, however, was to me the most heartening and exciting result of all this haranguing and bargaining; it was agreed that Seven Arts would rent me a villa in Mougins, as close as possible to Picasso's home! Dominguin also could stay there if he wished, in order to transport Picasso back and forth, or whatever arrangements Picasso himself would prefer; wherein I would then teach Picasso the craft of animation *for as long as it might take*, be it half a year or whatever, in preparation for the film, and all at the agreed expense of Seven Arts. Need I say that I was in ecstasy?

This was all to begin in January 1966. But the blackest day was yet to come, when one evening in the December preceding the blessed January, I turned to the news on my car radio as I was driving home, only to get the tail-end of a news item saying that "the great artist is in fair condition after major surgery." Who else could they have been talking about? I was devastated!

What happened was that Picasso had gone to the American Hospital in Paris for a gall bladder operation. At the ripe old age of eighty-three this, of course, could be extremely dangerous. Naturally, this also meant that the project was finished. Dominguin called from Madrid in near tears to tell me that although Picasso would probably be all right (he recovered beautifully after a year of rest), the film would have to be shelved. He also sent me a letter to this effect.

I could not accept this, because it had become my life's obsession; in fact, my life itself. I remembered hearing somewhere a quotation: "You're not finished when you're defeated—you're finished when you quit," and this expressed my feelings completely. I was determined not to let my anguish suffocate me, and I held out for some sign of fresh air. Dominguin made several visits to Picasso on my behalf with the intention of broaching the subject of the film, but backed down each time, so that Picasso would not think that this was the sole purpose of his visit. He might have considered this a selfish request, since it had been agreed with Seven Arts that Dominguin would appear as himself in the film.

After several more anguished phone calls back and forth with Dominguin throughout that unbearable year, I decided that it was once again time for me to take action, though I was not sure just then what that "action" should be.

19

Return to Cannes—December 1966

IN EARLY DECEMBER 1966, IT BECAME CLEAR WHAT I HAD TO DO; AND although I recognized it as an act of desperation, I was determined, out of a combination of this desperation and sheer willpower, to see it through. With money for plane fare generously loaned to me by my brother Bruce, I took off once more for Cannes and Picasso. I took with me the short animated film Picasso had requested me to do. Instead of merely one minute, in black and white, as he frugally suggested, I had done four minutes, in color, using as a musical sound track the Concierto *Aranjuez* by the blind contemporary composer Rodrigo. The subject of the film was the Bullfight. I had managed to capture in the animation what until then had been merely an elusive idea of unborn rhythms.

The difference between this journey and my first was the difference between night and day. Whereas my first trip was made in a burst of positive, spontaneous optimism and sheer elation, born of a feeling of inevitable sureness in my own artistic destiny, this trip was made with a heavy sense of overwhelming despair and a sick feeling in the pit of my stomach, which I was fighting every minute to conquer.

Even the stewardesses of Air France, who on my first flight were nymphlike angels in attendance, seemed to me now like mocking, time-worn symbols of my own defeats. I disliked them down to their red nail polish, so uniformly manicured on each and every finger, which on my first flight had so pleased me.

The plane landed at the airport in Nice where I was to take a bus to Cannes. It was a dismal Sunday night, and gloom pervaded every atom of the cold and empty atmosphere. To make matters worse, my loneliness was compounded by my being the only passenger on the bus! And, as if to emphasize my own fate, I sat myself in the center of the empty vehicle and looked out into the blackness of the night, while the bus driver, a woman, occasionally attempted conversation. I could not help comparing to myself the differences between this journey and my first trip from Nice to Cannes two and one-half years earlier. At that time I had rented a Volkswagon and drove through the lush green countryside in the glorious sunlight of late springtime; oddly enough, then too, my only companion was female—an attractive young French woman I had met at the Nice airport and who directed my way along the road to Cannes—a far cry from the burly woman bus driver on this dismal night. However, the driver was not without sympathy for my dismay at what I saw upon our entry into Cannes. For Cannes was absolutely barren; a stark contrast to my original entry into the wonderland of bright festive sunshine heralding Picasso's Mediterranean mythology, when the city swarmed with half-naked goddesses and the kaleidoscopic colors of the Film Festival madness! Now, everything was boarded up! Not only were all the hotels closed till Christmas, but, horror of horrors—my beloved Walsdorff-Victoria bore a sign stating that it was to be torn down to make way for a large apartment complex!

"Ah, oui," the lady bus driver sympathized, after translating the message on the sign for my unbelieving ears, "that is the saddest blow of all!"

The only hotel open was the Hotel Majestic, more expensive than I could afford, but I was forced to check in anyhow. As a further blow, the night clerk was a sarcastic young fellow, who not only hated Americans, but having lived for a year in Los Angeles, felt that this qualified him to hate Angelenos especially. He thought, of course, that he was a most amusing fellow, but I (unfortunately) had left my sense of humor in L.A.

After checking into my room and looking about disconsolately at the four luxurious walls, I decided to get out and take a walk through the town, with the hope of finding Claude at home, and with the double hope that she would welcome me after so long an absence with so little communication from me. I had telephoned Duncan from Los Angeles several weeks before leaving, and he had told me that it would probably be a good time to come, for Picasso was now being seen on the streets once again, and fairly regularly; but he himself, unfortunately, would be out of the country, and Sheila would be with her family in New York. And so I took myself into the streets. And yes: what two and one-half years earlier had been a paganlike eruption of color and joyous celebration; of warm good health and the shimmering fireworks of Day itself; sun, open blue sky, smiling sea, swarms of people in love with people—now was a morgue of invisible corpses sheathed in the cold of Night and the hollowness of an empty eye socket. Everywhere I looked my gaze was returned by the emptiness. What a barren place I found, returning to a lover of yesterday to find her prematurely aged, wrinkled, dead in all those aspects that before were bursting with the sap and flow of good life.

Half frozen, I walked the old familiar streets and rounded the old town a dozen times, approaching again and again the Rue d'Antibes, the avenue that brought the Galerie Art de France into sight; each approach certain that *this* time the light above the gallery, the light from Claude's upstairs apartment, would be lit—and, instead, met each time by a mocking darkness. There was no answer to my ring, the gallery window was clothed with the iron gate, and inside was blackness and a despairing stillness, barren like the rest of the city.

How brave I had felt that first time when Cannes had catapulted herself forward to greet me in that blaze of daylight colors, and I had fallen instantly in love with this mythic goddess, bronzed and sensuous; sure that those gleaming twin domes of the Carlton were no less than her proud breasts full of the richest and most forbidden of promises! They were in blackness now against the night, almost unseen, and it was with a great, despairing heaviness that I could even bring myself to look.

Then, as I passed between two buildings where on the left the dark sea spread beneath the sky, equally black and friendless, I saw, walking along the stretch of pavement that preceded the beach, a slender lady in a long heavy coat, collar turned up against a head of curly brown hair. She was walking slowly and as dejectedly as I was walking on the sidewalk of the city. She seemed at first not to be real, and I made no effort to turn left toward the beach for a closer look, though I was hungry for contact and fought stiffly against the ever-growing nightmare thought that I made a macrocosmic mistake in returning to Cannes! But several minutes later, between two buildings further along, I caught another glimpse of her, this time standing still with her head gazing downward in an attitude of despair that surpassed my own. And how much colder she must have been, so close to the sea, which seemed to be noticing her with a curiosity much less friendly than mine! Without hesitation I turned swiftly to my left and walked toward the beach where the lady was still standing, frighteningly alone. With each step nearer she came more sharply into focus, her beautiful fragile features troubled with an inward intensity that startled me into slowing my pace and approaching more casually. She raised her head and turned to me, and the curve of her long lovely throat emphasized the vulnerability of her demeanor, so that it was with the most gentle manner I could summon that I bid her a good evening, accompanied by the most benevolent smile it was within me to produce. Before I knew what was happening she was walking swiftly away from me, looking back over her shoulder with an expression of such fear that I myself became afraid, and watched with amazement as she disappeared into the night.

And so, I made my way back into the street, feeling (if possible) more sorry for myself than before. I continued circling the town in the

162

unbearable coldness, hoping like some desperate freezing madman, each time I came once again to the Rue d'Antibes, that *this* time I would see the light on above Claude's gallery!

Finally I returned to the hotel only to find that I was accidentally locked out of my room, and all attempts by the hotel management at opening the lock to get me back in were unsuccessful, and I was given the neighboring room—with all of my belongings locked up in the original room! How many times have we learned, through bitter experience, that despair begets despair, just as joy begets joy; and that the hammer never hits just once, but with a succession of blows. But all things pass, or at least abate—and it was to the sound of a different sort of hammer to which I awoke the next morning—the pounding of the locksmith working his way into my original room next door; and I dressed quickly in order to get my things and to feel some semblance of order.

After a hurried breakfast, I rushed outside full of hope that this new day, Monday would bring me better luck. I had already called the Duncan residence, after resituating myself in my own room, to check whether they were still out of town and was informed by their housekeeper that they were, indeed, gone for the holidays.

I had a better feeling approaching Claude's gallery in the light of day, though the sky was a dismal gray, and I was momentarily elated when, upon ringing the bell of her upstairs apartment, I heard footsteps approaching the door. My hopes plummeted when Claude's housekeeper Rose answered, only to tell me that Claude was out of town and would return in a few days; for to my weary mind a few more days would seem like years, Claude being the only one to whom I could turn for assistance and advice. Rose further informed me that Claude had a new gallery, better situated, on a corner along the Croisette, which she called "Wonder's Corner", using the English wording, and that her gallery Art de France was now vacated.

I walked to the Wonder's Corner gallery and saw that it was open, and that its location and situation on the corner was indeed advantageous, and that it was a most attractive and bright little place. A brilliant selection of colored Chagall lithographs dominated the display in the windows, which faced out on the intersecting streets, separated by the door. Inside sat an attractive young girl with dark red hair, who turned out to be Claude's new assistant, Colette. She spoke painfully little English, equal only to my painfully bad French, but we managed to communicate, and she accepted me as a sort of fixture for the next couple of days; for I used the gallery as a home-base where I could sit looking at art books and watch the colorful traffic of curious customers and art connoisseurs, as a substitute for my aimless wandering.

It was with a sense of enormous relief and gladness when, approaching the gallery's entrance on Wednesday morning, I saw Claude's face through the window, watching for me expectantly, as Colette looked on smilingly. It was a warm and happy reunion, but much had changed. Claude chided me, explaining that when I had stopped writing her and had not answered her cards and letters she assumed she would never see me again. She now had a new lover named Robert, a prosperous jeweler. However, our friendship was undamaged and the old warmth glowed as generously as ever it had before, and I was soon to find that Claude's loyalty to me was as strong as ever. She had called my hotel as soon as Colette told her I was in Cannes, but I was already on my way to her gallery.

She told me that this was the worst possible time I could have come to see Picasso, because there was presently, in Paris, a one-man show of his works—the largest one-man show in history—and that Picasso was incommunicado to *everyone*. She said that a week before my arrival the director of the exhibit himself came from Paris to talk to Picasso about the show, and that Picasso was out even to *him*! I told her that when I had spoken to Dave Duncan the previous month, in early November, and told him of my plans to return to Cannes, he had told me that this would be an excellent time to come and that Picasso was once again being seen out walking in the town.

"Ah yes, my poor Wes," Claude replied, "had you come *then*—but wait." She got up and walked over to a small cabinet from which she took a large Picasso book. Opening it to the title page she brought it over to me. There, scrawled across the entire page was a vigorous sketch of a clown's face made by Picasso for Claude's children, with an inscription to them dated November 14, 1966, only *weeks earlier*!!! Yes, Claude confirmed that had I arrived but two weeks earlier, I would have seen Picasso at almost any given time in Claude's gallery, for this book had been inscribed there, in this very room, sitting upon the very chair in which I then was sitting, reading the inscription!

"He came every day into town," Claude said, "to see me, like the old days, before Jacqueline puts to eet a stop!"

To see Claude! Every day! My sense of frustration soared and swelled till I thought it would burst through my head. For with Claude, I could have accomplished more with Picasso in five minutes than in five weeks through anyone else.

She told me that one day after she began going with Robert she walked with him into the outdoor terrace of a restaurant where Picasso and his Jacqueline happened to be seated. When Jacqueline caught sight of Claude with her new friend Robert, she cried out loud enough for the entire assemblage to hear, "Huh! She certainly changes her lovers often enough!" Picasso then became furious, and remonstrated his wife in tones even louder than her own, and Jacqueline stormed out of the restaurant in tears.

It was too late, now, however, for my own tears, and Claude advised me that the best thing for me to do would be to send flowers to Jacqueline to let the Picassos know I was here, and where I was staying, and then to wait a few days for some reply at my hotel. As expected, from what Claude had told me of the Picassos' complete "disappearance" during this exhibit, there was no reply, and my hotel placed a number of calls for me to the Picasso residence, but to no avail. Supposedly, they were out of town.

In desperation one night thereafter, I called Dominguin, only to find that he was not in Madrid, but was in Versailles. I contacted him in Versailles, and he was distressed to learn that I had made this long trip to France without first checking with him on the wisdom of such a move at this time.

"Oh Wes," he said, "why you don't call me first to tell me you go to France to see Picasso? Ees very bad time; Picasso sees no one now because of the great exhibit een Paris!" He then told me he would call Picasso immediately and tell him that I was in Cannes to see him, and that the following day I should call Picasso's home again, informing whomever answered that Dominguin told me to call and that Picasso was expecting my call. I was elated, and the following afternoon I had the hotel phone the residence once more, explaining to the servant as Dominguin had directed. But *still* the same answer!

Dismayed, I called Dominguin back that night and told him that it did not work, and in a rather hurt tone he told me that he *himself* was not able to get through, and that the servant told him the same thing—that the Picassos were out of town. He told me he *knew* that they were home, and that it was the first time ever that Picasso would not come to the phone for him. He said that he would try one more time, and that the next day I should call again, with the same message.

So the next day, instead of having the hotel call for me, I explained the whole thing to Claude and asked her to do it. With my limited French it would have been impossible to do it myself in a matter where proper communication was of such importance. However, Claude replied that it would be disastrous for me if she called, in the event that Jacqueline answered, because Jacqueline hated Claude with a venom—not merely because of Picasso's repeated visits to her gallery, but more especially because of that incident in the restaurant where Picasso had humiliated Jacqueline on Claude's account. I entreated with Claude to call anyway, figuring that Jacqueline would not recognize her voice, and that probably a servant would answer.

Against her better judgment Claude called for me, and Jacqueline *did* answer! Maintaining her cool, Claude explained to her that Dominguin had asked Monsieur Herschensohn to call Picasso, and before Claude could finish, Jacqueline shouted, "It's none of your business *what* M'sieur Dominguin told M'sieur Herschensohn!" and banged down the receiver. Claude looked at me wide-eyed, blowing simulated steam from her mouth and shaking her hand back and forth from a limp wrist, as from a burn.

"My poor Wes," she said. "My poor Wes!"

That night Claude and Robert invited me to dinner, giving me a written address of a restaurant where I was to take a cab and meet them at nine o'clock, in a mountainous area above Cannes where they would be horseback riding till just before dinner. When my cab drove up at the designated time its headlights shown directly on my two friends who stood waiting for me in their riding clothes—boots, jodhpurs, and all—in front of an elegant secluded restaurant that was obviously exclusive. It was to be the first and last decent meal of my entire dismal winter visit. We discussed the remaining possibilities of my getting to see Picasso with my film and came to the conclusion that there were none. I had come to Cannes on a two-week group charter flight and could not return sooner than the specified date without a considerable increase in cost, and my financial reserve was being rapidly depleted.

Claude, therefore, saw to it that I was situated in an apartment—inexpensive but attractive—through a woman friend who managed the building. It was far more charming and comfortable than my lushly extravagant and expensive room at the Hotel Majestic, and I set about trying to work out some sort of budget for myself.

I would spend most of my days in the Wonder's Corner gallery with Claude and Colette and, not wishing to impose further upon Claude, would leave just before closing time.

The gallery, however, was hardly a bad place to while away the time, for Claude had quite a number of illustrious clients, including Marc Chagall, whose lithographs she was handling, and the old painter Pignon, who would come in often with his wife and sit and chat in the grand French style. And often, too, Claude would take me along to the various homes or apartments of prospective clients, especially of those who imagined they had something quite special to sell, which was rarely the case.

One man in particular wasted a good chunk of Claude's afternoon, having called her over to see some fabulous paintings he had recently acquired in Brittany. First, upon answering the door, he was obviously displeased to see that Claude came accompanied by myself; second, his apartment was ill-lit and unkempt, with many tiny rooms that seemed to form a narrow, half-circular curve—a most peculiar place; and third, the paintings were so unbelievably amateurish, the sort made by school children but without the charming naivete of such paintings—only sticky-pretty paintings without muscle or bone. Each time the man would hold one up for viewing, Claude would step behind him as if to get a closer look over his shoulder, and then would look at me and cross her eyes and grimace wildly with her tongue hanging out.

With my finances in such a deplorable state it was inevitable that I would soon form a pattern of "dining" that was less than enviable. For dinner I would go to one of the smaller shops and purchase one or two cans of sardines, return to my apartment and attempt to make a meal of it, usually washing it down with a coke. Afterward I would walk down to a certain refreshment stand on a remote part of the beach where I would buy myself a particular treat in the form of a candy bar. But a word about this candy bar: it was called a "Mars" bar, though it bore no relation to the American candy bar of the same name, nor was any connection intended. This "Mars" was, without any doubt, the most delicious hunk of sweet stuff one could ever imagine. First of all, it was large and bulky with a layer of chocolate that concealed the tastiest, meatiest, juiciest, nuttiest concoction that was ever clothed in candy bar wrapping. That walk at night, after the sardines, to that magic refreshment stand far out along the beach near the dock was filled with as much delightful anticipation as anything in life can hold, and as the lights of the distant stand became brighter and loomed ever nearer as I approached, the mere thought of this magnificent delicacy made my very heart beat the faster!

The first night of this new dining pattern was, however, a near disaster. I had returned to my apartment with my can of sardines that I had just purchased from the not overly friendly shopkeeper, and partook, rather forlornly, of my supper. After finishing, the can retained so much of the sardine smell that I was determined to dump it outside somewhere, rather than disposing of it in my own wastebasket. After a thorough search of the apartment grounds I found no trash bin or garbage receptacle of any kind, and walked disgustedly along the rather darkened but charming side street behind the building, sardine can still in hand, inside a rumpled paper bag.

I must emphasize that at this point of my many frustrations I had reached a state of mind bordering on paranoia, and having directed all my thoughts to flow along a single track (to see Picasso again), in all other aspects I was not in the most rational or reasonable frame of thought. At this moment the most important problem at hand was how to dispose of this rumpled bag containing the smelly sardine can.

Then, through the rear gate of a hotel just a few doors from my apartment building I saw a large dark trash bin in the area of some considerable foliage of the hotel's back yard, next to the long concrete driveway that led to the hotel. I attempted to open the large gate of ornate iron railings through which I had seen the dark trash bin, but it was locked, and in a fit of real frustration I threw the sack over the top of the gate toward the trash bin. However, the sack landed with the most hideous CRASH on the concrete driveway, at which time I fancied that I heard a sudden stirring in the foliage. With the unreasoning fear of a madman I lunged back into my apartment building, raced up the stairs, and locked myself in the room, where I lay upon my bed awaiting the loud knock of the gendarmes! After five minutes or so, and still hearing no footsteps coming up the stairs, I began to form an explanation that I would offer the gendarmes when they arrived, and also began reflecting on the irony of getting into such trouble when I had only recently decided to return home to Los Angeles as soon as my charter-discount flight ticket allowed.

On the subsequent nights (having obviously eluded capture and arrest) I simply disposed of my sardine cans (always in the paper bags in which they were purchased) in a large maintenance closet near the head of the stairs. After a few days, as you can imagine, as one reached the top of the stairs, or in fact approached the maintenance closet from any direction what ever, a curious and overpowering stink pervaded the atmosphere, though of all the tenants on my floor I was the only one who *knew* the origin of this soon much-discussed mystery.

One late afternoon, in a state of solemn quietude, I was strolling the length of the Croisette—to my left was the long row of luxury hotels boarded up for the winter, and to my right the cold Mediterranean echoed the barrenness, both of these deserted edifices and of my spirit. Further-more, the melancholy aspect of the whole scene was accented by an occasional roll of distant thunder. A blanket of chilly blues and pinks infused the atmosphere as sunset was near, and I hardly noticed the automobile that was slowing its pace as it approached me on the street to my right. As it slowed to a stop I noticed a middle-aged man behind the wheel tilting his head to attract my attention, and an attractive young girl sitting beside him rolled down her window as the man called out to me.

"American?" he smiled. I nodded, and he asked me if I could use some company. Smiling in return I got into the back seat of the car and the man introduced himself as Arthur Penrose. The girl was his eighteen-year-old daughter Marsha. After briefly explaining, in response to his inquiry, the reason for my being in Cannes at this godforsaken time of year, I learned that Penrose was a long-time resident of Cannes, as a self-exiled refugee from the McCarthy "blacklist" era, an ex-screenwriter and an admitted member of the Communist Party. Though this revelation hardly endeared me to him, I nevertheless welcomed the sudden distraction of his conversa-tion and felt a tinge of amusement at the almost comical aspect of my new situation.

"Listen," he said, "I can help you get in to see Picasso!"

"How?" I asked. "Even his close friend Dominguin, the man who introduced me to him a couple of years ago, can't get through to him, now that he's in temporary hibernation on account of that gargantuan one-man show in Paris!"

"Ha ha ha!" chided Penrose. "All the 'party' has to do is snap its fingers and Picasso will come running!"

This remark made my stomach flip over a couple of times, and I reminded him that when the Communists offered Picasso the Lenin Peace Prize, he not only twice refused it, but also on two separate occasions refused to see the Russian emissary who had come all the way from Russia

168

to present it to him. "Picasso only became a 'Communist,' if you can call it that, in support of the so-called republican faction which fought against Franco's fascist takeover of Picasso's beloved Spain during the 1937 Civil War," I reminded Penrose. "And even then, it was only at the insistence of the 'intellectual' group in Paris which had attached itself to him."

"Ha ha ha," said Penrose again. "Just give me the word and you'll see how much you know about Picasso's politics!"

"You mean," I asked, "that you have that much authority with the party here in France?"

"I like you," said Penrose, tilting his head toward the back seat to cast a smile my way, "and I think your project is a worthwhile one. A snap of the fingers from the right source, and he's all yours."

"Oh come on," I said. "Even if that were true I wouldn't want him that way. It's *you* who know nothing of Picasso's politics. He's against suppression of any kind, a human artistic being, misguided at times maybe, but not a political being. And certainly not a subservient robot. Good Lord, don't you see how fascistic you sound saying all the party has to do is 'snap its fingers'?"

"Listen," said Penrose, "I want to hear more of your fascinating story, and what kind of movie you're planning to make."

Allowing the conversation to take this more pleasant turn I told him in capsulized form of some of my experiences and thoughts on the film, only to be interrupted by a long and loud roll of thunder, which prompted Penrose to turn his head fully around to look at me, eyebrows raised and grinning from ear to ear. "Thunder over Cannes!" he exclaimed. "It has a good sound, doesn't it?"

"Yes," I replied. "I love the sound of thunder."

"No," said Penrose, "I mean *thunder over Cannes* has a good sound! Doesn't it? Are you going to write a book about all your experiences?"

"I hadn't thought of it," I responded, slightly confused at his odd train of thought.

"Well," he said, turning once again to look at me in that wild-browed way, "if you *do*—call it—*Thunder over Cannes!*"

"Yeah, it's a great title," I nodded.

"How about a cup of coffee?" Penrose asked, pulling to a stop in front of a little cafe on a side street off the Croisette. "We'll talk inside."

The cafe offered a modicum of bright warmth and escape against the melancholy darkness that was now overtaking whatever had been left of the day, and the three of us sat at a round table near the cafe window sipping our coffee.

"And besides," I continued my assault, "if you recall, Picasso signed a petition protesting the Russian invasion of Hungary, and was very active and vocal in that protest! Were *you*?"

"Oh, bosh!" sneered Penrose. "How can you call the crushing of a fascist-inspired uprising an 'invasion'?"

"Oh," I laughed facetiously. "Is that what you call it? A simple label makes it so?"

"Enough of politics," replied Penrose. "I don't often get to enjoy the company of a fellow American at this time of year, and although our talk has been stimulating I can see you don't want my help, and I have no desire to alienate you."

"Fair enough," I agreed.

Upon which, at the conclusion of our little refreshment, Penrose invited me to his apartment to meet his wife Brenda, an encounter for which I could not have been less prepared.

The apartment was tiny, ill-lit, and unkempt, the major contribution to this disarray being the presence of a bed in one corner of the room in which languished the person of Brenda Penrose, attractive enough in her untidy way, but whom, from all I could manage to gather, was a self-proclaimed invalid, on a permanant basis.

"Mr. Herschensohn is an artist, here to see Picasso," announced Penrose to his wife, who acknowledged this statement with a wide-eyed nod in my direction. "Wouldn't it be nice if we showed him your paintings, dear?" He smiled. This remark explained the remainder, at least in good part, of the apartment's unkemptness, for I became aware of the multitudes of canvases, boards, and papers stacked and strewn throughout the room; and it was with a feeling of dread that I watched Penrose smilingly approach the first stack for my inspection.

So completely charmless and amateurish were these works that it took all I had in me not to beg the Penroses to allow me to take my leave instantly, but I feigned enough interest to carry me through the entire repertoire before excusing myself and bidding a fond farewell to the family Penrose.

After a week and a half of this terrible frustration I was longing, aching to return home; and one night I lay awake determined that before leaving I would make one last-ditch attempt at presenting to Picasso the reel of animation he had requested of me. This whole situation was becoming so inconceivable to me that I had to dig ever and ever deeper into myself to find the will-power to see it through.

So the following morning I asked Claude what she thought about my going directly to Picasso's home and telling my story to the housekeeper when she came to the gate, with the hope that she would relay the story to Picasso and I would be allowed inside. Knowing that there was little else left for me to try, Claude reluctantly acquiesced to drive me over, but suggested that the nighttime would be the most advisable, since Picasso is at his peak of affability at that period of the day, being a late riser and retiring in the small hours.

That night around 9:30 Claude drove me about halfway up the hill that led to the iron gate and waited as I went on ahead. I rang the bell and was surprised by a sudden burst of static as a loudspeaker overhead, to the left of the gate, brought forth a loud query from inside. Evidently, it was the voice of Lucienne, the housekeeper. Suddenly two large hounds charged up to the gate and barked at me angrily as I introduced myself over the speaker. There was a quick reply, accompanied by the static and the barking, and though I failed to understand exactly what had been said, it was the last response I was to hear from the box; and upon returning to Claude's car I told her that I would spend the entire next day in front of the gate if I had to. Before heading back to the city, she pointed out a small cafe on the road just near the Picasso home, from which I could call a taxi to pick me up at day's end, since she could not make the trip herself at that time, nor had I any wish to impose upon her further.

Therefore, the following morning I returned by taxi to the Notre Dame de Vie on that hill in Mougins where two and one-half years earlier I had been so warmly received. But after the occurrences of the past week and a half, and especially those of the preceding night, there was no way that my natural optimism could not give way to the heavy cloak of futility on this gray and bitter-cold morning as the taxi wound its way along the road to Mougins.

I dismissed the driver at the bottom of the hill and went the remainder on foot, carrying with me the briefcase containing the animation reel. I was prepared to wait out the entire day, if necessary, and play the whole thing by ear, hoping that somehow with all distance removed from me and the object of my destination, that eventually something would give—and that "something" would most definitely not be me. Ignoring the taxi driver's final assurance to me that the Picassos were "out of town," I waved him off with a weak smile and started up the hill. How different it all seemed, trudging along, observing every bush and pebble on the road, from that first time when Picasso's chauffeur Janot had whisked me up to the gate in the limousine!

I rang, almost as a formality, receiving a similar response to that of the previous evening, and I then deposited myself on a small ledge, almost at ground level, beside the gate, fully prepared to wait it out. My reasoning was that certainly during the course of one entire day there was a chance that this mighty gate would swing open for someone leaving or entering—and that hopefully, that "someone" might provide the solution I was seeking.

Throughout well nigh a whole day of this desperate vigil, freezing almost to the bone, I received the warm and friendly sympathy of the mailman and several delivery men, all of whom assured me that it would be fruitless to wait—that Picasso was definitely "out of town" to the whole world.

Then suddenly, the chance I was waiting for—the chauffeur Janot drove up the hill and stopped at the gate! As he got out of the car to open the gate I walked smilingly up to him and quickly explained the situation. However, he pretended to speak no English, and shrugged his shoulders as if he had absolutely no recollection of who I was; continuing to shake his head even as I mentioned the name of Dominguin and dinner at the Felix Restaurant, and so on. He waited "patiently" as I wrote these pertinent bits of information on a slip of paper, including my name, Dominguin, the date of our meeting, the film, and asked him to give it to Picasso. He took it silently and drove in through the gate, closed it behind him, and drove on behind the cluster of trees to the house. I half expected not to see him again, but within three minutes he reappeared with my note, shaking his head. "Picasso paints," he said politely. Then he turned and walked back toward the house. I knew that he had not bothered to disturb his Maestro and that all hope was now gone.

Disheartened and thoroughly dejected, I sat back down upon the ledge to think. I began trying to analyze my reasons, my purpose in all of this. My answer was simply that I wanted Picasso's approval of what I had done, as he had so enthusiastically approved of my presentation on that happy day in June of 1964, in order that I could return to Los Angeles with the news of his reception and thus woo a producer into financing my film. Having previously vowed that I would do anything "short of murder" in order to give birth to the child of my brain, I decided, as guardian of this unborn art form, that it would make little difference whether Picasso actually saw the film or not, if by merely saying that he did would provide the necessary financing; for not only would he then eventually see the film, but I was positive that his approval would be as jubilant as it had been at the earlier presentation. And so I left the hill with a newborn confidence in what lay before me.

The following day, at the office of American Express in Cannes, I was told that I could not return home that day on my group-charter ticket and would have to wait till the weekend unless I wished to pay an additional amount, but had hardly enough left to see me through the week.

"Did you ever get through to Picasso?" a familiar voice was inquiring.

Looking behind me, I saw the smiling face of Arthur Penrose, who was leaning against the counter, waiting his turn behind me.

"No," I replied. "Not this time."

"Well, you see," chuckled Penrose. "You should have let me do it for you my way."

For one brief moment I hesitated; then chuckling in return I said, "Thanks anyway."

20

Campbell, Silver, Cosby

HOME AGAIN, I SAT IN THE MELROSE AVENUE OFFICE OF MY BROTHER BRUCE. I told him everything, and of my resolution on the hill at Picasso's gate at the Notre Dame de Vie in Mougins.

He thought a while, and then, eyes ablaze, told me of the good fortune of our mutual close friend of many years, Bruce Campbell. Bruce Campbell is a mercurial, natural-born promoter in the greatest and most classical tradition of Hollywood showmanship, clothed in a rainbow suit of charming eccentricities that would have caused Charles Dickens himself to take pen in hand. Campbell's father had been a vice president of the powerful Hollywood agency, MCA, and Bruce could have followed in his footsteps, but chose instead to follow his own independent and more magical path to glamour. Coming close to success several times, including his own company in San Francisco, which contained twenty or thirty telephones in one room, a couple of million dollars slipped through his fingers and bankruptcy followed. But now, my brother was informing me of Campbell's new success—a partnership in the motion picture firm of Campbell, Silver, Cosby; "Silver" being the shrewd talent manipulator Roy Silver, and "Cosby" being the great black comic of television and nightclub fame, Bill Cosby.

"They're looking for material for films," Bruce told me. "Why don't I call Campbell and tell him about your project?"

It sounded like a great idea, and in a day or so the three of us met for lunch at the Hollywood coffee shop, Carolina Pines, Jr., now relegated to the chain gang of the Copper Penny. Campbell was ignited by the idea of a

173

movie containing sensuously rhythmic animated sequences bringing the work of Picasso to life, combined with a script by the great Ray Bradbury, which provided endless possibilities for a live-action film with locations in France and Spain. He was bursting to present the whole idea to his partner Roy Silver and to arrange a meeting between us. My brother and I shared a strong feeling of certainty that this was the break for which I had so long been waiting, and we drove back to the office with a happy sense of buoyancy, and irony—that after searching half the world for the key to the final door, I should find it in the hand of an old chum; and further, that my brother himself had pointed the way.

The transition from dream to reality, the *realization of a dream*, can be a very frightening thing. Imagine the characters of a sleepful night's dream suddenly taking over the workings of your subconscious fantasy, turning bliss into nightmare. In our heads we conceive—unimpeded by the intrusion of others; but bring that conception into the waking world, a world populated by beings as real as yourself, attempt (if you can) to hold that conception together like a large, fragile, transparent bubble that would burst to the slightest wrong touch—and all the while, those other very real beings not only wanting a piece of that dream, but claiming it as their own property, like a doctor keeping the infant he pulls from the mother's womb.

In this way, a dream no longer in the warm, protective womb of the brain in which it was born is the naked prey of every grabber and kidnaper and clodhopper in sight—if the newborn is not luckless enough to wander off into the swarming, horrendous cross-traffic of the avenues of Commerce, to disappear or evaporate before it has a chance to grow and become a part of reality. Society is a large fish that eats its young, and for every dream or idea that manages to survive and become a part of reality, the face of that reality becomes that much more altered or changed; for what we know as the *real world* is (by and large) the shape and summation of past dreams and ideas that have managed to survive. The trick is to expose your sweet night's dream to the hot, glaring light of day without its instantly dissolving in the open air—for if it survives this vulgar shock, the chances are it will make the light of day brighter and the open air freer; however infinitesimally. But that, after all, is how we have come as far as we have—though not really far at all. Man still has one foot in the cave. It will take another millennium and a whole earthful of dreams turned to action before that second foot is wrenched free. But what a moment in the mystical clockwork of the universe *that* will be!

But for now, we who plod forward in motionless splendor toward that glorious event an eternity away find that—now that we've convinced everyone our idea can make money—we must fight like demons to keep them from taking it from us! Or, to put it another way:

What I have related so far, those things I have laid bare on the printed page, were the events and circumstances that composed that portion of my cerebral pregnancy which started with *conception* and flowed along in a succession of blissful hopes and nightmares-within-a-dream; on to the agonizing labor pains to the almost inconceivable horror of a near stillbirth. And now, finally, my dream has been born alive and vulnerable to the whims and callousness of other real creatures, who care little or nothing for the intensive and loving nurturing that had given it life, many of whom have come forward with instant *adoption papers*!

The corporation of Campbell, Silver, Cosby was located in a little two-story brown brick building on Canon Drive in the heart of Beverly Hills. It was presided over by Roy Silver, a dynamic young man from the Bronx who was finally making it "big" as the manager of the famous comedian Bill Cosby. Roy was an impeccable dresser—tailor-made suits, high starched collar, an intense, darkly outgoing face with black eyes that gazed searchingly from behind large steel horn-rimmed glasses, and an imposing nose that curved outward and downward. His voice was commanding, with an unconsciously affected halting manner of speech. The star, Bill Cosby, trusted Roy implicitly and left the business pretty much in his hands. My friend Bruce Campbell had charmed his way into partnership through his engaging and disarming talent for showmanship; even to getting top billing in the firm's logo.

The CSC offices were, from stem to stern, the lushest and most extravagantly furnished imaginable—almost garrishly ostentatious in the grand Hollywood tradition; and cluttered, as well, with nostalgic memorabilia of the ghost of Hollywood Past. Gorgeous young girls were everywhere—secretaries, starlets, girl friends, office workers, career girls—all as if selected by a fashionable interior decorator, so that the furniture, the girls, the memorabilia, were all of a style.

Bruce's secretary, Sandy Kaplan, was a level headed, highly capable, very ambitious, and pleasantly attractive young lady; she was selected not by the "interior decorator," but by Bruce himself. I liked Sandy, but I enjoyed her more when I was less conscious of her monomotored ambition, and we got along well enough.

But I am allowing the memory of that quixotic, Camelot-like corporation to get the jump on me, and I am getting ahead of myself.

It was a day or so after my brother Bruce and I met with Bruce Campbell in the Carolina Pines coffee shop that I went, in the late afternoon, to the offices of Campbell, Silver, Cosby for my first official and fateful meeting with Roy Silver; Campbell, of course, was in attendance. It was an exciting,

Roy Silver and Bruce Campbell. (COURTESY
OF BRUCE CAMPBELL)

electric three-way confrontation, for we all knew immediately that we were
about to embark on an enterprise that required the ultimate in audacity—a
quality lacking in none of us. I was thrilled, and sparks must have shot in all
directions from my head when Roy said, "*We are going to make this movie!*
With whatever it takes, *we're going to make it*, if we have to finance it
ourselves, and from this moment on, it takes precedence over everything
else we're doing!"

Now, at last, in no uncertain terms, this was it!

Prior to and during the filming of *The Picasso Summer*, there were many
conflicts and misunderstandings that were each in its turn, resolved. The
following letters constitute an example of one such conflict, and they were
written at a time when the film was temporarily planned as a one-hour

television special sponsored by Eastern Airlines (merely one example of the roller-coaster ride this endeavor was becoming), but on terms that were highly unsatisfactory to myself and Ray Bradbury. I think that poor Bruce got stuck in the middle of our hot tempers, and after this incident boiled over and everyone got to know one another better, a great mutual respect was born.

However, these letters reveal a small part of the reason I hold Ray Bradbury in such high esteem, disclosing a great strength of character and self-respect; which, coupled with his dazzling genius with the English language, and the sheer poetry of his work, combine to make him one of the great astronauts of the human imagination.

As for the misunderstanding, I can hardly describe the pain that accompanied it, and the relief I felt when it was resolved—to the satisfaction and good humor of everyone concerned.

Dear Wes:

The enclosed is self-explanatory. I think all three groups of people involved haven't the courage of their convictions. I see no reason why you or I should work free or half-free for any of them. We have the talent. The least THEY can do is put up the money! I regret all of this immensely, only because of you. I won't waste time or regret on any of the other people involved. They are almost beneath comment. Best of luck to you and the project. I hope you can get it going on your own will power, strength, nerve, and imagination.

Signed/ Ray

July 28th, 1967

Mr. Roy Silver
Mr. Bruce Campbell
Campbell-Silver-Cosby Corp.
Beverly Hills, Calif.

Dear Roy and Bruce:

I take it, from Peter Thomas, that negotiations on the Picasso project have fallen through. This is shameful news. Above all, I feel for Wes, whose project this, in the main, is. If Wes were doing this on his own, on a shoestring, he would have my utter cooperation, gratis.

177

But, the picture I see is as follows:

Three large rich corporations: 1. Eastern Airlines. 2. Young and Rubicam. 3. Campbell-Silver-Cosby, want two poor chaps, Herschensohn and Bradbury, to contribute their creative talent to a project that nobody except Herschensohn and Bradbury believe in. Most importantly, at this time, a script for an hour show must be provided, almost gratis, by said Bradbury to said corporative trio. In the pinch, Young and Rubicam and Campbell-Silver-Cosby were not able to put up an additional three thousand to match two thousand from Eastern Airlines. So, I can only assume, two of the three corporations don't believe in the project.

Gentlemen, when rich people can't afford poor people, it is time for poor people to back off and find the exit. It is most unfortunate that many weeks ago I wasn't informed that poor-mouth time was coming up. I refuse to be a beggar in the street asking for crumbs. I would, please believe me, rather starve. It is easier to turn down an entire project rather than work for the pitiful beans offered by the triple corporative powers.

I wish only the best to Wes. As for Eastern Airlines. . . Santa Fe still remains my best bet.

Yours,

Ray Bradbury

21

Madrid and Dominguin, III

IT WAS A BRIGHT MORNING AT L. A. INTERNATIONAL AIRPORT, AND MY parents waited cheerfully with me for the arrival of Bruce Campbell, who was to be my companion to Paris and Madrid. They were cheerful because the occasion was a happy one compared to my other journeys of almost morbid intensity. This time all expenses were paid by Campbell-Silver-Cosby, who were committed to financing and co-producing my film, and all appointments in Europe were set and verified in advance.

Bruce arrived at the L.A. International waiting room followed closely by Sandy Kaplan who appeared to be picking up bits and pieces of Campbell as he approached the lounge where I sat with my parents. It was impossible for them not to laugh with amused admiration for, interspersed with the warmest of greetings for us all, he was dictating last-minute edicts and errands to Sandy, who was patiently writing it all down, trying at the same time to appear informal and cordial. There was the matter of tickets vanishing, unimaginable boxes with straps of every description, valises and paraphernalia beyond recalling—all adding to a sense of mysterious urgency that adorned the aura of incredible charm that surrounded Bruce Campbell. When things were going badly, Bruce was as calm and amusing as a master of ceremonies, but when things were going well, he was a nervous wreck, albeit still in charge.

It was Bruce's first flight to Europe, and my fourth, but this time I had little of that terrible sense of desperation which had been eating at me for such a long time, and it was with the most exhilarating sense of relaxation and fun that I gladly handed the reins over to Bruce; though in due time I

179

was to find myself in possession of a new and harder-to-handle set of reins than ever before.

The takeoff was sunlit and dazzling, and we were on our way to Madrid and Paris. Madrid, to see Dominguin in order to discuss the many arrangements for the film regarding Picasso and regarding himself, and to show him my four-minute sample film of animation. Paris, to see Truffaut, to show him the animation also, and hopefully to sign him as director for the feature, with Renoir now definitely unable to participate.

We were met at Madrid airport by Miguel's chauffeur, but only after the most incredible mixup and wait; I recall that we all separately disappeared from one another for great lengths of time, and after the most irritating confusion finally arrived at Dominguin's office. We were greeted with such open-armed warmth by Miguel that all other thoughts vanished, and after a round of introductions Bruce found himself as charmed as I had been three years earlier.

Pedro Rodriguez, with the blond hair and the blue eyes, was still with Dominguin. He was later to be known by Bruce (affectionately?) as "Hans," though my own friendship with him and his lovely, live-in girlfriend Lorita was to grow with time. For Pedro was also, for me, the savior whose voice I had come to depend upon so desperately during those many confusing and important long-distance calls to Madrid throughout these past years; and whose understanding of the urgency of this project did much to make it possible.

We all talked of many things regarding Picasso and the movie. Dominguin offered his ranch as a major location, and guaranteed that Picasso would appear in the scene on the beach in Cannes. Miguel liked Ray Bradbury's script, a Spanish translation of which had been sent to him a week or two earlier, and we discussed some contract points and provisions. There were some questions raised, but, in all, the meeting was quite congenial and as pleasant as had been all my contacts with the Matador.

Miguel had some further appointments before he could close his day, but intended to spend as much of it with us as possible, for Bruce and I were leaving that night for Paris and Truffaut.

First, his niece Maria was to take us to lunch, and afterward on a tour of Madrid's motion picture studio. Then Miguel would pick us up and the four of us would go to the projection room to look at my four-minute sample film of the animation of a Picasso corrida.

We were driven to Maria's office in which she was engaged in some capacity or other of Miguel's rather complex network of business affairs.

Maria was a joy—to watch, to hear, to talk to— to know. Small-boned and slender, she had a curvaceous figure, her hair was a dark blond with a lustrous sheen, her skin was tan, her eyes were blue, her smile was warm, her voice was sure and sweet, and she spoke English with only the slightest accent. Her poise was impeccable; a sophisticated child-woman in her early twenties. In every way, Maria was a beautiful person.

"We will join Miguel later," she said, "but first I have the pleasure of taking you both to lunch, and then on a tour of Madrid's motion picture studio."

Images flash before me of the lunch, the delightful food, the restaurant, the people, but all as if on a screen behind the gentle image of Maria herself, whose warm conversation flowed easily and humorously. At the movie studio we were impressed, first, visually, by the incredible modernity of its look. Three or four of the highest executives, in impeccable business suits, guided us personally through the whole elaborate maze (which often had the acoustics of an echo chamber), although at one point I drifted off alone and got lost for about five minutes, after which I was relocated by a large women behind a refreshment counter within the studio.

Bruce and I were treated like big Hollywood producers, and of course the executives were on familiar terms with Maria, who in their eyes (and in fact) was representing Dominguin, whom anyone in Madrid was most eager to please.

Although at first Maria was introduced to us as Miguel's "niece," it soon came out, first in bits and pieces, and finally through Maria's own candor (as well as Miguel's), that instead she was his mistress, having been brought up in his home since the age of twelve by Miguel's wife, Lucia; but she vowed, as she grew older, that the time would come when Miguel, with whom she had fallen in love, would some day belong to her. This information, oddly enough, did not diminish her in our eyes, nor did it enhance her, but only crystallized what had been certain amorphous and premature thoughts. One was not critical of such beauty—her loyalty to Miguel captured our admiration, and that of anyone who knew her.

Dominguin picked us up at the studio and drove us to the projection room to see my animation. Not at the motion picture studio, oddly enough, but at a screening room that belonged to a friend of Miguel's. Of course, there was the usual mix-up, with the projectionist not being on time and the place being locked when we got there; but soon enough the four of us were seated comfortably inside, and the projectionist, having made his proper apologies, started the film, which I had scored with a recording of the Concierto *Aranjuez* by the great contemporary Spanish composer Rodrigo. It worked beautifully with the animation.

I was nervous about the fact that I had long ago told Bruce that Picasso had already seen the film, so I simply told him that I wanted Miguel to think that he would be the first to show it to him. I knew that however it all came out, Picasso would be as enthusiastic over the film as he was about my work when I met him three years earlier, and that all would work out happily enough.

As it was, Miguel and Maria were ecstatic. The forms filled the screen,

181

swelling, dancing, roaring and ever changing in colors and with movements and rhythms I knew none of them had ever seen before. Dominguin was issuing gasps of wonderment in Spanish, and Maria leaned over to look at me, shaking her head in solemn amazement and admiration. Bruce, who had seen it many times before, told me that it never failed to thrill him, and Miguel and Maria were engaged in excited conversation at the short film's end.

When the lights went up, Dominguin looked at me as though with a new respect. "Dias, this weel scare Picasso," he said (and I thought of how Duncan said the identical thing when I first showed him my work, and I thought I was dreaming). "Thees ees Picasso *come to life*—but een *such a way* even Picasso could never eemagine!" He shook his head. "Do you know what I am going to do?" Miguel continued. "When I go to hees home in Mougins, I weel say nothing, but I weel hook up this feelm to the projector, and I weel say, *Pablo, I'ave a surprise for you*, and I weel bring heem into the room, seet heem down, turn off the lights, and run for heem thees feelm!"

As we all left the projection room, Miguel was saying how important it was that Picasso see the film, how it would change his life, and the direction of all art. Maria kissed my cheek and took my hand and said, "This is genius," and my heart began to pound again with that old sense of urgency to start things moving and to create the animation properly, in its totality of movement and to the fullest stage of completion possible. I was frustrated again, overwhelmed by that awful wave of urgency that ravaged me and all but drowned me in a sea of helpless, quiet rage.

Bruce and I were in the cramped back seat of Miguel's small car, Miguel at the wheel and Maria beside him, as Miguel was attempting to take us on a capsule tour of Madrid. We were driving through the busiest intersection of the city, in the center of what apparently was a classic Madrid traffic jam. Miguel and Maria were shaking with laughter as Bruce and I continually adjusted and readjusted ourselves to the stops, starts, bumps, and jumps. Everywhere the streets were being torn up and were in the midst of some kind of construction. "Madrid will be a beautiful city," Miguel laughed, "when they finish it!"

"Yes," I said. "So will Los Angeles!"

Miguel drove us through Madrid on his own personal tour of the city, and after one or two hours had passed we all became thirsty; Miguel was starving, and Bruce and Maria and I were even a little hungry again. We stopped and went into a restaurant that looked ordinary enough on the outside, but was, on the inside, a slice of Old Spain itself. It was dominated by one large room, into which one took several steps down, dark even in the afternoon light, with walls of ancient stone, from which hung wine caskets, cooking utensils, fish, and fowl.

We all had beer, and Miguel, Maria, and Bruce ordered some lobster. I ordered a loaf of salami, having never acquired a taste for lobster, simply because I could never reconcile myself to the horror of actually putting such a hideous crawling thing into the *mouth*! Miguel, of course, was hysterical with laughter as soon as he learned this, and feigned a sort of mock incredulity. Tauntingly he held a lobster leg to my mouth and laughed, "But you don' like thees? How can you not?" Then, in a more serious way, he tore off a piece of the meat and implored me to taste it, promising that I would find it delicious. "Eet's not so bad, een this shape, no?" he smiled encouragingly. I tasted it, and—predictably—liked it, but only in that shape.

"Now," I waved my hand, "let me eat my salami in peace!" Beer and salami are great on a hot afternoon. I wouldn't know about lobster.

Back once again to the peaceful and relaxing elegance of Dominguin's home, my attention was drawn, as it had been on the occasions of my previous visits, to the large, ornate room with the mantelpiece over which were displayed on the wall that incredible set of ceramic dishes. I speak of those large plates that portray in silhouette that seemingly endless ballet of the Bullfight, which Picasso had choreographed so lovingly in his ceramic workshop in Vallauris. This particular set he had presented affectionately to Dominguin, and the afternoon sun, which was brilliantly flooding the rooms of Dominguin's magnificent house, seemed to take pleasure in imitating that peculiar sunlight of the arena as it shone upon this almost unearthly display.

I felt, as I stood looking up at the plates, a mixture of delight and anxiety about the gnawing acknowledgment of the ever-present sense of responsibility that I had taken upon myself in calling together all of these various and incongruous personalities, the large sums of money, and so on in order to pursue what at best was still only a partially realized dream on a four-minute sample film.

I therefore felt obliged to look at them not as a bemused spectator, but with some sense of purpose regarding my intentions to transpose them at some date in the near future into animation. I was only vaguely aware of Dominguin's entrance into the room as I stared with forced intent at the familiar drama that spread itself before me.

The plates seemed, then, to roll into one another as my glance moved successively from left to right, and the accumulation of movement was dizzying. I began to see how I would use these silhouettes in the animation, and the bulls, matador, picador, and the arena itself became a swirl of undulating rhythm.

"Yes," smiled Dominguin, sensing my rapture, "Picasso sees every-theeng een motion."

Startled, I replied that motion was not enough—not enough at all. "All impassioned artists see their visions in motion," I said. "Rubens, Van Gogh, Rembrandt—certainly Michelangelo; but the thing I'm straining toward and dreaming of is to transform the movement into *rhythm*."

Dominguin nodded, wanting to understand.

"Only in *rhythm* does movement have any meaning," I said. "Movement is life, but rhythm is life in relation to the universe. With rhythm we have the fusion of Apollonian order with Dionysian joy, as in Beethoven, to give the highest example."

"Si," said Dominguin, "one must go beyond painting for thees—even beyond Picasso heemself."

"Picasso has stretched painting to the limits," I said. *"He's made the way clear*—no one else could have done it. I mean the way he's summed up the entire history of painting—all the periods of art unto himself, doing endless variations on all of it in his own language! As if to say, 'so much for that—*next!*' "

Out conversation was interrupted in a most Picasso-like way by the sudden appearance in the room of Manolo's chimpanzee, bounding about and looking in all directions at once. Manolo, a house-guest of Dominguin's, was a close friend of Picasso, and a sculptor of note.

"Enter Picasso," Dominguin laughed. "He has sent hees emissary!" This thought brought to mind the hundreds of portrayals Picasso has made of the chimpanzee, especially those in the series called *The Human Comedy*, where chimps are shown with the most fetching nudes, the prettiest in Picasso literature; where the little apes become the willing playthings of these sensitively drawn beauties. Suddenly Dominguin roared with laughter, and I turned to see the chimp attempting to raise the skirt of Maria, who was sitting in a chair on the other side of the room.

"No!" she yelled, pushing the chimp's hand away and drawing one knee up tightly above the other.

"Picasso ees everywhere!" laughed Dominguin.

Manolo ran into the room and chastized the poor animal in furious Spanish, and the chimp bounced off shrieking in reply. Manolo walked over to us shaking his head, and soon Dominguin was relaying to him in Spanish the conversation we had regarding the plates, gesturing to them quickly one by one. Manolo nodded slowly, then shrugged, said something in his language, and walked off again in pursuit of the chimp.

"Manolo says een sculpture ees no such complications," smiled Dominguin.

Dinner that night was in the most elegant, yet rustic, Spanish tradition. We all sat at the long, large table with Dominguin at the head, in the role of the charming, amicable host. The lighting was subdued, lending emphasis to the glow of the long candles at the table and contributing to an overall atmosphere of rich dark-orange that was unsurpassable in its romantic effect.

At bedtime Bruce and I were shown to our room, which contained, along with the usual chest of drawers, two good-sized beds separated by a night stand with a lamp. We were exhausted and ready for a good night's sleep. When we turned off the lamp, the room suddenly became a tomb of total darkness, for through the single window of our second-story room the night outside was black, there being no moon or neighboring lights of any kind.

After several hours of sleep I was awakened by the sound of footsteps near the foot of my bed, and wondered what Bruce could possibly be doing moving about in this blackness. I reached for the lamp to the right of my bed and in so doing met a set of fingers! Two cries of surprise rent the air—my own and Bruce's, who had reached for the lamp at the exact moment I had, and upon turning the light on we both sat up in bed staring at one another in amazement. "You mean that wasn't *you* walking around?" we said to each other simultaneously. For we had both lain awake for several minutes listening to the loud footsteps walking about our room before deciding at precisely the same moment to turn on the light. The door to our room and the second-story window were closed tightly—as we had left them upon going to bed!

It was with an uneasy mixture of dread and amusement that we turned out the light and waited for the return of the footsteps, but they never came and we once again drifted off to sleep.

The next morning we awoke to the visual noise of the bright Spanish sun that now filled our room, and laughingly we puzzled about the event of that nighttime interruption.

We dressed hurriedly and with an immense hunger, wondering if we were on time for breakfast or if the others had already eaten and were long since about the day's business.

Whether we had come down to breakfast early or late, it seemed it would make no difference, for there was always someone sitting at that large, sun-drenched mahogany table eating rolls and sausage, coffee or tea, eggs or whatever one wished, and we had only to ask of the ever-present servants.

Bruce and I were in a constant state of jubilation, albeit subdued, as would befit the occasion of early-morning breakfast as guests in the sprawling ranch house of a host so elegant, but we fell ravenously to our meal. Maria, having already eaten, joined us in coffee, and we told her excitedly of our bizarre experience of the night before. To our amazement she nodded with a knowing smile and told us that we had been visited by "the ghost that haunts the ranch house!" She said that on one occasion she had been awakened by those same loud footsteps, and with brave determination decided, once and for all, to track the ghost down. So, rising from her bed, she lit a candle and upon leaving her room heard the footsteps descending the stairway. Candle in hand she followed the footsteps down the stairs but saw nothing! When she had reached the bottom of the stairway the footsteps trailed off quickly across the room and disappeared before Maria could make chase, and she never bothered with pursuit again, though the "ghost" returned many times.

22

Paris—and Truffaut?

BRUCE AND I HAD TO CATCH THE AFTERNOON PLANE TO PARIS, AND AFTER OUR goodbyes to Dominguin and the assurances that we would soon all be working together, Maria accompanied us to the airport and we were off.

That night in Paris was, again, pure Gershwin. Walking through the streets of this town with Bruce Campbell was like participating in a wild ballet with oneself as second billing and Bruce as the star.

He charged through the streets and boulevards of Paris chattering constantly with me as he lunged ever forward, and I literally lost him three times, since, as he "strolled" like a Chinese rocket, he would gradually gain one or two entire blocks on me. Other times, when we were more in sync, we had an insane game, the origin of which totally escapes me, wherein I would imitate Cary Grant calling out to Dyan Cannon (his then newly divorced wife) in a frantic effort to find her, which would make Bruce hysterical and which we would do at the most unexpected times. I am sure there was more to it than that because it sounds as boring as anything I have heard, but I would write that off as the insanity of two young Americans sharing their first night abroad in Paris together. Ah, but the best was yet to come!

We decided to have dinner at one of Paris' most exclusive restaurants, but before ordering we had cocktails at a table while we watched the show. There was a beautiful girl singing at the microphone, and Bruce and I simultaneously fell in love with her. Bruce mentioned something about inviting her to the table, a suggestion I passed over, and the next act was another beautiful girl with a magic and mind-reading act. The suave master of ceremonies spoke in English as well as in French as he extolled the mysterious powers of this lovely young lady magician. I was the first to be drawn into the act, and before I knew what was happening she was using my wristwatch to establish mental rapport with me, and while I was writing things such as my birth place on little pieces of paper, she was simultaneously reproducing this information on a large blackboard, after which the master of ceremonies would reveal my handwritten verification to the uproarious applause of the dinner audience (after the proper assurances of no mirrors or trickery). My wristwatch was returned to me with a magnanimous flourish by the emcee, accompanied by a tantalizing wave of thanks from the lady magician.

A short time later I observed a sullenly gorgeous girl sitting in a chair between our table and the wall, just behind Bruce, and off a bit to the side. When Bruce noticed that she was eyeing him he lost no time in inviting her to our table and ordering her a drink; and she lost no time in proclaiming her great hunger, and so the three of us ordered dinner and a bottle of champagne to go around. By this time the beautiful singer was doing her number again, and I turned around to watch her. To my astonishment, when her act was finished she walked straight up to where I was seated, and introduced herself. It's a startling thing to see—a strange, beautiful girl walking with such deliberation straight to you. One thinks, *She's making a mistake?* and suddenly she is inches from you and addressing you, her face almost silhouetted by the bright lights behind her. So suddenly we had a fourth for dinner, though I must admit that I was reluctant to give in to that; although I ordered her a drink, and even though the dinner was being charged to expenses, I still did not like the idea that she could walk right up and take it so for granted. But Bruce was very convivial about it, the other girl was dining already, and my singer friend did more than hint about her own hunger.

So, for an hour or so, we were a jovial group, having devoured a delicious meal and going through our third bottle of champagne.

We invited the girls to pass the evening with us, and of course fully expected it, after this; but both said that they had to work in the club till 5:00 A.M., and that it was out of the question. After which, Bruce's girl disappeared and my girl went back to do her act. Disgruntled, we called for our bill.

"How much," said Bruce, staring at the bill, "do you think it is?"

"Well,' I said, "four dinners and three bottles of champagne—a hundred? A hundred and twenty?" Remember, this was 1967, and prices were then not nearly as astronomical as they are today.

Bruce lowered the bill slowly and looked at me with an incredulous half-smile. "Four hundred dollars," he said.

"Four hundred dollars!" I said.

"Four hundred dollars," he said. "What do you think is fair?" Bruce asked me.

"Well," I said, "one hundred—one hundred and twenty, I suppose would be fair, but I. . ."

"That's what we're paying, then," Bruce said. "I'm going to leave one hundred and twenty dollars on the table and we're going to get up and walk out of this place. . ."

"But," I said, "we won't get away with that!"

"We can try," Bruce said. "After all, we've been taken, and fair is fair!"

"Okay, then," I said. "Fair's fair. Let's get out of here."

I don't think we were three feet away from the table when my well-fed singer friend stopped her number right in the middle and announced something in French over the microphone to an unseen friend, for all the astonished diners to hear, and by the time we made it to the little hallway exit we were met by three giants (rare in France) courteously blocking the doorway.

Bruce insisted that they call the police and put us in jail, and as they were more than willing to oblige, I reminded Bruce of our appointment the next day with Truffaut, and suggested a settlement.

"But your bill was fair, M'sieur," said giant number one. "This is Paris, not the United States."

"Exactly why we don't want to sit here in jail," I whispered to Bruce.

When they saw it was better to get *something* than lose us entirely to the police they (still courteously but firmly) agreed to settle for only one hundred dollars more. We felt that it was still outrageous, and Bruce was eager to hold out, suggesting once again that they call the police. As giant number two obligingly opened the door to the street and looked left and right with a determined air, I said "Truffaut" to Bruce, followed by forty dollars I pulled out of my wallet. "It's all I've got," I announced to whomsoever it concerned. This broke the ice all around, and Bruce produced the follow-up sixty. Back on the street we laughingly gorged ourselves of the pure, brisk night air of Paris, and our almost-lost freedom. It was the best thing we tasted all evening—and it was free.

We met with Francois Truffaut the following morning in the small Paris projection room in which he was to view my animation, the four-minute sample film. He was a small, wiry man with a pleasant and somewhat rumpled countenance and unassuming manner entirely disassociated with his worldwide fame as one of Europe's leading directors. He spoke no English at that time, and so for matters of interpretation was aided by his gigantic American female secretary and associate, who by the very contrast to her boss, created such a Dickensian climate to the interview that I found it hard to concentrate on the flow of what was being said.

At any rate, he loved the animation and even asked what music I had used, expressing great interest in it, and when I told him it was from the Concierto *Aranjuez* by Joaquin Rodrigo, he made a note of it. He was, he told us, about to start a film of his own and was regretfully unable to get involved in ours, much as he revered Picasso as a man and an artist, and as fascinated as he was by the idea of the strange new animation.

So, we were unable to obtain the director whose fame had brought us to Paris, and we had no intention of returning home without a "name" to enhance our film.

That afternoon Bruce and I returned to the hotel and sat in his suite, trying to sort everything out and determine our next move. "The first and most important thing to do," he said, "is to get a star. We need a *star!*" I agreed with him wholeheartedly, as Audrey Hepburn's face flashed on and off in my mind. Bruce then suggested that due to my friendship with Deborah Kerr we should have no trouble signing her. Again I agreed, but saw at last my opportunity to meet Audrey Hepburn, recalling my strange meeting with her husband Mel Ferrer three years earlier in Madrid, and how I had come close to it then. I told Bruce to let me fly to Switzerland to meet her and that I was *sure* she would agree to it.

"Oh, Wes!" Bruce cried, rising to his feet. "Let's be realistic!" and began pacing back and forth through his entire suite of rooms, as if to shake off any attempt at self-delusion on our part.

"I know I can do it," I yelled, so that he could hear me in the next room.

Reappearing through the doorway he raised his arms imploringly. "Be *realistic!*" he pleaded once more.

"All right," I said. "I promise to see Deborah Kerr if Audrey refuses. Is that so much to ask?"

Bruce reluctantly agreed that it was worth a chance, and the matter was settled.

I remembered, then, with silent amusement, a letter I had received from my sister Vi, after my meeting with Picasso. "Well," she wrote, "now that you've met Picasso I have *no doubt* that you'll eventually be meeting your other idol—Audrey Hepburn!"

I then called Dominguin, who knew Audrey well, and told him of my plan. He all but whooped with delight, and thought it a splendid idea. He said he would search for Audrey's address, which he had misplaced somewhere in his files, and telegraph it to me at my hotel, as soon as he found it. He said also that he would telephone Audrey to tell her of my impending arrival the following day. The telegram from Miguel arrived only a matter of hours later, and all was set. Bruce had a plane reservation for New York that afternoon and everything seemed to be happening in an orderly sequence.

I accompanied Bruce to the hotel desk as he checked out and prepared to leave, when suddenly my "sometimes" sinus condition caused me to choke on an absurd case of postnasal drip, and I thought it was my farewell to the world. Everyone stood by helplessly, and I could not help but take cognizance of the odd relationship between victim and observer, as if suddenly all links of communication with the outside world were irrevocably severed. Wanting desperately nothing more than a drink of water, I was overjoyed to see a pitcher of liquid on the floor of a nearby doorway, and made a savage lunge for it. Four hotel waiters with aprons who had come out of the dining area to watch my impromptu decline, and who had been standing together with their hands folded behind their backs, suddenly came to life and beseeched me not to drink the liquid; all the while trying not to laugh as they explained apologetically that the pitcher contained urine; and in any case, my choking spell had ended as suddenly as it began.

Bidding Bruce farewell, we shook our heads in helpless amusement at the entire day, and it was with a look of near desperation that Bruce wished me the best of luck on my venture in Switzerland.

Early the following morning my plane flew over Geneva toward Audrey's home in Burgenstock, near Lake Lucerne, and I observed the charming pleasantness of the friendly green and blue landscape below. With Miguel's telegram and the knowledge that meeting Audrey Hepburn was now a certainty—not of the future, but of that *very day*— I was in a state of headiness nothing could dispel.

In Lucerne I showed a taxi driver Miguel's telegram with Audrey's address in Burgenstock. He looked like the actor Oscar Homolka, thick-set and solid with a large turned-up nose, thick dark eyebrows, and a warm, friendly humor beaming through a pair of wise-looking eyes framed by a network of laugh-wrinkles. He was thrilled by the mention of Audrey's name and talked of her incessantly as we drove. He warned me, however, that it was a long trip up a fair-sized mountain to the address I had given him, and we had a jovial time of it along the way. It was about ten o'clock in the morning when, halfway up our mountain, my driver decided to inquire of a small group of local residents standing outside their home along the road. To our great dismay we were told that Audrey had moved from that address *ten years ago*, but with great good luck my driver was able to find out her new address through her old neighbors. It was in the small town of Morges, near Geneva, which my plane had bypassed on the way to Lucerne!

So now, no plane being available, I was forced to take the train, on what would amount to practically a full day's journey, arriving in Morges by late afternoon. On the way to the train depot my driver was full of remorse and sympathy and—to my utter disbelief, as well as to the reader's, I'm sure—refused to accept any fare whatsoever! And so, as I left his cab I dropped a bill by his seat and waved him a cheery and affectionate goodbye.

That train ride was one of the happiest events of my adult life, having always wanted to take a long ride in a "real" train, journeying through a strange and cheerful land. And here I was doing it, finally, under circumstances even my train-ride dreams had not been greedy enough to include! The seats of the train were of a sturdy wood, finely crafted, and painted to a glossy bright orange-tan. The windows were immense, so that the compartments were flooded with blazing sunshine, and all the greenery of the country seemed to be waving greetings to me as it whipped by. The sound of the wheels over the tracks and the hypnotic rocking of the train soon relaxed me a bit, and I smiled to myself, with confidence in the meeting that was soon to take place.

Let me say a word here on behalf of Swiss taxi drivers! Considering the law of averages alone, who would ever guess that the cab I hailed in Morges would be driven by a man of a niceness and empathy comparable to that of my driver in Burgenstock? And yet, it was as though a member of my own family had been waiting to take me to Audrey's home. Our conversation, of course, was mostly about her, or should I say Her, with a capital H—for this man spoke of her as one would speak of a saint, rhapsodizing endlessly of the veneration in which she was held by the entire town, including his own family. Then, his face darkening, he told me of the great contrast between Audrey and her husband, Ferrer; with story after story of his cheapness, his treatment of laborers working at one job or another at his home, of his ugly temper and jealousy of his wife. I mention this (without detail) not knowing with any authority the validity of anything I was told regarding the man; just as I am sure that one could find any number of people who would say otherwise, and praise him as endlessly as my driver was damning him. I mention it only to lend a certain perspective to the events I will be relating later in my narrative.

It was now nearing five o'clock as we approached the vicinity of Audrey's house, and I began to feel concerned about my hot and sweaty condition, imagining my appearance to be that of a disheveled maniac. Maniac or not, within minutes my driver was to make the final turn that would be bringing me to—*Audrey!*

191

23

Audrey

THERE, IN THE LATE AFTERNOON SUN, STOOD THE LARGE WHITE HOUSE THAT marked the end of my full day's journey. My cab drove into the small driveway and parked facing a two-car garage. One door was open, revealing a small Ferrari, and I prayed that this meant that Audrey was home. We were greeted by the sound of two barking dogs. I got out of the cab, and a small, heavy-set Latin girl who had poked her head out of an upper window upon our arrival, came down to see what I wanted. I had difficulty communicating with her, except to find, to my great relief and excitement, that Audrey was *home*— and on the back of Miguel's telegram to me in which he gave me Audrey's *Burgenstock* address, I scrawled this note; "Audrey! as you can see, Miguel gave me your *old* address and I've been looking for you all day! Can I *please* just have five minutes of your time! Thanks, Wes Herschensohn."

To my left, at a right angle to the garage, was a small white picket gate, beyond which was a large, pleasant yard with green lawn. It was already just past 5:00 P.M., and the evening shadows were beginning to signal their appearance, though the sun was still shining brightly. I stood waiting for the servant girl to reappear with an answer to my note, and I smiled and shrugged occasionally to my cab driver who would nod back confidently that all would be well. Just as I was checking my disheveled reflection in one of the small garage-door windows, there suddenly appeared from behind the wall a little tan face, accented by the white picket gate above which it stopped, like an upside-down exclamation point. I heard myself exclaiming, "Hi!" and the little face beamed. It was Audrey, so incredibly beautiful and warm and bright-eyed, beyond all expectation. She opened the gate

192

and held out both hands, one of which held my telegram-note.

"I'm sorry you had such trouble," she grinned sympathetically (and that voice!). "I don't know why Miguel gave you that old address, but he called me here and told me to be expecting you, so I've been *waiting* all day!"

As we strolled toward the patio, I felt such confidence in her closeness that I had no doubts of the outcome of this meeting. She wore a white dress and white shoes that enhanced her charmingly slender body and accented so becomingly her smooth tan skin and black hair.

"You ask for five minutes of my time," she smiled. "And now unfortunately, that's literally all I have left to give you—I have to take my little boy Sean to the doctor, and in fact when you drove up I thought it was my cab coming for me. Can you capsulize it for me?" she smiled as we sat down at a small white patio table, leaning her cheek on her hand and smiling her great, full-lipped smile. "I know it's awful to ask," she said, "but I'll listen carefully."

In five minutes I told her *everything*; and yet I must have looked and sounded like a raving madman, trying to fit it all in without losing the importance of any detail: how, in my recent lifetime I'd wanted to meet only two people—Picasso and Audrey Hepburn—and that now I'd met both! I told her that one was as important as the other for my film, in order to set the style of beauty the animation itself must take, and I explained to her about the new type of movement I envisioned in the animation, and how Picasso himself was excited and stimulated by the thought of it.

She sat there the whole time, never taking those incredibly bright dark eyes off of me, never once losing that warm, wide smile of the full red lips. But to my surprise she would occasionally *blush*, turning redder through her tan and constantly following with her entire expression every word I poured out to her. Never had I said so much in such a short time, and never had I had such an audience.

Finally, when I finished, she looked away and breathed deeply. "Well," she said, "first of all I must tell you your story amazes me and I admire you greatly. But sadly—and I mean this, sadly—I recently promised my husband and my son Sean that I would retire for one year and devote that entire year to Sean. I also made this promise to myself. I've already turned down some good roles I would have liked, and I'm now several weeks into my retirement." She looked at me sadly. "You can't expect me to break my promise to my husband and my son, can you? Or especially to myself?"

I asked her if her husband (Mel Ferrer) was home, and she said that he was in Los Angeles.

Here's where memory fails me, because I only know that for the next five minutes my naked soul did all the talking, and something comparable within her listened. My next recollection is that she smiled strangely and looked at me sideways. "It's true," she said, "that if I do it, I might get to meet Picasso, isn't it?"

"Of course it's true," I said.

193

"I can't very well pass up such an opportunity as that, can I?" she smiled.

"No," I said, "you can't."

"All right," she looked at me squarely with a mixture of elation and timidity for what she was about to say. "I'll do it!"

"You will?" I yelped.

We were jubilant together and laughed with joy. Suddenly she became quiet and looked down at the ground. "I'm sorry we have only this short time together," she said. "But sometimes great things come from crazy little meetings." The quiet, musical way in which she said that, coupled with the fact that she kept her eyes downward all the while, had a strange, unreal effect on my exhausted imagination, and to this day chills me with unfulfilled expectations when I think of it.

She took my hand and walked with me to the gate, still maintaining this new strangely subdued manner. "I must tell you," she said slowly, pressing my hand warmly as we stood by the gate, "never in my whole life have I been so flattered. I know that sounds phony and corny, but I mean it—I'm *truly* flattered." Again she looked down, but when she looked back up I tried to lock her eye in my own gaze, and managed it for an instant—but she looked quickly away. "I'll give you my address and number," she said, and went into the house for a card.

Her cab had long since arrived, and the two drivers were standing together, engaged in coversation, and my driver looked over at me and winked. Then Audrey appeared with the card, telling me she would be talking with her agent, Kurt Frings, and thanked me warmly again; and once more she said how sad it was that we couldn't have spent the whole afternoon together in the house—talking, and listening to music, and having tea—with lots of time.

As I walked toward my cab she shouted something in French to her driver, and with a final goodbye wave and a final look, she disappeared again. I was powerfully aware that I had just encountered a creature of great charm and beauty unequalled in our time.

In sheer ecstacy over the results of my meeting with Audrey, everything seemed to me as some incredible and beautiful dream. Before embarking on the all-night train ride back to my hotel in Lucerne, I took myself on a short tour of Geneva, treating my palate to a fine dinner, and taking in an outdoor jazz festival in the style of the old park bandstands, with hundreds in attendance. I was driven to the railroad depot by another in the long line of great Swiss taxi drivers—a younger fellow this time, but equally friendly, eager to be of service and loaded with informative conversation. It was a great, clean, exceedingly attractive city.

The railroad depot was awe-inspiring. Massive beams intertwined in the curved ceiling far, far overhead; trains puffed side by side, having recently arrived or about to leave; and so exciting was the overall feeling of good life on the move, of orderly bustle and activity, that I temporarily lost sight of my reason for being there, and almost missed my train.

With the train lit from within, and the darkness of night outside, there was little scenery save one's own reflection and that of the compartment's interior staring back through the window as one looked out; but the warm feeling prevailed, and after two hours or so I began to doze off, in a reverie of Audrey.

I was rudely awakened as the train came to a stop at a small junction very late into the night, and I and the other passengers had to disembark and switch trains. It was to be a good half-hour's wait in the small station, and I could barely keep my eyes open. Soon several of the other passengers, all men, began dozing off; so, spreading myself out on one of the benches, I followed suit. The next thing I knew, I was being awakened by a gentle but very definite tap on the bottom of my feet. Looking up I saw a policeman with his club, shaking his head at me instructively as he walked off. Sitting up, I noticed the others also rubbing their eyes as if newly awakened.

On the last half of my journey I was joined by a bright young blond Swede in shorts, with a pack on his back, who informed me that he was making his way across Europe on foot, and that this train ride was one of the few times he was allowing himself to cheat a little. He was criminally awake. However, without his conversation I would have missed that mystic predawn blueness that pervades just before sunup, with all the accompanying sights of village and farm. I was weary and bleary-eyed as the train finally chugged, slower and slower, to its stop in Lucerne. I descended almost hypnotically, as the morning light gradually seemed to be bringing the view more into focus, and, half-awake, I took a cab back to my hotel, a charming country-cottage type of place, and climbed happily into bed. As I did so, I turned on the radio, to hear the strains once again of Haydn's *Trumpet* Concerto, which I had been hearing at such strategic points in my journey to Audrey ever since leaving Los Angeles! Hardly a romantic piece of "traveling music" with which one would be inclined to identify amorous or even adventurous thoughts, but it became my "traveling music" nonetheless.

Picking up my phone from the comfort of bed, it was with great relish that I called Bruce Campbell at his hotel in New York. It was nighttime there, and my call woke him up.

"Hi, Bruce!" I said.

"Tell me what happened!" he cried.

"Remember," I teased, "you were telling me to be realistic?"

"Tell me what happened!" he cried again.

"Well," I continued, "I have a piece of realism for you!"

"Tell me what happened!" he persisted.

195

"Audrey said *'Yes'!*" I shouted, interrupting another "Tell me what h——" as with a *thump* he fell out of bed at my news.

With Bruce and I both back again in Los Angeles, we met with Roy Silver at the offices of Campbell, Silver, Cosby, and I filled them in on the details. They were both wild with joy and wanted me to return immediately to Switzerland with a letter of agreement for Audrey to sign.

"Not a contract," said Roy, noting my dismayed reaction, "just a letter of agreement."

"But it would seem so *gross*," I argued, "after such a beautiful meeting, to shove any kind of legal paper under her nose so quickly!"

"Wes," Roy smiled patiently, "we're in the business here of making a movie, not promoting tender little romantic meetings! Either she was serious or she wasn't, and if she said she'll do it, then *believe me*, she understands these things!"

"I know, I know," I said. "All right—I'll call her tonight."

The day before, I had sent Audrey a telegram thanking her for the visit, and reminding her of her cryptic remark that "Sometimes great things come from crazy little meetings." That night, sprawled atop my bed in my apartment, I called her in Switzerland, and was surprised at how easily I was able to reach her; shocked into a brief siege of nervousness at the sudden sound of her warm, friendly voice.

"Thank you for your telegram," she laughed. "It was most welcome."

"Oh, you got it already?" I replied, trying to keep from sounding like Henry Aldrich.

"Yes," she said. Then, rather falteringly: "There's been a change since I saw you."

"Is it your husband?" I guessed.

"Yes," she answered. A pause—then, "He doesn't seem to approve of my decision to be in your film."

"Oh no," I moaned. "Why not?"

"Well—," she hesitated.

"Is he there with you now?" I asked.

"Yes," she answered.

Silence.

"Things—," she continued, "things aren't all that well here." Her voice, at least to my mind, took on a tearful tone.

"I was going back to Switzerland this week to see you—to talk some more about the film," I said.

"We won't be here," Audrey answered, still in a hushed tone. "We'll be on vacation in Southern Spain. Marbella!"

"Marbella!" I cried. "That's in Malaga where Picasso was born!"

"He was born there?"

196

"Yes! Well—is it all right if I see you there then, instead?"

"Oh Wes," she replied. "I can't promise you anything—he's pretty insistent—but if you want to come—I won't try to stop you."

"I will," I said. "I'll see you in Marbella!"

She gave me the address where they would be staying, and we said our goodbyes. I lay on my bed for an hour afterward, not knowing whether to be crushed at the new turn of events, or just to be amazed at the wonder of such a conversation having taken place at all, in the confines of my own prosaic bedroom!

I flew to Marbella several days later with a letter of agreement, two copies of Ray Bradbury's *Picasso Summer* script, and high hopes, after sending Audrey a twelve-page letter, detailing what it was I intended to create in the animation and the events leading up to my meeting with her; also I wrote of the importance to me, and the overall feeling for the film itself, that it be *her*, my own concept of Beauty, who graces the film. (Bruce Campbell told me later that when Roy Silver read a copy of the letter he actually cried, saying that *this* should be the story they were making into a film!)

With my earphones on the plane plugged in, as usual, to the selection of symphonic music, I was astonished to once again hear the familiar strains of Haydn's *Trumpet* Concerto, until I realized I was flying the same airline on which I had heard it before; but still, hard as it is to attribute anything significant or mystical to such a piece—odd to believe—I did hear it on my own radio in Los Angeles the night before leaving on this very trip!

It was a hot, sunny afternoon when the plane landed in Malaga, far from the airport terminal; so that all the passengers were driven in buses to the airline buildings for customs inspection and baggage retrieval. Sitting in the seat just ahead of me were two enormously talkative young American girls from New York. They were attractive, but I felt no inducement to join in their conversation as a fellow American, for my mind was actively engaged in its own thinking match pertaining to the purpose of my journey to Marbella.

However, it was inevitable that we would meet, for the buses from the airport to Marbella had all taken off by the time we had cleared customs and claimed our baggage, and the next bus due was a guaranteed hour's wait. It had been arranged for a limousine to meet me and take me into Marbella (an hour's drive), and I invited the girls, who were now visibly distressed and disheveled from the scorching, unrelenting heat, to join me. They were delighted, and we were on our way.

The most talkative and older of the two girls was Brenda; the quieter and more attractive one was Jenny. Brenda was extremely protective of Jenny, and to my great annoyance made this very clear from the outset. But I held my peace, and the trip was very pleasant, due mostly to the richness and color of the scenery through which we drove. The Mediterranean was a lush, dark blue; the sky blazing with sunshine; the hills alive with greenery; and even the yellow-white sand mounds were abundant with colorful growth sprouting from the richness of the soil. Truly, southern Spain was the other side of the Iberian coin, and there was no wonder that this was the land that gave birth to Picasso and nourished his genius to fruition.

But surely enough, that old question of hotel reservations and availability was ever, ever the same! I had gone with the girls to the hotel at which they had reserved rooms—a beautiful place on the outskirts of town—to be sure they were checked in and safely settled; but when we approached the lobby it was literally swarming with tourists trying to get a room—all of whom had "reservations"! The girls were near tears till I assured them there would be plenty of room in Marbella itself, and we continued the journey together into town. Our driver told us that we would be lucky to get one room between us, for Marbella was fast becoming the most "in," the most chic vacation resort in Europe.

Well, it was the same at my hotel; my reservations were not honored. The three of us traipsed from hotel to hotel, finally jumping with joy when told that there was one suite available, with one bedroom, a living room, and bath. We took it, embracing each other in a delirium of relief—but not so wild a delirium that I could fail to read the message of warning in Brenda's eye as she yelped with joy with Jenny and me—and we hurried to our little suite to purge ourselves of the oppressive heat that by now had us almost prostrate.

There was an attractive little balcony just off our living room (which was to be my bedroom, with the couch as my bed), overlooking a beautiful view of the hotel grounds, which were expansive and picturesque. The girls were to share the large, comfortable bed in the boudoir, with the bathroom just adjacent to it.

They were enthralled with my reason for being in Marbella and begged to go with me when I saw Audrey on the following day, but I assured them that this was out of the question. However, in the evening after dinner they walked with me to the exclusive colony of summer cottages at which Audrey was staying with her husband and young son Sean. To gain entrance one had to have clearance through the security office in front, but we got a good view of it by walking around the grounds from the outside. It was impressive by any standards, and housed only the world's most wealthy scions of industry and society, and celebrities of the first rank.

Jenny turned in early, succumbing to the exhaustion which had begun to overtake her in the late afternoon, and Brenda and I watched a colorful and sensual Flamenco dance in the garden of one of the neighboring hotels. The husky, sonorous tones of the savagely beautiful dancer filled the summer-night air with its suggestive haughtiness, but did little to stir any romantic urgings in my companion's firmly immovable bosom; and soon enough we, too, were overcome by the day's wearying pace, and returned to our hotel to retire for the night.

I awoke at midnight to the heavy call of nature, and walked through the bedroom toward the bathroom to answer this urgent call. The girls were sound asleep in skimpy white negligees, with the covers thrown completely back, almost to the floor. They looked like angels, so different from the chatty, gabby little "yentas" of their waking hours, and I had to smile at the sight. The bathroom was just to the left of the head of the bed, and it embarrassed me to imagine with what dreadful noises I might be awakening them. To my great dismay, I noticed that there was no water in the toilet, and when, to test the plumbing, I turned on the tap of the sink I discovered that, indeed, the plumbing was totally dry! With a toilet that would not flush I had no intention of leaving any sort of despicable sight for the girls to discover upon arising in the morning—but what was I to do?

Returning to the living room I picked up the telephone to inform the desk of my plight, only to be casually informed that the plumbing was turned off every night until *three in the morning* to conserve the water! How could I survive for three hours in this condition? All but bursting with gas, I stepped out onto my balcony and disturbed the night air instead of the girls. Then, back in my couch-bed, I lay awake in agony for three hours until finally I heard, after what seemed the most unbearable of eternities, the most beautiful sound imaginable—the slow but certain *drip, drip* of the hotel plumbing, returned to working status!

The next day was a crucial one for me and all my dreaming, for this was the day on which I intended once again to see Audrey, but knowing full well that this time in order to do so I would first have to pass that most troublesome of barriers—her husband! I went to the Colony around two o'clock in the afternoon and called her from the phone in the security office. A servant answered and told me she was taking a nap. I told her who I was, informing her I would call back in an hour or so. When I called back, Audrey herself answered the phone, on the first ring.

"Oh, Wes," she said sorrowfully. "I'm so sorry you made this trip now. I can't see you."

"Why not?" I cried.

"Ohh," her voice became choked and tearful. "Same thing as before. I read your letter, Wes—it was so beautiful; I admire you so much and wish now more than ever that I could work with you and be a part of it all!"

Suddenly, another voice interrupted rudely; it was Mel Ferrer, having taken the phone from Audrey: "Listen, you goddamn pest," he screamed, "I want you to leave Audrey alone, do you understand? I happen to know that you're just using her name for publicity and exploitation purposes! I saw that 'blurb' in the Hollywood trade papers saying that Audrey would be starring in *The Picasso Summer* and—"

"What?" I yelled. "That's absolutely untrue! There never—"

I was stopped in mid-sentence by the sound of a receiver banging down.

I was absolutely incensed, enraged, crushed—it was over! He had lied about the "blurb" in the trade papers, but, in any case, it hardly mattered. It was over. It was to be another three months or so before I was to accidentally discover the true story behind Ferrer's deceit, through a chance meeting with the bodyguard who was staying at the cottage at this time. But more on that later, in its proper place.

Brenda and Jenny were sympathetic, but totally incapable of penetrating the black shroud of rage and disbelief by which I was now completely engulfed. Instead, I called Dominguin and told him what had happened, and he told me to come to Madrid right away and we would figure out what to do. The girls were delighted and grateful to find that the two days they had spent with me had been charged entirely to my expense account, for with or without them, my room was paid for by Campbell, Silver, Cosby; and so our parting was sweet and sentimental, and I was on my way, numb with frustration, shock, and anger, to Madrid.

24

Actor, Actress, Director

MIGUEL MET ME AT THE AIRPORT, AND FRANCISCO (SHADES OF TOM TANNEN-
baum) drove us back to the house. At dinner Miguel consoled me with his
own opinion of Ferrer, and asked me if he could be of any further help. I
told him of my promise to Bruce Campbell to ask Deborah Kerr if she
would star in *The Picasso Summer* if Audrey could not do it, and he smiled
confidently that he was sure she would love to do it, and that he would call
Peter Viertel and Deborah right after dinner.

"They are vacationing now een San Sebastian," Miguel smiled, "and weel
have plenty of free time to read the screept."

I expressed my very real concern that Deborah might feel slighted that
she was only my second choice, when actually I felt that she was in no way
second to anyone, on any level.

"It's just that, with me, Audrey Hepburn had always been a sort of
personal romantic ideal, ever since I fell in love with her in *Roman Holiday,*"
I explained. "I in no way compare the two women to the detriment of
either!"

Miguel laughed heartily. "I assure you, Wes," he said, "Deborah
understands these theengs. She ees not a woman with complexes or
pettiness of any kind. You need not say a word about eet, she weel know
you are een love weeth Audrey. We *all* are, no? Even Deborah. Ees okay,
believe me!"

After dinner, Miguel put in the call to Peter and Deborah in San
Sebastian, as I sat anxiously by.

"Hello, Peter," said Miguel, with a wink in my direction. "Thees ees

Dominguin. I 'ave here weeth me our friend Wes. You talk to heem an' then I weel say hello after."

Miguel handed me the phone and I told Peter, briefly, what had happened in Marbella.

"Don't worry about a thing, compadre," Peter said jovially. "You just get on down here to San Sebastian tomorrow and Deborah and I will take a look at the script. And we'll have some interesting stories to tell you that I think will make you feel a little better about the whole thing."

At bedtime Miguel gave me the room that Deborah and Peter had used during my very first visit to the Dominguin home in May of 1964, and I slept in Deborah's bed—the one under which she had deposited my large portfolio for safekeeping before we all had left for the bullfight. I was beginning to feel better already, knowing full well that once again I was in good hands—the old, familiar hands that had given me such a tremendous lift at the beginning of my journey to Picasso. I lay awake for a long time, thinking of the comments Miguel had made during dinner regarding his personal opinions of Ferrer, substantiating all I had heard from the cab driver in Switzerland. It was impossible to be depressed in the company of Dominguin, and my recent brush with Ferrer and the memory of Audrey's sad voice was soothed over now in the bright anticipation of my trip to San Sebastian the next day, and the incomparably joyful company of Peter Viertel and Deborah Kerr. I slept well, and awoke refreshed, rejoicing once again in that confident feeling—almost childlike, I suppose—of door after door opening, with a smile behind each one.

San Sebastian is a beautiful border resort town between France and Spain with pleasant, tree-lined streets—languishing in its own romantic charm under the southern sun. Peter and Deborah were vacationing in the rented home of the actress Anabella, Tyrone Power's first wife. I was to meet them at a designated spot: a most appealing little hotel that had a tree-shaded patio-restaurant on the front street. It was about two o'clock in the afternoon, and I sat sipping a cup of coffee while awaiting the arrival of my friends. I was completely alone, until presently a lovely young lady sat down several tables away. I was trying casually to catch her eye when I noticed her looking with great interest at something just over my shoulder. I turned in time to see Deborah sneaking up behind me, just getting ready to cover my eyes with her hands.

"Oh, rats!" she cried. "I never am successful with that sort of thing!"

I laughed, and embraced her happily. "Peter will be along in a minute," she said. "He's with our daughter and his secretary, getting ice cream cones. You like ice cream cones, don't you?"

"Oh, one will be plenty," I said.

"That's all you get!" she laughed.

Soon Peter and the girls showed up with the refreshments, and after a hearty exchange of greetings we all squeezed into the car and drove to the house.

Deborah and Peter sat on the back patio of Anabella's beautiful home, each reading a copy of the Bradbury script, which I had brought for them. I lay down to rest on a couch in the room which was separated from the patio by a large sliding glass door. As I peacefully watched them both reading intently, my eyelids began to feel heavy, and I was soon fast asleep.

I was awakened gently by the form of Peter standing over me. "Hey, compadre," he said. "I can't let Deborah do this part! You're just using her for publicity and exploitation purposes!" The three of us roared with laughter, and in the laughter was the knowledge, for me, that Deborah would, indeed, do it—so that my mirth was part amusement, part hysterical relief and appreciation for the manner in which the acceptance was given.

We all returned to the patio outside, and sat discussing the script. They were both very impressed with it.

"And don't worry about money," Deborah reassured me. "I know your budget is negligible. I want to do it because I think this is the most worthwhile project I've ever come across." Then, to my surprise, she told me a story that boggled my senses.

"Don't feel alone in your experience with Mel Ferrer, Wes," she said. "He's treated Peter and me in an equally boorish manner."

"*You?*" I exclaimed.

Peter nodded smilingly, as Deborah continued. "Yes, *us*," she said. "At one time we had planned on buying a home in Switzerland near Audrey, whom I consider one of my closest and dearest friends. Then one day Mel called and told me that I was using Audrey to further my own career, for cheap publicity purposes! He said that he had just read a newspaper item stating that I was taking a home near my friend, Audrey Hepburn. Of course, I was shocked and horrified with disbelief, and had Audrey known about this incident she would have died."

I shook my head incredulously, and told Deborah what my Swiss cab driver had said about Ferrer, in comparison with Audrey.

"Well you see," said Peter, "Mel has just recently produced and starred in an art film of his own, called *El Greco,* which has, literally, been laughed out of all the theaters in Europe at which it's been shown. Had he allowed Audrey to star, now, in an art film of this stature, I'm sure he felt it might make him an even bigger fool, should any comparisons be made!"

Early that evening it was decided that we would all go out for dinner, and while the others were bustling about in preparation, I once again (to my great surprise) fell asleep on the couch. Lord, I must have been tired! I awoke this time to the sound of Peter charging heavily down the stairs, calling my name cheerily, and off we went.

We sat at a table in the outdoor terrace of a charming restaurant, with Deborah sitting directly across from me. To her left sat Peter, with their young daughter seated between them. Peter's beautiful secretary sat to my right, and she and Peter talked business while Deborah and I were engaged in a most amazing conversation, in which I discovered that she had one of the most hilarious and charmingly *outrageous* senses of humor I had ever encountered. It was still early in the evening, and the San Sebastian twilight bathed the whole scene in an aura of mystic blue-violet. But back to Deborah's humor!

Somehow we had found our way, most incongruously (considering our delicious seafood dinner), to the subject of nose-picking, nose-pickers, and all the various nuances and aspects; with description after disgusting description we became more and more hysterical. My hysteria was more pronounced than hers, for each time she would say something on the subject, the incongruity of what she was saying, coupled with her inalterably feminine and ladylike demeanor, would throw me completely; Peter and his secretary would be interrupted in their own conversation to find themselves laughing automatically in response to our hilarity, and Deborah's little girl was beset with giggling.

The subject then took a dive for the worse, funnier in that we now had control of our laughter, and the stories and examples of people passing gas under various circumstances now took on a sobriety that only underscored the uproariousness of it all; for there was respectable and royal manner in which Deborah said the things one never speaks of at dinner.

"Now I *know* you're just using Deborah for publicity and exploitation purposes!" Peter laughed.

By the time we had our tea and dessert, night had (entirely unnoticed) made its appearance, and the city lights were glowing enchantingly. We left the restaurant filled to capacity with the hearty meal and heartier merriment; and that, coupled with the fact that my day had included two incompleted naps, caused me to sleep even sounder that night than I had the night before, and I was content that the problem of finding a star for our film was solved.

Back in Los Angeles, Bruce and Roy were intrigued and delighted with my news, but as the days passed, and Roy contacted Deborah's agent to consolidate the deal, my contentment soon turned once again to anxiety. For it seems Deborah's agent was disturbed by her offer to do the film for the small sum she was more than willing to accept, and was unable to contact her in Europe in order to discuss it with her. I tried calling her, and even Dominguin tried for me, but he told me he assumed that she and Peter were junketing off somewhere on a continuation of their vacation. So meanwhile, Roy and Deborah's agent haggled, and precious time was passing.

When it looked as though this haggling between Deborah's agent and Roy might go on indefinitely, Roy wasted no time in hopping the first plane to London when he heard that Albert Finney was interested in doing our film, and he returned in several days with Finney's signature on a letter of agreement.

This meant that Deborah would not play well as the wife in any case, because of the age difference between her and Albert Finney.

With Renoir definitely out of the picture as director, due to his infirmity, we finally decided to send for Serge Bourgignon, the popular young French director of *Sundays and Cybele,* which had just recently won an Academy Award for Best Foreign Picture and had received much acclaim throughout the world. I had suggested his name in remembrance of my promise to Christine long ago (that first springtime in Cannes), and Roy and Bruce were interested anyway because of the excitement his film had been generating at that time.

Serge agreed to it on several conditions, the most pleasant one being that his ex-sweetheart, Yvette Mimieux, play the female lead opposite Albert Finney.

That first afternoon when I saw Yvette, in all her golden-blond magnificence, mounting the stairs in Campbell, Silver, Cosby to Roy's office, I was struck by the aura of *niceness* that emanated from her, obvious even through her visual sensuality. She was accompanied by a tall, very pleasant, if not conservatively square-appearing man who turned out to be her manager and publicist Jim Byron, who had discovered Yvette, as well as the great sex goddess Jayne Mansfield. Things were beginning to fall into place very swiftly.

During the weeks Serge Bourgignon was in Los Angeles to sign with Campbell, Silver, Cosby as director of the film, part of his deal was that he stay at the Bel-Air Hotel (with all expenses paid)—an extravagance to which CSC generously but tearfully yielded. Each afternoon Ray Bradbury and I joined him at poolside where the three of us discussed the *Picasso Summer* script while Ray jotted down all ideas that seemed to hold some promise, before he was to get heavily into the writing. This was great fun, and we all got along beautifully; from the joviality of these meetings no one could ever sense the great rift that was eventually to come between Serge and Ray.

One afternoon when we finished early, Serge told me that he had some clothes and accessories he wanted to buy and asked me to accompany him on his shopping spree. I was soon to learn that he was shopping not so much for clothing, but for women—as many as he could collect with the sensual glance of his heavily lidded brown eyes: the prototype of the "sexy French look." He came back loaded with clothes (compliments of Campbell, Silver, Cosby!) and phone numbers (compliments of a dozen flustered young ladies), and I was exhausted from laughing at his audacious antics, little suspecting that someday these antics would lose all their humorous effect, thanks to the persistent and overbearing ego from whence they originated. But we enjoyed one another's company, and for a while he was an amusing and entertaining companion.

When I suggested to him one day that part of the reason he was chosen was because I had promised Christine that I would definitely consider him for director of the film, he took great exception to this, insisting that Roy and Bruce had picked him on the basis of his talent alone. I acquiesced promptly, and never mentioned it again. For sure.

Christine was the subject of many of our conversations, and Serge apparently still felt a good deal of affection for her, and smiled dreamily when I told her how she spoke of him so often, with a love that seemed virtually undying. He told me of his two-year romance with Yvette and how great it was that they could still be such close friends even though all feelings of passion and romantic love had passed for both of them. How nice if all romantic affairs could end so cordially!

One afternoon, soon after Yvette had signed for the film, my four-minute sample animation reel was screened in the plush projection room of Campbell, Silver, Cosby. Yvette, Serge, and Jim Byron were in attendance, as well as several of the CSC regulars. It was such a rousing success with them that they requested that it be rerun several times. Jim Byron gave me the ultimate compliment, when he said (after the lights came on) that he had never understood Picasso before, and hated all of his work. But now, he said, after seeing my version of Picasso-in-motion, he not only suddenly understood Picasso, but could not wait to get his hands on a Picasso art book so that he could devour all that he had been missing before in his ignorance.

One afternoon Serge and I sat at a long table in a room at CSC, which was stacked with every available book on Picasso's work, with the intention of going carefully through every one of them in order to select the best and most appropriate subjects for the animation of *Picasso Summer*.

In a very short time we were in a hushed state of virtual awe, as in reproduction after reproduction we witnessed the unbelievable versatility of this master Picasso; the refined, almost painfully beautiful tenderness of the fragile and sensitive line with which he would draw a mother and child; the bold, masculine, aggressive strokes with which he would portray a bull or minotaur in action, with an incisive mastery seen before only in a Michelangelo or a Rembrandt. We looked at page after page with an ever-growing humility, watching as satyrs and fauns pranced before us in bacchanalian innocence and sensuality born of the Earth's beginnings; matadors and picadors and bulls locked in glorious and bloody combat in distortions that were not distortions but dramatizations of the reality of life's struggles and endless battle with destiny, as in his soul-searing portrayals of war, wherein one could imagine the sounds of screaming and moaning actually spiraling up out of the book's very pages.

After several hours of this silent spectacle that paraded itself before our eyes, in book after book of life itself captured in paint and line by an imagination and creativity unequalled in any century, even in prolificity alone, no one could convince us that Picasso was not *the* master, *the* artist, *the* genius of those regions of vision that go beyond the surface of all that presents itself so superficially to the overworked and ordinary eye. In both hands Picasso held out to us his boundless spirit as reflection and potential of our own—and the chillingly wondrous thought that we were to work with him in any way on the production of our film caused us to look at one another with a brief look of egoless disbelief and vertigo, as we closed the final book and all but staggered from the room.

Bruce and I met Albert Finney at the airport and were struck by his relaxed friendliness and humor, as if we had been friends for years. In his hotel room, when he learned how close we had come to getting Audrey Hepburn as our female lead, he laughed and said, "That would have done it! You know, everyone was linking us romantically when we starred together in *Two For The Road,* and had we been together in *Picasso Summer* the rumors would have been flying stronger than ever!"

Much later, however, Albert confided to Bruce that he actually had been in love with Audrey, and would have married her, had that been possible. Similar statements have been made since by Cary Grant and a half dozen other leading men who have fallen for the irresistible charms of the bewitching Audrey.

Shortly after Albert's arrival, Roy Silver threw a party for him at his home in the hills above Doheny and Sunset. This was attended by many celebrities and was predominantly a very pleasant affair. Roy's neighbor, the recently divorced Tommy Smothers, was entertaining small groups of appreciative guests in his amusingly shy way, and Marty Ingels spent most of the evening dancing with my date, the beautiful Marj Dusay; while I in turn spent that same period of time chatting with his gorgeous wife. Later, we all stood in line to have our fortunes told behind the closed door of a room in which sat a famous woman psychic who was renowned for her accurate readings. Behind me in line was Ray Bradbury, who was as excited by the whole idea as a young boy in line for a Saturday matinee.

The woman predicted only the very best for me, apparently intentionally refraining to predict the great headaches and heartaches that were yet to come, packaged with the good!

June 6, 1967

Senor Pedro Rodriguez
Segre 8
Madrid 2, Spain

Dear Pedro:

As stated in last week's cable, I will be coming to Madrid the 24th of June. However, I will call you shortly after you receive this letter to verify the date.

I will be accompanied by Mr. Lee Phillips, attorney for the Campbell, Silver, Cosby Corporation and will bring the contract as well as the script for the approval of Luis Miguel.

We will try to accomplish as much as possible this trip so that we can do the necessary filming within the first two weeks of August, if this is convenient to Luis Miguel's schedule.

Thank you again for your kind assistance, and I'll be talking to you soon.

Respectfully,

Wes Herschensohn
WH/slk

Serge, who had returned temporarily to Paris, flew into Madrid to meet with me. I had been involved in negotiations with Miguel, accompanied by the Campbell, Silver, Cosby attorney Lee Phillips; and now I was to introduce Serge to Dominguin.

Serge met me at my hotel and together we went to Dominguin's office. All the way there, and the whole time we waited in Dominguin's outer office until he was free, Serge kept bombarding me with the threat that if he did not like Miguel he would not work on the picture, despite Picasso; such was his artistic sensitivity, or so he incessantly insisted.

I knew, however, that both of these characters contained such a sense of "macho," and that they would recognize this quality so instantly in one another, that there was no way these two lusty male egos would not hit it off; each would see in the other the opportunity to further his own legend of masculine camraderie. Serge insisted on first talking to Miguel alone, after I introduced them, so that he could gauge the measure of their rapport without outside interference.

While I waited in the outer office for Serge's "interview" with Miguel to come to an end, I began gradually to hear their voices become louder and more jocular, increasing subsequently to a crescendo of manly laughter, and I knew my evaluation of the manner in which they would come to terms with one another was true, if not absolutely on target.

And so, one "crucial" step in Serge's terms, insofar as accepting the directorship of our film, had been met with flying colors.

Haunted by the exquisitely French face of Anne Dussart, I was determined to see her again, and on a stopover in Paris, before returning to Los Angeles, I cajoled Christine, one bright afternoon, into calling the Dussarts' home for me to arrange a visit. We called from a phone booth in the midst of the city, and the maid answered, saying that the Dussarts had gone away for several days but were expected back in a day or so.

Disappointed, I thanked Christine, who laughed and said, teasingly, that it served me right; and we proceeded to cross what was undoubtedly the busiest intersection of Paris, with endless streams of cars racing madly in all directions, so that Christine and I became trapped on an island in the dead center of the intersection with no hope of getting across the boulevard. Suddenly a small car drove up to our side of the island, with a smiling, familar face behind the wheel. It was Gicky Dussart! Although this was but one in a series of almost psychic happenings, I was nevertheless astonished at Gicky's sudden appearance, for not only was it timely in relation to the phone call, but we were badly in need of rescue. Christine was devastated by it, especially when, while driving us to our destination, Gicky invited me to visit Anne and himself at their home some day that week! He said they were returning from a short trip and he had just dropped off Anne and her sister and the baby at her mother's house.

The Dussarts, who lived in the fashionable, shady suburb of Nuilly, had a two-story apartment studio bathed in sunlight, and when I arrived Anne was still upstairs. When she descended the stairway she was in silhouette and I saw that her hair was long and came down to her waist, a fact that I had never considered when I first had seen her in Cap d'Antibes with her hair up in curls. She was like a vision, like music, after all my dreaming of her.

Hardly knowing, myself, what it was I wanted with her, what I expected of her, I asked her and Gicky if she would like a small part in my movie. Gicky said that it would be up to Anne, and she looked up at me from the sofa where she sat and said in reply, *"Porquois Pas?"* This surprised Gicky, who told me she was usually very shy. Then he showed me some of his paintings and photographs and, later, offered to drive me back to my hotel. As we left, Anne looked at me from behind Gicky's towering figure and said, in her soft, musical way, *"A bientot!"* This was the last time I ever saw her. Gicky was such a good-natured fellow, large and handsome with an almost naive manner, so reminiscent of Pierre in *War and Peace,* that I felt guilty for my innocent infatuation for Anne. (Innocence due to lack of opportunity is nonetheless innocence, alas.) Although upon my return to the States he sent me several black-and-white photos of her, with an offer to send others in color if I desired, I was nevertheless unsuccessful in convincing Serge, as director, to make such an unnecessary and out-of-the-way casting, since all of our actors came either from the USA or from those location spots where we did the actual filming, such as Madrid and Cannes. Nor did I ever respond to Gicky's welcome communications, so shamefully neglectful of the niceties was I during those harrowing preproduction days of the film.

Such was my love affair with Anne Dussart, whose face dominated my thinking as the personification of that girl whose image had appeared mysteriously throughout the history of French painting, up to and including those dazzling little femmes who materialize as echoes of Ingres and Boucher and Fragonard and Delacroix and in the later erotic etchings and lithographs of Picasso himself.

When I was a little boy lying on the green grass of our back yard watching a butterfly or grasshopper while my mother hung freshly laundered sheets and linen on the clothesline to dry in the morning sun, I would often hear the distant sound of a vacuum cleaner and these simple sights and sounds made the whole Universe smile for me for the rest of my life. It was the security and warmth of innocence, but more so, of *an awareness of the beginnings of things.* This feeling pervaded everything that was happening to me in Cannes. When I would be awakened in the morning by the sound of the vacuum cleaner outside my hotel door, I was once again that child on the grass. And Anne Dussart was a butterfly at which to marvel. "Roxanne! Roxanne!" Cyrano said.

"Anne Dussart! Anne Dussart!" I was constantly saying, with an endless flow of sketches and water-colors, that will tell you—if you see them—everything.

The 24th of June was a banner day, for it was not only the day I arrived in Madrid with the contract, but halfway around the world, at The Hague in Holland, a man was writing an inscription in a book. When I returned from Spain I found a package waiting for me at the post office. It was a copy of David Douglas Duncan's new book *Yankee Nomad—A Photographic Odyssey,* mailed from the Netherlands.

Opening the book, I found this inscription inside:

For Wes—   24 June 1967
We await you!   The Hague
   Saludos,
     Dave

25

Madrid—and Fernet Branca

I WAS THE FIRST TO ARRIVE AT THE HOTEL PALÁCE IN MADRID, TO BE JOINED IN a week or so by Bruce Campbell and Joe Juliano, our Paris-based production manager, and finally by Serge and the entire French film crew. During my solo stay, Dominguin invited me to his home one afternoon, suggesting I bring a girl—so that in the evening we could all go out on the town. This was great with me, because for several days I had had my eye on a bright-eyed little switchboard operator at the hotel named Amalia, who was very shy and reticent, but who blushed appealingly whenever we spoke. This was my opportunity, for no little Spanish working girl was about to turn down an invitation to the home of the great Luis Miguel Dominguin!

Fortunately, she got off work at two in the afternoon, and we went straight to Miguel's home. Everything went well, and Miguel was impressed with Amalia's beauty and shy femininity. However, around five-thirty, when the afternoon sun was making way for the appearance of evening, I noticed that Amalia's eyes were beginning to fill with tears! Stunned, I asked her what was the matter, and she replied that she was afraid her mother would be worrying about her, for she always returned home by this time. I suggested she call her mother and explain that she would be out for the evening, when she began to cry in earnest!

Miguel laughingly chastised me for picking such an innocent, explaining that this was obviously a family girl in the old Spanish tradition. Sending Amalia home in his limousine, Miguel then called the girl he had invited for the evening and told her to bring a friend.

Miguel's girl was ravishingly beautiful, by any standard—mine was wanting considerably—but we had a great evening, and Miguel surprised us all by his prowess at dancing rock and roll at one of the posh Madrid discotheques.

The next day at the hotel, when I went to the switchboard to say hello to Amalia, she was full of apologies and said that she would love to go out with me again—any *afternoon*.

Once our film crew arrived at the Hotel Palace it seemed the whole place came alive, especially since the crew of *Villa Rides* took up residence at the same time. The massively spacious lobby became the focal point of all activity, and I took special enjoyment in this as a sort of private counterpoint to the many weeks I spent in solitude at this same hotel on other occasions.

Just prior to the arrival of our crew, I was entering the hotel one evening and noticed a small flurry of activity at the far end of the lobby on the stairway that led to the dining room. A fat lady was sitting in a semisprawling condition upon the middle of the stairway and her leg was in a cast. She was wailing and moaning in a loud English accent that she had just rebroken her leg, and her young, effeminate son was running about frantically in search of a doctor, and apparently the hotel management was having a difficult time locating one. The whole scene was right out of an engraving by Rowlandson.

I positioned myself in a large leather chair toward the left of the stairway to observe the excitement with what I confess was a totally detached attitude, for I could feel little sympathy for this woman who was precluding all possible sympathy for herself by her ear-splitting shrieks of lamentation, interspersed as they were by softly voiced commands to her son each time he ran past her in his fruitless search for medical attention. After several minutes Robert Mitchum, who had just entered the hotel, approached the lady on the stairs and bent down to speak to her. After apparently informing him that the management was trying to locate a doctor, Mitchum appeared about to continue on into the dining room when the woman grabbed his hand with a shriek and held it in a vicelike grip.

"Ohhh please, Mr. Mitchum!" she cried. "Don't leave me! I'm in such pain—stay with me until the doctor arrives!" Upon which she resumed her repertoire of wails and moans.

What could poor Mitchum do, with all eyes upon him, but consent to stand by this injured flower and comfort her in her dark hour of tragedy? How was he to know that a full half-hour was to pass before professional aid was finally to come? And for half an hour he stood there holding the hand of this fat woman who was sprawled upon the stairway engaging him in constant conversation, so that each time that he assumed she was all right and gave any indication of leaving her, she would let out another volley of screams and tighten her grip on his hand. What made the incident all the more comical and Rowlandsonian was that the string orchestra, which was stationed in the dining room for the dinner hour, just above the stairway, was conducting business as usual, and the tuxedoed musicians were flailing away at their own repertoire, which consisted of Strauss waltzes, Cole Porter medleys, and the usual sophisticated dinner-hour divertissements.

The following evening, when Serge arrived with the crew, all hell broke loose when Serge discovered he could not be placed in a particular suite of rooms he desired, even after he informed the hotel manager that he was Serge Bourgignon! It seems that the suite had been reserved for Mel Ferrer, and later, when Ferrer arrived, Serge solicitously gave way to him, and the two became engaged in that all-too-familiar repartee of false camaraderie that seemed to be the stock-in-trade of the whole bunch.

When later I noticed Ferrer's eyes glaring at me from under his hat in what seemed to me a darkly hostile manner, and in what must have been for him a moment of sudden recognition, I mentioned it to Serge, reminding him of the Audrey Hepburn episode.

"I know, I know," he said with some irritation, "but keep your voice down—we can't afford to start anything!" At which point I suppressed a loud guffaw in the direction of Serge's face, for what Serge meant was that if anyone was going to start anything, it was to be Serge himself, and *only* Serge. Little did I know how soon that was to take place, and that I was to be the victim, albeit foolishly on my own part.

Once our French film crew was all settled in the hotel, we decided to go out and celebrate our first night together. Our group consisted of Serge, Bruce, myself, Joe Juliano, and the entire crew of seven or eight French film technicians, headed by the internationally famous cameraman Vilmos Zsigmond, known as "Ziggy," and including the great cinematographer, Henri Alecan. We arrived in separate cabs at the designated restaurant, a lavishly appointed two-story white building in an exclusive section of Madrid. We were given a long table on the second floor with the room all to ourselves.

Serge and I sat opposite each other at one end of the table, and to my left was Bruce and to his left was Joe, followed by some of the crew to Joe's left. Ziggy sat at Serge's right, and to Ziggy's right sat the remainder of the crew. The room was rather brightly lit, and we were attended by an appropriately large group of waiters.

I was feeling in particularly festive spirits for having come this far along in the realization of my dream; I could hardly feel otherwise, and I was determined to establish warm and cordial relationships with this willing group of Frenchmen who at this point were still strangers to me. It was in this frame of mind that I listened, in mock seriousness, to Serge's amusing account of the "Fernet Branca Club" of which he was "president," and Ziggy was "vice-president." Fernet Branca, he explained, was a potent drink, which because of its medicinal attributes, was possibly the most horrible-tasting drink in the world; and because Serge had at one time been able to drink seven in a row, this (without question) qualified him as president of the Fernet Branca Club, while Ziggy, who followed a close second with five glasses in a row, naturally qualified as vice-president. Maintaining the spirit of mock seriousness I expressed my great interest in the concoction, much to the merriment of the crew, and Serge, at my request, ordered the waiter to bring me a glass to sample.

And true, it was unquestionably the most horrible-tasting liquid I had ever drank, but to the astonishment of all present, I downed the entire contents of the glass, feeling absolutely no ill effects. After my third drink Ziggy began to realize that his vice-presidency was being threatened, and with that most important post at stake he implored me to end my challenge. This, of course, raised the pitch of merriment to a new peak, and I overheard Joe telling Bruce that he had never seen a group of Frenchmen take to an American so fast and in such a warm way as this crew was taking to me, and quoted to Bruce some of the kind remarks that they had been making to each other about my remarkable cordiality. Of course, with this unexpected encouragement I was determined to depose Ziggy, and it was not long before I became the new vice-president of the Fernet Branca Club, to the mighty cheers of the entire group.

Still feeling absolutely no effects, except for the headiness of my victory and newly established power, I challenged Serge head-on for the leadership of the club. Serge laughingly admonished me to stop while I was ahead, but at the same time signaled the waiter to refill my glass. After I became president of the club, to the deafening applause of the incredulous Frenchmen, I decided to insure my presidency for all time by surging so far ahead of any future challenger as to discourage any attempts at usurping my newly established position. By now the waiter no longer stood by for a signal, for having himself become an active participant in the joviality, he would simply (with a look that was a mixture of amusement, wonder, and respect) refill my glass each time I emptied it, often without my realizing it.

Soon I was vaguely aware that the word "douze!" was being uttered in hushed tones by the crew, and it was with only a slight difficulty that I mentally translated the word to its English equivalent: twelve!

And with that I stood up to acknowledge the reverent look on the now strangely serious faces of all present, which I assumed was obviously a reflection of the fact that I was now indisputably . . .

All I remember after rising from the table was a brief flash of being helped into an elevator, held up on one side by Serge and on the other by Bruce—and after that, an eternity of intermittent flashes of my lying in my jockey shorts on my hotel bed in an agony of nausea and vomiting. To my right, on the night stand, I saw as in a dream an open box of Alka-Seltzer, and sitting in a chair near the foot of my bed the vaguely discernible form of Serge Bourgignon. Such was my first and brief awareness of what was to be a seemingly endless nightmare, accentuated by the faint presence of Serge, who at one point of my sporadic spells of consciousness seemed to be calling my name frantically, as if from some great distance, accompanied by loud and dreadful knocks at the door.

When I awoke the next morning, like the survivor of a shipwreck sprawled out upon a life raft in the middle of a tossing sea, I saw six or seven cigar butts on the floor between my bed and the chair—the only remaining evidence of Serge's night-long vigil, and the cause of my constant awareness through that awful night of a sickening stuffiness that contributed to my already unbelievable nausea.

My phone rang then, and after one or two unsuccessful attempts at answering it, and finally managing to do so, I heard Bruce's voice inquiring after my condition. It was then I learned that Serge, probably more out of guilt than compassion, had undressed me, tended my constant spells of sickness, and having left my room on only one occasion during the night had inadvertently locked himself out. When I failed to respond to his calls and desperate knocking he feared for the worst, and in a fit of panic summoned the night clerk to come and open my door.

"He was afraid you had died," said Bruce. "He kept vigil at your bedside through the night to be sure you stayed alive. Otherwise—well, he'd have had no Picasso movie!"

In an hour or so Bruce called my room again, to inform me that Dominguin had invited him, myself, and Serge to come up that afternoon to his home on the outskirts of Madrid, and asked if I would be well enough to go. I replied that I thought I would be all right, and shortly after the noon hour we were on our way in our company limousine, driven by our company chauffeur.

No one could have been more amused by my condition than Dominguin, who suggested that the best cure for it would be a glass of wine. He went to fetch it for me while I sat, almost prostrate, on a lounging chair by the pool in the warm afternoon air. He returned in a few moments and handed me the glass.

"Thees weel be the best theeng for you," he smiled gently, suppressing a grin as he looked at my agonized expression.

"Take it away, Miguel!" I cried. "Just the smell of it is making me sick all over again. It'll be weeks before I can bear even the smell of alcohol!"

"But eef you can drink eet," he replied, "eet weel be like plunging back eento the ocean after almost drowning, you see!"

"Yes," I moaned. "That's what I'm afraid of!" And with that I lunged into the nearby dressing room and threw up.

It was possibly the world's worst hangover, and, in fact, a good two weeks passed before I could tolerate even the slightest whiff of alcohol. I knew positively that my title as president of the Fernet Branca Club was secure.

26

Lois, the Brynners, and Production under Way

ONE EVENING, WHILE BRUCE, JOE JULIANO, AND I WERE HAVING COFFEE IN THE restaurant of our hotel in Madrid, discussing the preparation of our production prior to the arrival of our crew, we noticed two extremely attractive young American girls at a nearby table—a little brunette and a slender blond, both in their early twenties. Joe enthusiastically called our attention to these girls, exclaiming that at last Bruce and I might have the female companionship we were seeking. They got up to pay their check, and I arranged to be standing by the door as they left. I introduced myself and invited them to join us, which they politely declined, due to the late hour, so I invited them to dinner on the following night. The little brunette said that they were leaving Madrid in a few days and that she had much to do, and therefore again declined; but the slender blond, the more beautiful of the two, said she would be delighted. Through her sun glasses I could see her dark eyes looking steadily and directly into mine, and they revealed a great gentleness, and a warmth and intelligence that made a powerful impact upon me.

The following night Bruce and I waited expectantly for the girls to appear in the lobby, our designated meeting place; for the blond, whose name was Lois, had assured me she would prevail upon her friend to join us. We watched as a dazzling blond beauty appeared on the main inner stairway, and in fact *all* eyes were upon her. We were still waiting for our girls, when to our great surprise this dazzling beauty waved at us! It was Lois, whom we had failed to recognize without her sun glasses, and whom was dressed more strikingly than her casual garb of the night before.

The three of us sat at a table in the lobby and had a drink, and Lois

Lois and the author—a beautiful relationship. (COURTESY OF BRUCE CAMPBELL)

explained that she could not persuade her friend to change her mind.
Therefore, the unspoken fact of the matter was that either Bruce or I, one
or the other, was superfluous. At one point, while Lois was laughing, there
appeared, as will sometimes happen, a small bubble of moisture at the tip
of one nostril, for which she seemed greatly embarrassed. Rather than
pretending not to notice, and thereby making it worse, since it was so
obvious, I decided to make a joke of it, and turned away with a cry of
disgust. This caused her to roar with laughter, and taking my hand she
said, "Oh, I love you—will you marry me?" Bruce took this as his cue to
leave, though she had only said it out of amused gratitude, and not at all
out of a decision between us; but Bruce, never one to extend situations of
discomfort, intentionally decided to simplify the matter in this way and
made a most gallant, if not unwanted, exit.

And so began my most serene and beautiful relationship with Lois

Segerman, a boon beyond my imagining, who became as a soothing salve for the wounds I was yet to receive.

As the production got under way in Madrid, I began to develop a warm friendship with Pedro Rodriguez, to whom I felt forever indebted for his constant encouragement via endless long-distance calls during those hard years when all seemed lost. There had been times when it was difficult to understand Miguel's accent with all the interference and static that sometimes accompanied these calls to or from Madrid, at godforsaken hours of the night or morning, due to the time difference, and Pedro's strong command of English was always somewhat of a relief when he spoke on behalf of Miguel; he always offered his own words of advice and optimism, and he encouraged me not to give up.

My own associates, however, grew to dislike Pedro, and Bruce Campbell and his assistants continued secretly to call him "Hans" (the nickname given to him in New York), due to his blond Germanic appearance and his quiet but insistent overseeing of Miguel's interests during production.

Pedro lived with a beautiful, young, brown-haired girl named Lorita, and one afternoon they invited Lois and I to their apartment for lunch. It was a delightful place, full of light, with an outside wooden stairway leading up to the front door. It was obvious that Lorita was totally responsible for the decoration of the apartment, which was predominantly feminine, with frilly curtains and an exquisitely colorful decor.

After lunch Pedro suggested that Lorita accompany Lois and I that afternoon to nearby Toledo to see the magnificent and world-famous painting by El Greco, *The Burial of Count Orgaz*. This was in response to my inquiry about the work and my desire to see it some day. Pedro himself had numerous chores to take care of for Miguel, regarding production arrangements.

It was a thrilling trip, and the country around Toledo was breathtakingly dramatic, so reminiscent of Greco's paintings of the area. The shrine containing the work we had come to see presented the painting at intervals throughout the day to the never-ending parade of tourists who made the pilgrimage daily. We were seated in a small room with chairs facing the painting, which was draped with a curtain, while music played. Then, after a brief introduction by a host lecturer, the curtain was swept back to reveal this awe-inspiring masterpiece that towered fifteen feet high and eleven feet across; after which we were left to sit and look at it for as long as we pleased—like Forest Lawn in Hollywood!

I had seen El Greco's *Burial of Count Orgaz* in countless reproductions since adolescence, and it had always made a terrific impact upon me and had been a continuing influence upon my own artistic thinking. Now, seeing it before me in all its true splendor took my breath away, as it did to all who looked upon it. The upper half represented a group of angels, topped by the figure of Christ, receiving the soul of Count Orgaz, who, in

219

life, had been a noble benefactor of a church in Toledo. The lower half of the canvas represented a group of men (portraits of Toldeo's aristocracy) witnessing the body of Count Orgaz being laid to rest by members of the church, some of whom were bearing torches. Despite the separation of the real and the supernatural, or miraculous, into two halves, there was a remarkable cohesiveness to the work, which was itself a miracle of the mysticism of the creative force at its best. Yellows, grays, and purples, combined with the dramatic placement of deep blacks, gave to the painting an unworldly, sublime quality, as if one were actually witnessing a real event of heaven and earth. There was a lyrical, almost musical effect of movement; even more so (oddly enough) in the ingenious placement of the row of aristocratic faces that looked down upon the body of Orgaz—those lean, aesthetic faces framed in their white ruffled collars, also ingeniously arranged.

It was for me a welcome restoration of faith in El Greco; for I found, upon viewing the great body of his work at the Prado museum in Madrid, and here again in the many smaller canvases at Toledo, that I could not *connect* with them, as I had done with the reproductions of these very same works! It had been a frustrating experience, not to say disappointing, to find that these mystically beautiful canvases had so much less impact upon me than they had in books! I had attributed this to the profound and very powerful effect I had experienced upon viewing the Goyas at the Prado, knowing full well that such comparison was odious.

But the work of Goya had made such a direct and immediate connection with something so innate and deep within me, that the work of El Greco, which I had learned to love and to emulate through reproductions, now seemed flat; and with all its lyrical movement and spiraling rhythms, it seemed somehow static, compared to the brutal sweep and forbidden syncopations of the titan Goya! I was determined not to let this happen, but the more I returned, staring, to the El Grecos, the more I remained unmoved by them. Now, here in Toldeo, El Greco was redeemed—and my eyes, which had been blinded by Goya's Olympian bolts of lightning, were once again opened to the sacred vision of El Greco.

Still, no one has managed, unless perhaps it is the sorcerer Picasso himself, to capture the essence of Spain as has the great Goya. His ingenious mastery of *asymmetry,* those off-balance groups of sardonically dancing forms, enveloped in counterpointed areas of mysterious dark-ness, are a lesson in rhythm itself, mirrored only in the swirling haughti-ness of Spain's very voice: the *Flamenco!*

That night Lois and I had dinner at a large restaurant in Madrid that featured a troupe of Flamenco dancers upon a stage that, fortunately, was close to the table at which we sat. I was dumbfounded! The performers, male and female, sat in a long row of chairs, and each, in turn, took center stage as if in competition, to outdo the others. The force and genius with which these dancers stomped and swirled, expressing the sum of a lifetime of experience, made one feel as if they had sprung up from the very soil of Spain itself, giving vent to the pride and secret mysteries of countless centuries. Somehow, too, I could not help comparing them to American prizefighters, in their physical capacity to express energy and rage through *form,* and their tireless efforts to outdo one another. It was an odd comparison, to be sure, but the dance seemed to me to differ from boxing only in that the competitors did not touch one another; and there was certainly a group camaraderie, in that the others kept time with the clapping of their hands while the soloist attempted to eliminate them by outperforming them, lending to the whole effect an almost unbearable sensuality that was undeniably symbolic of the more savage and erotic aspects of the sexual relationship. The Flamenco *was* Spain, in the way jazz *was* America. And, to make a point, it was *Goya.* And all this, I vowed, I would capture in my animation, in the sequence titled *The Bullfight,* which was, after all, simply an extension of Flamenco and the ancient drama of Spain.

Serge Bourgignon directing on horseback.
(COURTESY OF BRUCE CAMPBELL)

Dominguin, player, and Serge in last-minute preparations for the filming of the stampeding-bulls scene. (COURTESY OF BRUCE CAMPBELL)

One afternoon, on the vast spread of Dominguin's ranch, we were shooting one of the film's most spectacular scenes. Albert (in the movie) has just arrived to seek out Dominguin, in the hopes that he will arrange an introduction to Picasso for him. We had the full complement of technicians, cameramen, and crew, and Serge was directing (shirtless and sans saddle) on horseback. In the scene, while Albert is wandering aimlessly but hopefully in search of the Matador, Dominguin suddenly appears a short distance away, atop his horse, and motions frantically for Albert to get out of the way—for he is in the path of an entire oncoming herd of stampeding bulls! Albert runs in a panic, narrowly saving himself by diving off a bridge

222

Albert Finney (with Dominguin in the background) also receiving last-minute instructions. (COURTESY OF BRUCE CAMPBELL)

into a pond, after which Dominguin rides up and laughingly fishes him out by extending a pole down to the floundering Albert and pulling him up onto the bank. At this point in the filming, Dominguin, to the surprise of us all, threw his head back and roared with laughter; for unbeknown to any of us, Albert (who had his back to the camera while being fished out onto the bank) had the fly of his trousers wide open.

This stampede, as one can appreciate, was a most difficult maneuver for Dominguin to properly manipulate for the camera, and it took, of course, a highly expensive chunk out of our dwindling budget. Therefore, it was most disconcerting, in the midst of one of the "takes" of this panoramic scene, to watch a *helicopter* appear overhead, slowly descending!

Serge was raging mad, understandably, and his horse reared and

A shot of the cameraman shooting Dominguin and his riders giving chase to the stampeding bulls. (COURTESY OF BRUCE CAMPBELL)

stomped accordingly—to most dramatic effect. Bruce and I, who were standing together by one of the production jeeps, looked at one another in wide-eyed disbelief, and then back again, hypnotically, at the ever-descending copter, as if in some bad dream.

Finally the craft touched ground, propeller blades slowing to a halt, and Serge and Dominguin rode from separate directions to accost the uninvited and most unwelcome visitors. From the great distance at which Bruce and I were standing we saw the whole thing from a hilltop view, and watched as three figures emerged from the helicopter. With even greater disbelief than before, we saw Dominguin and Serge, now both dismounted, throw up their arms and rush forward to *embrace* these figures!

Soon enough we learned, as the figures came closer and closer into view, that we had been blessed by the appearance of Miguel's old friend, Yul

Brynner, his wife, Doris, and their pilot. Brynner, it seems, was shooting a film nearby on the life of the Mexican bandit Pancho Villa, called *Villa Rides!* and, hearing about our film being shot on the Dominguin ranch, decided to pay us a social call, Mexican bandit outfit and all.

Serge, of course, was now in a delirium of joy and solicitousness, flattered by the drama of the visit, and delighted by this opportunity for a whole new display of macho camaraderie and manly laughter, superseding even the hard-to-take, tongue-biting fact that the great Bourgignon had been upstaged—with a vengeance!

Soon other actors, also filming nearby, made their appearance as well, and the faces of Robert Mitchum and Charles Bronson were to become familiar sights during this stay at the ranch, with parties, lunches, and

Trying to stop the bulls . . . (COURTESY OF BRUCE CAMPBELL)

. . . but to no avail . . . (Courtesy of Bruce Campbell.)

dinners including one and all—but at whose expense? And this is where Bruce Campbell and Luis Miguel Dominguin began to have a real parting of the ways—with Pedro Rodriguez as Miguel's "secretary of state," and me as the man in between, being asked by both sides, especially by Dominguin, to act as intermediary. "Eet ees all for the sake of the peecture," he explained. And Yul Brynner graciously volunteered to appear in one scene, dialogue and all, *gratis:* an afternoon scene at the table of the outside patio where Albert Finney, now dry from his rescue from the pond, is explaining to Miguel and a small gathering (Brynner, Doris Brynner, and Lucia Bosé) why he wants to meet Picasso, and how he had hopes that Dominguin might arrange an introduction for him.

For an almost unexplainable reason I disliked Doris Brynner on sight—something about the troublemaking look in her eyes, perhaps— and Sandy Kaplan and I privately came to the conclusion that, through

. . . for Albert must dive into the creek to escape them. (COURTESY OF BRUCE CAMPBELL)

Dominguin, Doris's ultimate intention was to meet Picasso, and (we speculated or fantasized) become his new young mistress, in sort of a back-door bid at immortality and international acclaim and prestige. Though we were never to discover exactly what she had in mind, we were nevertheless astoundingly accurate in our overall assessment of this woman's secret ambitions; and my unexplainable fear of her presence and hatred for those private thoughts I saw reflected in her eyes (eyes that were

Albert is then "rescued" by a sympathetic Dominguin. (COURTESY OF BRUCE CAMPBELL)

A very wet Albert being pulled out of the creek. (COURTESY OF BRUCE CAMPBELL)

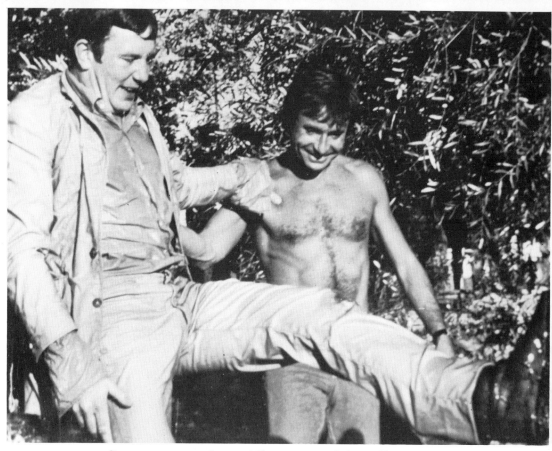

Serge congratulates Albert on a job well done. (Courtesy of Bruce Campbell)

And Yul Brynner helps Albert to dry off. (Courtesy of Bruce Campbell)

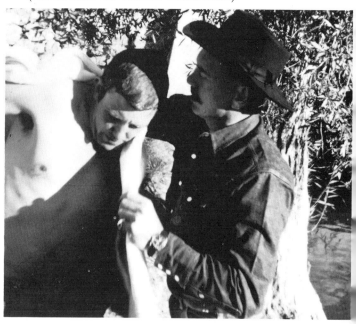

Sitting at the table, *from left to right:* Lucia
Bosé (Dominguin's wife), Albert Finney,
Doris Brynner, Dominguin, and Yul Bryn-
ner. (COURTESY OF BRUCE CAMPBELL)

constantly avoiding mine) were no less than premonitions of a very real
disaster to come.

From that moment on, she and Yul Brynner were everywhere, each
doing their own thing separate from the other—a marriage of "understanding." And Doris and Miguel were soon to become almost inseparable.
Everyone was having a great time. Except Bruce and myself. We wanted to
make a film.

27

"Bullfight"

ONE NIGHT WE ALL ASSEMBLED IN WHAT COULD PROPERLY BE CALLED THE den, a small room compared to the immensity of the house but intimate and comfortable, and warmed by the flames of a beautiful rustic fireplace. Lois and I sat in a casual embrace upon one of the two sofas, Dominguin was in a chair, Albert Finney and Serge Bourgignon sat on the floor, Sandy Kaplan and Doris Brynner sat on the other sofa, and Bruce Campbell was mobile—here and there at different points, enjoying it all immensely. And all of the attention was focused upon the thick, masculine, gypsylike figure that sat silhouetted in front of the fireplace, guitar poised and waiting for Yul Brynner's fingers to bring it to life. The first chord was followed swiftly by the strong, deep call of his voice in song—rather startling in this small enclosure, and we were helplessly and willingly riveted. Occasionally, one of the men would glance at Lois, and I realized that she must have cut a striking figure, with the red flames of the fire reflected on her long, bare legs.

The fire was the main source of light, save one small lamp in the corner of the room, and those lights which remained lit in the adjoining rooms. This made a dramatic glow behind Brynner's strong barbarian profile and accentuated the almost primitive and gutteral sounds of his deep-throated singing:

> *De tanto mirarme en ti*
> *Como tu me estoy volviendo.*

232

Albert among the crowd of local people
watching the bullfight especially staged by
Dominguin for *The Picasso Summer*. (COUR-
TESY OF BRUCE CAMPBELL)

In the stands watching the bullfight, *from left
to right:* Serge, Doris and Yul Brynner, and
Robert Mitchum. (COURTESY OF BRUCE
CAMPBELL)

The beginning of the bullfight. (COURTESY
OF BRUCE CAMPBELL)

Dominguin in action. (COURTESY OF BRUCE
CAMPBELL)

(COURTESY OF BRUCE CAMPBELL)

(COURTESY OF BRUCE CAMPBELL)

The end of the bullfight. (COURTESY OF
BRUCE CAMPBELL)

Porque la mar es azul
De tanto mirar el cielo.

He sang, and all present were hypnotized. For Lois and me it was
romantic, and her head rested warmly upon my shoulder, but for the
others the romance had to be restricted to imagination alone, for she and I
were the only "couple" there—except for the questionable arrangement
between Yul Brynner and his wife, Doris, whose vibrations continued to
strike me in a negative way—albeit at a minimum, in this convivial and cozy
atmosphere.

Once or twice Finney or one of the others joined briefly in chorus, only to
fade off soon enough against the strength of Brynner's voice. Dominguin
clapped his hands in tempo during certain Spanish songs, but mostly it was
Yul Brynner in concert, solo. Even Serge made little attempt to pit his
identity against Brynner's presence during this performance.

Then after half an hour or so, Yul put down his guitar for a smoke, and we began talking quietly among ourselves. Suddenly Dominguin, Doris, Serge, and Albert walked toward me, and before I knew what was happening I was being lifted off the sofa by my hands and feet and carted into the next room by this merry quartet. When I was slowly released, laughing but curious, I got up and, after rearranging myself, went back to the den, where Lois had been screaming in protest as I was carried off. But when I got back, Dominguin, Finney, and Serge were all embracing Lois who sat stiffly, wondering how to take it, with a look of fearful uncertainty on her face. She looked almost tearfully relieved when I walked back into the room, and the three men roared with laughter, joined by the rest of the assembly.

"We were jealous," Albert explained. "You've got this lovely blond lass

Dominguin taking his well-deserved bows.
(COURTESY OF BRUCE CAMPBELL)

237

(COURTESY OF BRUCE CAMPBELL)

all to yourself, and we've got no one! Blast it, I'm sendin' for Jean straight off!"

I took my place once more beside Lois and laughingly assured her that it was all a joke; but she replied that the sight of me being carted off, even in jest, was not funny to her, and she admitted a certain apprehension when the three men approached her in that way. Still laughing, I reminded her how most girls would have given a lot to have the attentions of any one of these glamorous men, and she kissed my cheek softly in answer.

It was decided that Miguel would stage a bullfight just for the movie, in his own private bullring, and invite all the townspeople to fill the grandstands. It was a charmingly rustic arena-in-miniature, and the local residents swarmed in, full of enthusiasm and excitement, for this was the event of a lifetime for most of them. The faces of these people are indescribable, for they were straight out of Velazquez; faces of the earth, of the Spanish soil itself, peasant faces with toothless grins, faces with the accumulated living of centuries. With what contrast the face of Albert Finney, who sat among them (for a scene in the film) stood out! His young, shiny, very wholesomely English face shone like a polished white stone among rocks and crags, and even the rugged faces of Charles Bronson and Robert Mitchum and Yul Brynner, who also sat among the townspeople, looked like inexperienced babes in comparison! Never had I seen such color, such an epitome of the *picturesque*, as that which constituted the soul of this crowd.

Miguel never looked better, visually—but his form in the arena was wanting; and realizing this when the corrida was over, and having performed the whole business for the cameras (the first time in years), he decided to do it all once again. So several days later the townspeople were called back, the cameras were back, Miguel was back; everyone returned but the bull, who would never again be returning anywhere, and the fight was restaged with a new protagonist, and the townspeople were rejoicing in the surprise treat of two special festive holidays, in an atmosphere of celebration shared by everyone except those poor souls who were responsible for the budget of the film.

28

The Moment Of Truth

WE WERE ALL GATHERED IN BRUCE CAMPBELL'S SUITE AT THREE O'CLOCK IN the afternoon to prepare for the stupendous event. That night Miguel was to bring Picasso to the festival building where he was to be met by Bruce, Serge, and myself. Then he would be shown some rushes of the film that had been thus far shot, and my four-minute film sample of the "new" animation. To avoid publicity and photographers, this was all to be done in secret.

However, this meeting of the entire crew was called for another reason as well. Bruce's partner, Roy Silver, the aggressive young chief of Campbell, Silver, Cosby, had just arrived in Cannes for this one day only (!) to see the movie in progress, and had timed his arrival by pure coincidence with the evening's forthcoming excitement. Campbell, Silver, Cosby had been pouring more money into the production of *Picasso Summer* than actually existed, and it was with a great deal of anxiety and concern that Roy had made this brief trip, and was returning the following day to Los Angeles.

All of us were crowded into the living room of Bruce's suite, except Miguel who was with Picasso. The handsome blond Pedro Rodriguez was there in his stead, and with him was a business associate whom I had never met before. Albert Finney was also not present, for Bruce did not wish him to be concerned with these urgent matters of business. Yvette Mimieux was due to arrive shortly in Cannes from Los Angeles for her part in the film, since her role called for no participation in any of the Spanish sequences. Vilmos Zsigmond, the cameraman, lent his distinguished presence, as well as Joe and the entire crew and production assistants of men and women, French and American. Since this was a business meeting, Lois was not present, and I found to my surprise that even in this large group I missed her. Dominating everything with his agitated presence was the sensual little Serge Bourgignon, who, as director, seemed to be ignoring Ray Bradbury's delightful script, and to be jealously vying with me for creative control of the film, as if by merely meeting Picasso his own reputation as enfant terrible of French directors would be verified for all time. Though he had shown moments of great charm and charismatic warmth to all of us when the mood struck him, his general attitude all along had been one of affected temperament and arrogance, and he had demonstrated several acts of childish belligerence to Bruce that had been done totally for show, with no thought or regard for personal feelings.

However, when Roy Silver made his appearance, shortly after we were all present and accounted for, it was very definitely *his* show, not only because it was he who at this point was providing the company's money for the film, but also because of his rather commanding presence. He took over as if he had been with us all along, or, rather, as if none of us had really left Los Angeles at all.

To add to the tension and excitement, Picasso, if he liked what we were to show him that evening, was to make an appearance on the following day, for his one scene in the film, the great climactic scene where he covers the beach with his drawings in the sand! Needless to say, with a scene like that, the value of the film would be enhanced beyond speculation. Ironically, Roy was hoping to see some of the film being shot, for he had never before seen a film in production, and such was his timing that this was the scene that, hopefully, awaited him. Miguel had already guaranteed us that he would have Picasso on the beach for us, and we had little reason to doubt him.

It was amid these heavily anticipatory hangings and trappings that Roy had made his arrival, and for those of the crew who had never before seen him they were made instantly aware that this expensively dressed fellow was the other third of Bruce's partnership and obviously the one who held the financial strings. His was a dark, bespectacled, large, and imposing face, which, because of the forward curve of the nose and large dark eyes that glared with such curious intensity over that curve, seemed to encompass everything at once, and to be in profile when full-face, and full-face when in profile—a disturbing simultaneity of angles underscored by an equally large and imposing voice, which resounded with an unconscious affectation of speech intended to place emphasis by way of pausing before the accented syllables—and in exact cadence to the movement of the hands—so that it seemed to resound while pausing, and pause when resounding; and, in all, created an impression of a somewhat annoying *force*, most adequate to its intent, but regretfully blinding one to an

241

otherwise very real yet untapped reservoir of warmth. There was no question that Roy Silver was here. *Now then*, his presence was saying, *where are we at this juncture, and what do we need yet to do?* And this was, in fact, the very question Roy had verbalized.

The response was Serge's, who suggested that since the old man would probably be very tired we should be careful not to show him too much of the unedited film, which would only confuse and bore him. Most important, Serge insisted, was that we should not tire and bore the old man, and therefore he should see only the best highlights of that which Serge had shot to date, and that we should not bother him with the animation at all.

Needless to say, this produced in me a bombshell that shook the room. "The animation," I said, attempting to keep my voice quiet and steady, "is the whole point of this film."

"Nonsense," Serge replied impatiently. "Why can't you acknowledge that this is no longer just your film? We are all involved in it now, and I am putting just as much creativity and art in the live portion as you plan to do with your portion of the thing."

"Yes," I said, "and tonight you will show him whatever rushes of your film your choose, and he will also see my animation."

"But he already saw it!" Serge cried.

"No," I said firmly, and then enunciating very clearly: "he hasn't seen it."

"But," Serge looked at me accusingly, "you said he had seen it and liked it and that's why we are all here!"

"Exactly," I said. "Without that, we would none of us be here. There would be no film being made at all. I did what I had to do to get this picture shot."

"But you *lied*!" Serge screamed hysterically.

The tension in the room was unbelievable, and all eyes were riveted hypnotically upon me. I told them how I had gone back to Picasso's villa in the winter of 1966 with the reel of sample animation that he had requested of me a year and one-half earlier, along with the original drawings that made up the film; and how, because of the incredibly bad timing due to the enormous exhibit of his work in Paris, he was at home to no one, including the director of the exhibit himself, and even to Dominguin, who had called him twice on my behalf, only to be told by the servants that he was "out." I told them how, after two weeks of fruitless waiting, with practically no funds, in the cold and dismally deserted town of Cannes in the winter, I had finally planted myself, early one morning, with my film and drawings, on the cold, damp ground on the high hilltop beside the electric gate that barred entrance to Picasso's villa. I told them how I had sent word inside that I was there and spent a day-long vigil on the hill, where I was told by the mailman and several delivery boys who periodically enlivened my lonely waiting, that Picasso was out of town; and then, finally, when

Picasso's chauffeur, Janot, drove up the hill to the gate, and I scrambled elatedly from my place to tell him that I was there with the film Picasso had requested of me, *only to have Janot pretend he did not recognize or remember me,* and in fact to be suddenly unable to speak English well enough to understand me!

It was then, as I sat staring bitterly out from the hilltop, over the view that spread itself beneath me in the gray light of this bleak December day, that I had come to the decision that would, within one year, take me back to Cannes with an entire film crew, a production company with financial backing, a cast of major film stars, and, most importantly, the chance to create my animation, and give birth to that which needed to be born. So angry had I become by the irony of being ignored by the man who just a year and one-half earlier had driven me up that hill to this very gate, that I restated to myself the vow that I would do anything short of murder to create the situation wherein I would be enabled to perform my art and have at my disposal the staggering financial means necessary to permit the creation of it—as well as the guarantee of an audience to see it. Therefore, since I had already met Picasso under the most beautiful of circumstances and since he had already seen my work and had proclaimed it, according to Dominguin, "*Magnifico,*" what then did I really need from Picasso now? I was sure that if, indeed, he *did* see my sample film he would love it, just as he approved so heartily of my other work, and so I would go back home and say to some potential financial backer that Picasso saw my film and loved it! If this, then, was all it took to interest a backer, what real difference whether Picasso saw the film now or at some later date, when, through a little fabrication, I could have the film *produced*? And, indeed, we had now, in Bruce Campbell's suite, come to that very point, and I had confessed all, come what may!

"Well," said Roy, who, after a considerable pause, had walked to the window for comfort, but without bothering to look out, "now, in effect, we're *all* sitting on that hill freezing our balls off—in this case, it's our *financial* balls."

I was quick to assure Roy that Bruce had never known the true story, and that it was *because* Bruce had been a close friend rather than in spite of it that I had to protect his integrity by lying to him as well as to Roy, since because of Bruce's relationships with me and with Roy he would have been on the spot had he known.

At this point, needing very much to be alone, I got up and, walking past Pedro who was smiling and nodding warmly at me, albeit with a slightly confused look, opened the bedroom door and walked inside. And there, sitting all by herself on the bed, was Yvette Mimieux! She had arrived earlier at the Nice airport where Anna Korda, our production assistant, had met her and driven her to our hotel, and having arrived in the middle of the meeting, decided to wait in the bedroom till it was over. However, before I could say a word to her, she exclaimed sympathetically about my dejected appearance. "Oh, Wes," she cried, "why the long face? What's the matter?"

This sudden, totally unexpected vision of exquisite beauty, coupled with this outpouring of sympathy and understanding, after having just left a room bristling with hostility and derision, produced an involuntary onrush of tears in my eyes, and I sat on the floor at Yvette's feet and told her the whole story. As I spoke she stroked my hair tenderly, and I could not help but note, objectively, the amusing contrast in my demeanor in this room with that which I had displayed in the other.

"But I think that's *great!*" Yvette said, after I had finished my story. "That's the *only* way to get anything done!" This made me feel so much better, and I was so encouraged, that I was ready once again to face the firing squad in the next room. Yvette went to her own room and said she would greet everyone later, at a better time.

When I went back into Bruce's suite where the others were engaged in active and varied conversation, I announced to Roy that I had just seen Yvette, told her the whole story and that she thought it was great, that it was the only way to get things done. Roy exploded in a verbiage of expletives for my having told Yvette and warned me that Albert Finney was not to know, since he had agreed to make the film on the basis of my "lie."

"What has that to do with it?" I cried. "Picasso is looking at our stuff tonight, and tomorrow he'll be doing the scene on the beach! What has my 'lie' got to do with Albert?" I laughed facetiously. "I have no intention of discussing it with him anyway, I only told Yvette because she took me by surprise, sitting there, and saw that something was wrong." I walked exhaustedly from the room, followed by Bruce.

Bruce closed the door behind him and the two of us stood alone in the hall. He stood looking at me with tears of sympathy in his eyes and a broad, understanding smile. He shook his head as if to say, *me, too*—and, without a word, embraced me with both arms. Here was a man who not only always knew *what* to say at all times, but also knew when to say *nothing,* and could say "nothing" more eloquently than anyone else.

After I told Lois the incredible events of the afternoon we decided to go down to the lobby lounge for a cup of coffee, only to find Serge doing the same thing. He was friendly now and smilingly shook his head. But soon, though still smiling, he began telling me once again that I had lied, and that Roy was absolutely right about Albert not finding out; and when Lois, in her gently firm way, began coming to my defense, Serge switched the conversation to the subject of creativity, for, thinking my line of defense weakened, he began pitting the superiority of his creativity against mine, or rather that of the director opposed to that of the "mere animator," and so on.

Picasso was to be at the Festival Building with Miguel at 8:30, and the

Doris Brynner—with Albert Finney and
Bruce Campbell. (COURTESY OF BRUCE
CAMPBELL)

projectionist was to let them in through the side door so that no one would see them. Bruce and Serge and I were to meet them then, but Bruce and I got there at eight o'clock out of sheer anxiety, having left all our friends at a cluster of tables at one of the outdoor cafes along the Croisette. They were all there, waiting for the results: Sandy and all the girls, Joe, Albert Finney, Yvette, and Lois—everyone except Roy, who decided to have a night on the town after having confided to Bruce his dread fear that I was intending to assassinate Picasso on the beach the next day in order to bring my animation to the attention of the world—and Serge, who was nowhere to be found, though we were all certain enough that he would be at the Festival Building at 8:30.

Well, 8:30 came and went. Not only was there no Serge, but no Miguel and no Picasso. Only Bruce, myself, and some distant projectionist, who kept shrugging his shoulders. Nine o'clock, nine-thirty; we were falling apart. Then suddenly the distant projectionist called to us to pick up the phone in the waiting room. Bruce picked it up. It was Serge, calling from the airport! Something awful had happened! He would tell us all about it as soon as he got back, within an hour, but we should know that he just saw Miguel and Doris Brynner off to Madrid and that it's all off with Picasso!

Many had been the shocks, the crushing defeats, and bitter disappointments I had encountered along the way in trying to get this movie made, most of them occurring just at that moment when sure success seemed the closest—but this was utterly devastating! Bruce and I were both dazed, if not totally shattered and confused. We returned to our friends at the tables and told them what had happened, all we knew, and awaited Serge's return while Albert did the most to keep up the spirit of the company.

Eventually, after a period of tortured waiting, Serge returned and told us this story:

That afternoon Miguel had gone to Picasso's villa—and with him he had brought Doris Brynner, with whom he had been sharing a suite at the Carlton, since their arrival in Cannes a few days earlier. Unbeknown to Miguel, word had reached Picasso of Miguel's tryst with Doris, and he had become outraged because Miguel's beautiful wife Lucia and their son were guests in Picasso's home, where Lucia had apparently flown for solace from the grief and humiliation of Miguel's new affair. Picasso loved Lucia as his own daughter, much in the way he loved Miguel as his own son. So that when Miguel showed up at Picasso's gate with that very woman herself who was the cause of all the misery, the servant was instructed to turn Miguel away. One can imagine the indignation with which Miguel received this response to his ring, and he demanded to be allowed inside. When the servant returned with a note from Picasso informing him that he was no longer welcome in his house, Miguel exploded, and scrawled a message on Picasso's note to the effect that Picasso could go to hell! With that, Miguel and Doris headed straight for the Nice airport to return to Madrid, after

246

informing Serge by phone what had taken place. Serge met them at the airport but was unable to convince Miguel to have a change of heart, and it was at this point that he had called Bruce and me at the Festival Building.

Later, we had heard from our production assistant, Anna Korda, who happened to be at the airport by coincidence and who was returning on the same flight to Madrid for a few days, that Lucia was also on that same flight! She had left her son for a while at Picasso's home and had decided to return that night to Madrid, little knowing that Miguel and Doris would be on the same flight! Anna related how, on the bus ride from the airport to the field, Miguel and Doris sat at one end of the bus while Lucia sat by herself at the other end, with no words exchanged at all.

The night before the meeting where I had revealed my "lie" to Roy Silver and all those assembled, Miguel had requested a meeting with Bruce and myself at a table in the Carlton bar, a gesture that mystified us. When he finally appeared after a fifteen- or twenty-minute wait, he entered *behind Doris Brynner* and wore a sheepish, embarrassed expression. My stomach sank, and Bruce turned white, and at that moment we knew that a wrench was being thrown into our best hopes. Doris first declared that Yul wanted to be paid for the scene he had voluntarily done with Albert and Miguel and others at his own suggestion, offering it as a gift to our project, free of charge. It was a happy, spontaneous scene and was a small if not somewhat unnecessary plus for the film. But now Doris said that we pay or the scene was out! Miguel avoided my glance, and I failed to comprehend why he was allowing her to use him in this way. One day several weeks earlier, in Madrid, Miguel had been having some disturbing financial discussions with Bruce and had been rather upset. That night, when we were going in three separate cars to meet at a certain restaurant for dinner, Miguel approached the car in which Lois and I were seated and asked if he could go with us. We were delighted, but Miguel asked if he could first talk with me a moment. He put his arm around my shoulder and led me to a spot where the others would not hear. "Wes," he said, "you know I do all thees only for you, because I love you, and for myself I do not need any of thees deefficulties. I am neglecting my business and reesk my friendship with Pablo to maneepulate heem to work weeth us." He went on to say that he wished the financial negotiations were not so constantly fraught with misunderstanding, that he had been putting up all of his own money to house and feed the film crew, and so on, and that he would appreciate whatever I could do to straighten things out with Bruce, which I assured him I would. As for Picasso, he assured me, all would be well, and he was sure it would be fine and that he, Miguel, was only momentarily upset; he then apologized. "Pablo and I," Miguel smiled, "we are both Spaniards, and we understand and love each other. He weel do anything I ask, I am sure."

Bruce, of course, explained to me the source of the misunderstanding

—the frighteningly accelerated depletion of finances due to such excesses as Miguel's parties and dinners, which really bore no connection with the production of the film, and for which Miguel was asking absurd sums to cover the costs. For my part, I preferred to play the role of mediator, to narrow those slowly widening rifts between certain people, not only Bruce and Miguel, but Joe and others who were beginning to buckle under the increasing tensions and ever-rising questions of finance, which were starting to surface more and more frequently. I was constantly in an agonized state of tension with stomach pains and headaches, and prayed only that the filming would reach at least a satisfactory conclusion so that I could begin work on the animation. I thanked God for the sweet angel in the person of Lois, whose continuously calm and encouraging manner was for me the most perfect and life-saving of sedatives, and whose mature and sophisticated character seemed so far beyond her mere twenty-two years. She told me that she had been that way since the age of twelve and could remember people remarking on it constantly as she grew up.

As for Miguel, I counted myself privileged to have been in such close contact with him for such an extended period of time, for here was a man who literally lived the role of a hero straight out of romantic fiction, and he played that role genuinely, making a truth, a reality, out of that fiction. He was Dominguin, the Magnificent Matador, who put his life on the line regularly in the bullring, and who had come through every time with grand style, making of the bullfight a true art, commanding the admiration of such titans as Hemingway and Picasso and the devotion of many of the world's most beautiful women. I treasured his many moments of counsel and friendship, his ready humor and warmth, and his constant assistance in seeing the project through, often to the neglect of other important business matters. He was always delighted to hear my voice on the phone at those odd hours when I might call him in desperation to see how strong or weak were the possibilities of my film ever going through at all, and conversely, his voice in response became a distant beacon of hope to my sometimes wavering moments of faith.

A year after this incident with Doris Brynner at Picasso's gate, long after Warner Bros. saved the day and bought *The Picasso Summer* for over 1.7 million dollars and I was well into the animation, I was browsing at a newsstand at the all-night market on Pico and Robertson in Los Angeles, when the cover of *Confidential* magazine caught my eye. There on the cover of this, the October 1968 issue, was the unmistakable face of Yul Brynner, with a large caption that read: "Yul's wife Bulled by Bullfighter." I grabbed the magazine and leafed through the pages, and there, beginning on page fourteen, was a four-page spread with photographs and spicy text dealing with the fateful incident at Picasso's gate. Though the article had some of the facts wrong, it was basically an amazingly accurate account, and I could not help but wonder who had leaked all these personal details to the magazine. And although Frank Sinatra had already divorced Ava Gardner by the time she had met up with Dominguin, I also could not help but be amused at the caption over the article's title, "The Bullfighter Bulled Yul's Wife," which read: "First Sinatra's Wife, Then Yul's, Luis Miguel Dominguin Has Struck Again!"

Viva Miguel!

29

The Filmmaking Life—and Back to the States

ONE AFTERNOON WE WERE ALL WATCHING SOME RUSHES AT THE PROJECTION room of the Studio Victorine, which was located between Cannes and Nice, at which Serge worked intermittently on the editing of his film footage. Albert had recently sent for his girlfriend from London, the actress Jean Marsh, having constantly joked with Lois and me about how lonely and jealous he was, seeing us together all the time.

Everyone was there; Yvette, Bruce, Joe Juliano, Ziggy, Henri, Serge, Anna Korda, Lois and myself and several others of the crew. Albert was to arrive shortly with Jean, after picking her up at the airport in Nice, to watch the rushes with the rest of us. Lois and I sat there expectantly, wondering what Albert's girlfriend would be like, not really knowing Jean Marsh by name at that time; for since then she has achieved a fame of her own as the cocreator and star of the British PBS Teleseries *Upstairs Downstairs*, in which she portrays the maid, Rose. We tried to imagine the type of woman who would appeal to Finney, and when she finally walked in with him we gasped in proud astonishment at how close we had come to accurately predicting, practically to the smallest detail, her physical appearance and her genuine manner; but we failed to predict entirely what we were eventually to discover was the full extent of her marvelous humor.

I soon recognized also that she was the talented and appealing young lady who portrayed (with dark makeup) the sensuous Tahitian native sweetheart to Laurence Olivier's Henry Strickland in David Susskind's production for television of *The Moon and Sixpense*, the great Somerset Maugham classic.

Lovely Jean Marsh. (COURTESY OF BRUCE CAMPBELL)

Finney was full of robust humor, and I somehow developed a kidding relationship with him wherein, for some reason, he took delight in laughingly pinching my cheek as if I were someone's amusing little son. Now, with Jean as his constant companion, the humor was boundless, and some of my fondest recollections were those dinners we ate together each night during the filming in Cannes. For dinnertime was always the climax of the day; no matter how fatiguing or how joyous the day's work might have been, we always looked forward to the evening's adventure—the selection of a new restaurant—and whether it was a seafood cafe by the harbor, or a picturesque inn at a winding street in town, or a far-off club in the hills, it was always a memorable and very special occasion.

On one such occasion, however, the evening was marred, but only slightly, by the presence of an inebriated middle-aged American lady who was with a young sailor, also American, who was embarrassed by her drunken behavior and was constantly hushing her. For a long while she sat, looking over at our table, not saying a word—when suddenly she shouted across the room to Albert: "Just because you speak with a British accent doesn't mean you speak perfect English! *He* speaks perfect English!" pointing, to my horror, straight at me.

"You're from the Midwest, aren't you?" she asked.

I nodded. "Originally, yes—from Milwaukee."

"I knew it!" she screamed. "Midwest Americans speak the *perfect* English! I could tell it from clear across the room—I can always pick one out. I can always pick one out!"

Albert turned and glared at her. "So can I, lady," he said. "So can I."

We were doing some location shooting around Castellaras for a few days, and we took rooms in the old "castle," the club owned by Christine's father, where Sheila Duncan had brought me to dinner on my first visit to Cannes. One afternoon when everyone had gone out to shoot, I decided to stay around the club to relax and think. I was sitting in a small room, sipping a cup of coffee, when suddenly someone sneaked up behind me and messed up my hair. Turning to look, I saw the laughing face of Christine herself, arms outstretched. "Mister Son-of-a-Deer!" she exclaimed. "Sexy-Mouth!" I shouted with a whoop of joy.

We embraced laughingly, and then, arms about each other's waists, we walked outside to the shady, green tree-filled grounds, and picking the shadiest tree of them all sat down to exchange stories about all that had taken place since we had last seen one another. And there we sat, for the entire afternoon, questioning and answering until we joyfully drained each other. She expressed her delight that Serge had actually become our director, and wanted to know if the affair between Serge and Yvette was really over. I told her that I thought it was, but that they certainly remained the best of friends.

"You know," Christine remarked, "I finally got to meet Yvette a couple of years ago, and we really liked one another. We became almost like sisters. She is the nicest lady I've ever met, and I really learned to love her. She was so nice to me, and sincere about it—nothing made up or phony."

I asked her about little Anne Dussart and Gicky, and Claudine, and Nissan and Armel, and the memories of those days flooded back over me like a warm wave of sunshine. We spoke for hours about everything and everyone, but before the crew returned from location, she was gone.

What a mad merry-go-round of whirling egos is this business of moviemaking! Everyone in competition for the spotlight, and woe to him upon whom that spotlight shines, in this image-adulating, undeclared war called moviemaking!

Serge was everywhere, dominating all, shirtless whenever possible, directing on horseback whenever possible, raving whenever possible, and ignoring Ray's script whenever possible *or not*. The result of this latter directorial liberty resulted in a quiet feud between Serge and Bradbury, in which Ray, back home in Los Angeles, managed to vent his hostility by shouting lustily, "*I hate Serge Bourgignon!*" whenever the urge hit him, which was quite often; and always to the great delight and resultant hilarity of whoever was within earshot.

Campbell was more often than not at odds with Dominguin and Pedro, over financial matters; and thus with Joe Juliano over procedure, and others against others, on down the line, ad infinitum, myself included.

One particularly hostile incident took place one afternoon in the dining room of the Hotel Majestic. I was seated at a table with Serge, Bruce, Yvette, Lois, and some of the crew when an argument started between Bruce and Serge regarding Serge's freedom with the script and the budget. Suddenly Serge reached across the table and pulled Bruce up off his chair by the front of the shirt, clenching his right fist in the air, and threatening to punch Bruce in the nose. This caused Yvette to leave the table and exit from the dining room, in a quiet attempt to shame Serge, which it did.

Serge and myself were the cause of another exit by Yvette on a similar afternoon in the same dining room, but for an entirely different reason. I was sitting with the two of them enjoying a light snack when Serge suggested we have a drink. "How about a Fernet Branca, Wes?" he said, jokingly referring to the near disastrous incident that had occurred on that first night with the crew in Madrid. Serge then began to recount the episode for Yvette.

"I know all about it," she interrupted. "That was a very silly thing, and I don't think it's a bit funny."

"Oh come on," laughed Serge. "What do you say, Wes? Care to join me in *one*?"

"Of course," I laughed. "Why not?"

"Now this is ridiculous," Yvette scolded, rising from her chair. "I refuse to sit by watching you two behave like little children!" And with that she left the dining room.

One day several of us, Lois and myself included, were invited to have lunch at the villa of Terrence Young, the distinguished English motion-picture director. He had directed Audrey Hepburn in the film *Wait Until Dark*, and so she easily became the main topic of our luncheon conversation.

Young described her fondness for great artists, her favorite houseguest being Arthur Rubinstein, who occasionally visited her home in Switzerland and played for her on the piano. I, in turn, related my experience with her and Ferrer. After lunch, Terrence Young's chauffeur (a professional Brooklyn bodyguard named Jack) took me aside and, slapping his head, said "So *you're* d'guy!" and then proceeded to explain that while Audrey and Ferrer and their little son Sean were vacationing in Marbella, he (Jack) was living with them as bodyguard and swimming instructor to Sean. He recounted how he overheard many fights between Audrey and Ferrer about a "Picasso film," and how Ferrer on one occasion abruptly left the dinner table in a rage. On another occasion, Jack said, Audrey tearfully pleaded with Ferrer to "at least talk to d'guy!" (Jack's phrasing), and how finally Ferrer made a deal with her.

There was a man whom both Audrey and Ferrer loved and respected, who was also vacationing at that time in Marbella, Harry Kurnitz, who wrote the screenplay for *How to Steal a Million*, in which Audrey starred with Peter O'Toole. Ferrer asked Audrey if she would abide by their good friend's decision as to what he considered would be the best thing for her. She agreed, obviously feeling that Kurnitz would know that this was certainly something in which Audrey should participate.

Albert Finney and Jean Marsh at the beach in Catalina. (COURTESY OF BRUCE CAMPBELL)

However, Jack continued, when Kurnitz arrived one subsequent evening for dinner he overheard Ferrer take Kurnitz aside, explaining the purpose of the invitation, and pleading with him not to yield to Audrey's "misdirected desire" to star in this "second-rate amateur undertaking" and so on, and that it would be for her own good if Kurnitz advised her not to do it. Therefore, when at dinner the subject was broached, and the unsuspecting Audrey, who had promised privately to Ferrer that she would abide by their good friend's decision, asked his opinion, he naturally advised her against it. Jack said Audrey was crushed; but that was that. And so the entire course of the film was changed, and several months later, as it turned out, Audrey and Ferrer ended their marriage.

Needless to say, I, too, was crushed upon hearing Jack's story, and walked off by myself in an effort to suppress a futile inner rage. Later, when Jack drove Lois and I back to our hotel in Cannes, he amused us with many tales of his experiences as masseur to the stars, telling us who among the leading men were and were not "queer."

"When you give rubdowns to as many guys as I have," Jack said, "you can tell pretty quick which ones are queer by d' way dey respond. For instance, some people t'ink Peter O'Toole is a little gay, on account of d' way he acts in some of his films, but I can tell you right now d' guy's *okay*. F'rinstance, when I massage him he don't react like ―――― ――――, who is definitely queer, reacts. I mean he gives no responses at all. An in d' second place, one morning while we was out on location doin' a film, I was supposed t' wake O'Toole up at 6:00 a.m., an' when I come into his room to wake 'im up, dere he is, sound asleep wit' two broads, one on each side of 'im!"

As Lois and I walked through the lobby of the Hotel Majestic, we ran into Finney's girlfriend, Jean Marsh, and the three of us decided to sit for a while and have a drink. She soon had us in stitches with her comments on anything and everything, and so I decided that with an incredible sense of humor such as hers, it would be all right to make a confession to her.

"Jean," I said, "remember, several years ago, you played the role of an exotic native girl in Susskind's television production of *The Moon and Sixpence* opposite Laurence Olivier? Well, I—"

"How can I forget it?" she broke in. "They smeared me all over with brown makeup for the part, and every time I washed it off I looked like a sickly white ghost; so when Albert called me to join him here in Cannes, the first thing I thought of was spreading myself out in the sun and becoming that native girl again!"

"Your tan looks great," I said, "but let me confess something to you. They had a three- or four-page color spread of that production in *Life* magazine, and there was a picture of you lying back with Olivier sitting next to you."

"Do you want me to leave?" Lois laughed.

"Anyway," I continued, "in this picture you had a bare leg exposed through your costume, and for some reason—I don't know what—that leg had such a sensuous impact upon me, the curve of the calf, the way it reflected the light, or whatever—that to this day, I still have that picture somewhere in my files."

"Do you want to see the real thing?" Jean said, moving her chair back.

"No," I laughed. "It's just the idea that if I had ever known that someday I would be sitting here *telling* you about it—do you know what I mean?"

"Lois," Jean said, "let's *both* leave!"

"I guess somehow it does sound kind of lecherous," I smiled helplessly. "But there was a certain satisfaction in telling you about it."

"But you spoiled it for yourself now," Jean said. "When you get back home and look at the picture again, all the magic will have gone out of it—just a stupid leg, after all."

"Probably so," I agreed. "And I'll become a cynical, sour old man embittered with life."

"You mean *Life* magazine?" Jean laughed.

"Lois," I moaned, "get me out of this!"

Suddenly Jean exposed her bare, tan leg, and there was something so *familiar* about it—the curve of the calf, the way it reflected the light, or whatever. . . .

That night a group of us drove, in two separate cars, to a local restaurant for dinner. Lois and I sat in the front seat with the driver and Jim Byron and Yvette occupied the back seat. Lois told them, laughingly, about my embarrassing confession that afternoon to Jean Marsh.

"Are you a 'leg man'?" Yvette asked.

"Yes," I replied, hardly failing to notice Yvette's magnificent pair of bare limbs exposed in all their glory, thanks to the brevity of her skimpy summer dress. "Can I pay a tribute to yours?"

"How?' Yvette asked.

"By drawing a nude of you on your thigh," I explained, as though it were the most logical thing in the world.

"I'd love it!" she said.

So, taking my black felt pen from my pocket, I leaned over the seat and picked up Yvette's leg from the under-thigh and set to work. Within a minute or so I finished a full-bodied nude of Yvette, to everyone's delight. Almost everyone. "I think," Jim smiled, "you had better put a bikini on it." I agreed grudgingly, and added the skimpy raiment.

We joined our friends in the restaurant and were delighted by their shocked reaction to Yvette's "tattoo." I sat across table from her, with Bruce sitting to her left and Jim to her right. "I love art," Bruce said, and his hand disappeared under the table, where it was slapped kiddingly by Yvette who said "I hate art critics!"

During the course of the evening I gained a new and lasting respect for Yvette's astonishing intelligence, which included among so many other things an incredible knowledge of classical music, with which she dazzled me completely; for I had hungered for years for the opportunity to discuss this subject with someone who had the same relish for it as myself. She attributed this encyclopedic awareness of the subject to her two-year affair with the brilliant young conductor Zubin Mehta, but her love of life and adventure and learning was entirely her own, and ranged in scope from subjects as diverse as photography and archaeology, to literature and all fields of art.

The following morning my drawing was gone from her thigh, but I noticed that the flesh was red and raw, as if from much rubbing, and it was with great anticipation that I approached her. "I hope your ears were burning all night last night," she said, "because that's how long I sat in the tub trying to scrub your picture off, and *cursing you* with every rub of the cloth!"

I apologized on behalf of all the "leg men" of the world, but never again was I to be satisfied by setting pen to mere paper.

As the filming progressed, the whole production seemed to take on the aspect of a swirling kaleidoscope of colorful egos upon a madly whirling merry-go-round during an earthquake, and only the calming effect of my sweet friend Lois prevented me from developing a case of ulcers.

There was our *Napoleon,* Serge, and his battles with Bruce; Miguel and Pedro and their well-meaning but unclear awareness of the limitations of the Campbell, Silver, Cosby financial situation; there was the ever-present dynamism of our production manager, Joe Juliano, upon whom everyone leaned in moments of stress, and who eventually numbered among those who were to fall from favor in the eyes of my associates; the marvelously strong-charactered production assistant, Anna Korda, the blond-haired European woman who could be relied upon for anything, and who was never to fall from favor in the eyes of anyone; and the beautiful little Algerian delight named Tchina, who became Bruce's companion after being sent for by Joe Juliano from Paris. Poor Tchina—who cried such bitter tears (out of love for Bruce) when the time came to send her back to Paris as production in Cannes neared an end. I saved her from that fate for a while convincing Bruce to keep her on a bit longer, for which I received a tearful embrace of gratitude from her, and an appreciative nod of thanks from the ever-concerned Anna Korda.

Finally, somehow, production in France reached a conclusion, and preparation was made for the journey home. After many sad goodbyes (and a few joyous ones), Bruce, Sandy, Lois, and I were bound for Paris aboard an all-night train. At Orly Airport in Paris we caught a plane to New

York. Lois's mother and uncle were waiting for her, and we repeated the emotional goodbyes we had begun on the train to Paris.

Back home in Los Angeles once again, the filming was far from over. There was still the opening scene in San Francisco, the beach scene to be shot in Catalina, plus three or four other scenes that could be filmed either on a sound stage or neighboring locations. Serge arrived, raring to go; and the madness began once again.

We had all regrouped, in fact; Albert, Yvette, Jim Byron, Bruce, myself, and a whole new group of faces constituting our American film crew. So, saying goodbye once more to family and friends, I was off with cast and crew for San Francisco.

In the opening scene of the film, a wild, afternoon party sequence at a simulated San Francisco art gallery, attended by George Smith and his wife (Albert and Yvette), we threw in the whole works: eighty extras, beards and berets, bizarre miniskirted starlets, sequins and feathers, sensuously tattooed seductresses, a Chinese girl in a tantalizingly slit dress, two beautifully gaunt old ladies in long black dresses and large floppy hats, an effeminate young fop in a pink velvet jacket with picturesque buttons, and the Sopwith Camel rock band, a shaggy group of wild musicians whose sound dominates the whole sequence, while a gorgeous black girl competes with them with a classical song at the piano. Champagne is everywhere, and every available wall is covered with the work of a talentless young artistic discovery whose work is being feted at this opening—a phony of the first order—and whose paintings are nothing more than a form of glorified calligraphy.

For the setting we rented the penthouse apartment of that flamboyant barrister, Melvin Belli, whose domain high atop San Francisco's Telegraph Hill overlooking the Bay was "atmosphere-perfect." This glass-walled suite of rooms, bathed in red velvet and lined with books of law, was filled to capacity with dancing, writhing, gaudy party-goers of all shapes, sizes, and ages, and the sequence took three dizzying days to shoot.

Serge was everywhere, shooting the scene alternately with the big Mitchell camera and the little hand-held job, which took him between gyrating dancers to the farthest corners of the penthouse. His barking, French-accented commands stopped and started the action constantly, regrouping the frenzied extras and zooming in on unsuspecting groups who forgot they were actually being filmed.

Serge had taken full advantage of his directorial authority in much of the casting for this sequence, for half of San Francisco's more glamorous starlets sat waiting their turn outside his hotel suite, the night before the shooting of this scene had began, to be interviewed.

The camera crew was headed by the marvelous cinematic talents of Dave Shore, and a thoroughly enjoyable bunch of San Francisco film technicians worked as well. We had a long stay in this town, for we were also shooting the bedroom sequence on a sound stage in the vast emptiness of the newly built Alcoa Building; so this meant many more enjoyable dinners reminiscent of our European evenings, when our little group went out daily in search of a new dining adventure.

My long-time friend, Karen Le Vine, who was bubblingly enthusiastic about my project since its inception, was a resident of San Francisco, and was a popular caricaturist at the famous Hungry Eye restaurant. She knew *everyone*, and introduced me to the entire city. She induced the famous columnist Herb Caen to mention me and the film in his column, and brought me to the bizarre office-den of the hip poet Lawrence Ferlinghetti who put "speed" freaks to work washing windows to keep them busy while he sat pouring out his wildly sensitive verse.

Friends were easier to make here than in any other town I had seen, and, in fact, I made several long-lasting and delightful acquaintances. The party sequence, meanwhile, dominated everything, like some ongoing, never-ending Roman orgy—the perfect setting for the young architect, played by Finney, to become fiercely disenchanted with the whole phony art scene, causing him to take off with his wife, impulsively, for France and Picasso—the real thing.

Two well-known reporters were in attendance—Judy Stone of the *San Francisco Chronicle*, and Kevin Thomas of the *Los Angeles Times*. I was taken aside separately by both, to be interviewed, as were Albert, Yvette, and Serge. These were very long "in-depth" interviews, and I was delighted at the results. The Sunday pink section of the *San Francisco Chronicle*, the "Datebook," devoted a huge spread in their March 10, 1968 issue, with a large headline that read, "I Got Sick of Doing Junk...I Got Tired of Being Funny." This was a quote of a remark I had made to Judy Stone regarding my work for so many years on the *Tom and Jerry* variety of animation. On the first page of the article was a still from the film of Dominguin riding elegantly on horseback toward the camera, with a small group of his ranch hands behind him, also on horseback. On the second page were two photos, one of Finney and one of myself. The caption beneath my photo read "An Act of Desperation," which is quoted from that part of the article which states "It was an act of desperation and aspiration that took Wes Herschensohn to Picasso's door in Mougins nearly four years ago. ('Don't come like pilgrims to Mecca,' Picasso once told a friend. 'Come because you like me, because you find my company interesting and because you want to have a simple direct relationship with me.') . . . . It would have been easier to reach Mecca."

She had begun her article by saying that love letters, real and fake, are nothing new to Pablo Picasso, and she quoted Picasso's remark that there is no such thing as love—there are only proofs of love. The *Picasso Summer*, she said, is a proof of love, "a tangible demonstration of the way genius can touch and change the most remote lives."

Kevin Thomas's article was equally enjoyable, referring to my years of effort as "Herschensohn's long and frustrating odyssey. Through a maze of intermediaries, including photographer David Douglas Duncan as well as Dominguin, he eventually did meet Picasso. . . ."

But all through the time these interviews were taking place, and long after they were completed, the party sequence raged on. Yvette was wearing my favorite outfit, the black velvet pants suit in the style of a man's tuxedo, which accented her blond loveliness and femininity. I remembered the first time I had seen it, when one night in France a group of us were having cocktails in one of the hotel suites, when I answered Yvette's knock and was so startled to see her standing there in this suit. It knocked me out, and I was delighted to see her wearing it for this sequence.

We had one mishap that scared us all. Marty Ingels, in a red turtleneck sweater, was pretending to be a matador; and in the midst of a crowded group of revelers was making passes at a man who charged him wearing a large, basketlike, raffia bull's head, as sparklers on the horns were spurting colorful stars. Suddenly, the basket bull's head accidentally caught on fire, with flames racing down the back of it, and billows of black smoke curling into the air. Nothing could have pleased Serge more, and it was an unbearably long time before he yelled "Cut!" while the extras went to the frantic man's aid. "Excellent!" cried Serge. "That will add just the right touch!"

I thought then, how wonderful for Serge if the whole place had caught fire! And I wondered afterward, in what condition could it all have been left, what degree of restoration was required when the shooting was finished, and what was the expression on the face of Melvin Belli when next he was to insert the key in his front door, to return once more to his beloved penthouse apartment on Telegraph Hill?

We had been searching for a large house to serve as a simulated version of the Picasso residence as part of a dream sequence for the film, in which Yvette goes wandering through the rooms in search of Picasso and his work; the balance of which we were to shoot on a sound stage in Hollywood.

A suitable house was finally located in San Mateo County, and that part of the cast and crew that was needed took off from our temporary base in San Francisco for a long day's shooting. Bruce's brother, Jim Campbell, was in charge of production for the day, as he was on a number of other sessions.

The mansion was huge and imposing, and would have been equally suitable for a horror-suspense film. The owner was a tall and dignified gray-haired gentleman in his late fifties; and a younger man, very plump and smooth-skinned, with a thin black mustache and black hair combed slickly back from a part in the middle of his head, walked around carrying a tiny infant in his arms. The older man kept pretty much to himself, but the younger fellow with the infant was everywhere, watching the filming and chatting incessantly, though in a very subdued tone.

The "lady of the house" was ill, and confined to her room upstairs. Both men confided to me separately that she was very beautiful and hinted at some mysterious "secret" that hung over "this house." Because of the great unintentional comicality of their manner, the whole thing seemed like something straight out of Charles Addams. Soon I was to discover that this comparison was truer than my wildest dreams would have dared allowed.

For, an hour or two after the filming was in progress, I sat in the library perusing a large rare edition of the drawings of Michelangelo, which the owner had taken, with great pride, from behind the locked glass door of a high and very imposing book cabinet. I excused myself after fifteen or twenty minutes of conversation about this book to go into the kitchen to get myself a glass of water. As I stood by the sink quenching my thirst, I suddenly found myself confronted by a beautiful young woman with long black hair. She began *whispering* to me, wide-eyed, that she did not want anyone to know she had come downstairs. This was the owner's wife, the mistress of the house, who was supposed to be ill. She confessed to me, still in a whisper, that she was only staying upstairs to "avoid suspicious speculation" as to what was "going on in this house."

Expressing my confusion as to her meaning, she went on to confess that the baby the young man was carrying around in his arms was her own, and that the young man was the *father*. It was an arrangement, she continued, that her husband only reluctantly allowed, and that the three of them lived under one roof (with the infant) in an atmosphere of unbearable tension. She was gone as suddenly as she had appeared, returning, apparently, to the confinement of her upstairs room. I must have remained standing there by the sink for at least a full minute, shaking my head in utter disbelief, wondering if Charles Addams had ever paid a visit to this home.

I was hoping that my parents would be able to watch some of the filming of the movie, and the chance finally came when we were to shoot the only scene to be made in Los Angeles. This was Yvette's "dream sequence," where Albert dreams Yvette is walking through a maze of large Picasso paintings, done in multiple exposure and other dreamlike effects. This scene had been partially shot at that mansion in San Mateo, and now the remainder was to be filmed on a sound stage in Hollywood. My parents were delighted with the chance to watch, and to meet Yvette.

After each take (and there were many!) Yvette would run back to the chair she had stationed between my parents and chat with them and entertain them, and we all had a grand time. I appreciated her attention and recalled that Jim Byron had told me how important Yvette's family was to her, and how devoted she was to her parents. The humor of my mother and father matched Yvette's sense of humor, and there was a comfortable and very lively rapport between them.

The set was actually nothing more than a series of walls covered with large reproductions of Picasso's paintings and drawings, through which Yvette was to wander, with trancelike awe, creating an eerie sense of wonder, within Albert's dream; the dream from which Albert awakens inspired, deciding to follow his impulse and leave with Yvette for France, to meet Picasso. And like all Hollywood productions, this dream sequence being one of the first in the picture, it was one of the last to be filmed.

30

Ode to Joy—Marla and the Sand Mural

IT WAS DECIDED THAT THE FINAL SCENE WOULD BE SHOT IN CATALINA, FOR WE needed not only a beach with a tide, but a beach that in all other ways would resemble the shores of southern France.

I was to cover a massive area with drawings in the sand, whereupon I would be replaced by Duke Fishman, who was to be doubling for Picasso, and who would appear to the camera as having done all the work himself.

We were doubly blessed in having discovered Fishman, inasmuch as he not only looked like Picasso—in face, height, and build—but he was somewhat of an artist as well, and was able to briefly continue my drawings for the camera with a degree of aplomb. Furthermore, he was a well-known, almost legendary citizen of Catalina and was really a natural "find" for us. With Perc Westmore's final touches of makeup one would almost have sworn this was the Maestro himself—yet, how my stomach would flip whenever I let myself think back on how close we had come to the real thing, and how we lost it, and for such a sickening reason!

George Smith looked down at the sand. And after a long while, looking, he began to tremble.

For there on the flat shore were pictures of Grecian lions and Mediterranean goats and maidens with flesh of sand like powdered gold and satyrs piping on hand-carved horns and children dancing, strewing flowers along and along the beach with lambs gamboling after, and

263

musicians skipping to their harps and lyres and unicorns racing youths toward distant meadows, woodlands, ruined temples, and volcanoes. Along the shore in a never-broken line, the hand, the wooden stylus of this man, bent down in fever and raining perspiration, scribbled, ribboned, looped around over and up, across, in, out, stitched, whispered, stayed, then hurried on as if this traveling bacchanal must flourish to its end before the sun was put out by the sea. Twenty, thirty yards or more the nymphs and dryads and summer founts sprang up in unraveled hieroglyphs. And the sand in the dying light was the color of molten copper on which was now slashed a message that any man in any time might read and savor down the years. Everything whirled and poised in its own wind and gravity. Now wine was being crushed from under the grape-blooded feet of dancing vitners' daughters, now steaming seas gave birth to coin-sheathed monsters while flowered kites strewed scent on blowing clouds . . . now . . . now . . . now . . .

—Ray Bradbury, "In a Season of Calm Weather"

★   ★   ★

Duke Fishman, Picasso's amazing double.
(COURTESY OF BRUCE CAMPBELL)

I came to the Mediterranean with my head already filled with those mythological beings of the sea I had learned from Picasso's work, and that Ray Bradbury had laid out so enchantingly in his story "In a Season of Calm Weather." I had known them earlier, sensed them, in the magnificently sensuous paintings of Botticelli; for in my imagination I had repainted all those erotic bacchanalian masterpieces that Botticelli had consigned to the fire, under the hypnotic influence of the religious fanatic Savonarola. Yet even in those paintings of the *converted* Botticelli, of madonnas and saints and angels, it is easy, through the magic of his forbiddingly delicious color and line, to see the invisible satyrs and nymphs swirling in their pagan rituals within the kaleidoscopic imagery of his flower-strewn foliage; and behind the ecstatic expressions of those beautiful madonnas it takes little imagination to smell the naturally perfumed body odors and aphrodisiacal aromas that emit themselves through the pure joy of the Nature in which they abound. Botticelli could burn his testaments to natural joy, but he could never destroy those true God-gifts which are self-resurrecting.

Beethoven, especially in his Seventh and Ninth symphonies, materialized these delirious joys better than anyone before or since. And Picasso, in the warm sunshine of his imagination, fostered by the magnetism of the mysterious Mediterranean, embodied them in a way I wish everyone could know and understand. This was what I wished to do in my animation; and in what ultimately became the *Erotica* sequence, I hope that I did. Much was cut from it by my well-meaning co-producers for the sake of time and economy, but the essence remained. In it my one goal was to capture a relentlessly driven joyousness that is the rhythm of life—the cosmic movement that embodies all things of the Creator.

It was, through an incredible act of good fortune, that just prior to the time I was to leave with the film crew for our hidden "Mediterranean" beach on Catalina to cover the shore with these Picassoid creatures, that I met one in person. Her name was Marla. She had about her a look of what can only be described as a *wholesome succulence*. She was in her early twenties, with short brown hair that fell loosely across her face at an angle from the right side of her forehead and coming to a point at the top of her left cheek. Behind her large, dark blue eyes it seemed as though charges of dynamite were being constantly set off. This, I think, was her most singular characteristic; and these dynamite charges were reflected in her downward-flaring nostrils, as if she were in a state of some continual inner excitement. Her full-lipped mouth was often curled up to one side as if in an attempt to ward off a naughty laugh, in an expression of sheer mischief. She had a paganlike power, a *real* power, and it frightened and put off a lot of people, for nobody knew how to take Marla. How does one handle a bacchanalian nymph transported from antiquity to modern times? And yet I felt a tremendous protectiveness for her and fell totally under her spell. For with everything else, Marla had such an inner largeness and goodness, and such a generous and sensitive and intelligent nature, that it was hard not to feel a softness for this child-woman. She had a humor that embraced everything in its tremendous positiveness. But most significantly, and probably the most charming and spellbinding thing about her, was that hearty gusto of a *laugh!* It could be heard certainly halfway around the world—easily the most contagious laugh I have ever known, and it melted a lot of hearts.

So, praise be, I met this strange bacchanalian nymph just in time to create my massive bacchanalian "fresco" in the sand for the film! So I took her with us to Catalina, and we were in love under this most unique of circumstances. Oddly enough, Marla's middle name was Joy, and I marveled at the appropriateness of it, though I, as well as she, was to suffer for this overwhelming aspect of her nature, which took a long time for her finally to harness. That is—if such a power can ever truly be harnessed!

Everyone came along—Yvette, Serge, Bruce Campbell, the entire camera crew (led by David Shore), Albert Finney's double (Albert was now back in England), a bevy of beauties for some equestrian shots Serge wanted on the beach (and which were not included in the final film cut), and Marla and myself. And on the island was, of course, the venerable Duke Fishman, who would be seen "finishing" my sand mural for the camera—as Picasso. Whenever I thought of this it pained me to think of how close we had come, that fateful day in Cannes, to having Picasso himself create the entire scene.

The problem in selecting a beach was this: in Bradbury's original short story, "In a Season of Calm Weather," the tale ends with the tide coming in and washing away Picasso's vast bacchanalian masterpiece on the sand. This was fine, for the story originally took place in Biarritz, France, where the wild Atlantic does, indeed, have a tide. However, the film took place in Cannes, where the benign Mediterranean has no tide. Yet without a tide coming in we had no ending. Therefore, after much exploring and searching a beach was discovered on the far side of Catalina, California, that bore an amazing resemblance to the Mediterranean shore of Cannes and yet did indeed, at day's end, have a tide. To add further to the convenience, it was surrounded by large hills and cliffs close to the shoreline where the camera crew could station itself for the necessary aerial shots of the mural in the sand, as well as allowing us the enclosed privacy required for the filming of the scene.

I had no inkling, at the outset, of the intense physical labor that was to be required in covering this shore, as far as the eye could see, with these immense Picassoid figures and scenes. Two days of shooting were necessary, not merely for the drawing, but because Serge got it into his head that he wanted several beautiful girls riding bareback along the beach; a sequence to be used elsewhere in the picture to add a touch of erotic

The author—drawing the world's mythology in the sand at Catalina. (COURTESY OF BRUCE CAMPBELL)

fantasy, never really explained, and in fact never used in the final cut of the film. Serge directed these scenes on horseback, and it cut annoyingly into the precious time needed for the sand mural.

Soon enough, however, the work was begun. This required a crew of men to sweep the sand flat in preparation for my drawing, for which I used a large stick I found along the beach, and which, happily, suited my purpose perfectly. Just prior to each drawing being laid these men sprinkled the sand wet from buckets of water they carried in their arms, so that the sand would be the right consistency for etching a strong, dark line that could be seen from the cameras on the neighboring hilltop. There were several spots along the beach where this procedure was not necessary.

After an hour or so, the stick began digging blisters in the palm of my hand, until it was covered with blood. At first I was unaware of this, so engrossed was I in the fantasy that seemed to be unfolding itself on the shore: the "satyrs piping on hand-carved horns," "the Mediterranean goats and maidens with flesh of sand," the "children dancing, strewing flowers along and along the beach," and all of the other creatures of Bradbury's story and Picasso's brain and my own now-fevered imagination. Marla, the little demon-ripe sea sprite, encouraged me onward like a Muse from the ocean depths, dancing alongside of me like one of the etchings in the sand come to life.

But soon it was necessary to find a glove for me to wear, since it became obvious that my hand would otherwise shortly be dripping blood on the sand. Then we proceeded joyously. Marla continued to dance alongside of me as I etched this love letter to her in the sand; to her, to Picasso, to Bradbury, to myself, to anyone who could find joy in these sensuous hieroglyphs. I drew a large portrait of Marla's face, possibly ten feet long, as were many of the figures now sprawled across the sand, and it was incredible how perfectly in context it was with the other figures of this visual mythology. There were immense families of satyrs and nymphs bouncing smiling little infants playfully into the air; and beneath the real sun and beside the real sea, in the ripe freshness of the ocean air, there was lent to these scenes an eerie feeling of some unknown reality returning to its rightful home.

At day's end, as the tide moved in, my job was to sketch a figure as quickly as possible on the wet shore where the waves had just receded, finish, and get out of the way as the waves returned, in order for the camerman on the hill (using a telescopic lens) to get a shot of the onrushing waves washing away the drawing. It became a real joke, because each time the crew would shout down to me from their post on the hill that a proper wave was coming, I was to draw a large figure or face as decently as possible in a matter of seconds and then clear out, and when I failed I got pretty wet; so that before long we were feeling, all of us, hilarious with laughter.

We had flown over from L.A. to the island on little seaplanes that seemed loaded down with the weight of its many passengers (the heavier ones were told to sit toward the rear) and then driven in huge buses from the main part of the island, over bumpy and treacherous roads (passing many bison on the way!), to the isolated spot at the far end of the island where we were to do our filming.

At the end of the first day's shooting almost everyone returned to the "civilized" part of the island the same way, to spend the night in one of the hotels, but a few of us luckier ones got to ride back in one of the three available helicopters. It was my first helicopter ride and I was thrilled, but on my second ride the next evening the thrill was gone and I was secretly terrified, and delirious with joy upon landing, to feel my feet on solid ground.

That night we were all awakened by a tremendous storm, and through our windows on the ground floor we could see the waves lashing out over the fence that separated the hotel from the beach, and roaring up toward the windows themselves. However, in the morning, all was calm again, and we returned to our little Cannes-on-Catalina beach.

Yvette and Albert's double (as George and Alice Smith of the story) had to be filmed walking along the shore, oblivious of the figures drawn in the sand, as George recounts to Alice his fruitless attempt with Dominguin in Madrid to get an introduction to Picasso. They fail, also, to see another figure at the far end of the beach stooping over with a stick and drawing in the sand, then dropping the stick and running off in the opposite direction from George and Alice, to a small group of people with children, which he joins, arms extended. As George and Alice walk off, unknowingly, into the distance, the tide comes in, beginning to wash away this testament to joy they never noticed in their disappointment at not having succeeded in meeting Picasso.

The little figure they failed to notice was, of course, Picasso—portrayed in this instance by Duke Fishman, although no one who has seen the film believes that this was anyone but Picasso himself. At any rate, thus the film ends as Picasso rejoins his friends after having covered the beach with his creation *as far as the eye can see,* and George and Alice disappear unknowingly into the distance, as the sun sets in a glorious and dazzling display of reds and oranges, and the waves wash over the last remains of that bacchanalian vision in the sand—all to the swelling sounds of Michel Legrand's thrillingly lavish music.

During the many breaks in shooting and drawing I had a chance to talk once again with Yvette, who never failed to astound me with her incredible grasp of art and music. However, at one point on the second day, as we sat together in a shaded spot, she took the opportunity to question me at great length on certain subjects, and we had an interesting conversation concerning Serge and Christine, and about Jim Byron, and Lois, and all the people we had each encountered both separately and mutually, filling in many blanks for one another.

Marla eventually tired of dancing and walking and standing beside me, and I found myself drawing alone and was beginning to find it very tedious. My back was aching and my arm muscles were getting stiff, not to mention the pain in my hand. Missing the great diversion that her merry presence had been affording me, I stood up and began looking for her, but saw only the crew and actors. Then I saw, far to the left, on the distant cliffs that extended out to sea, two figures—Marla and Don (our still-photographer), she having her picture taken and exploring the seascape. I called to her, and though she seemed too far away to hear me, she must have had one eye on me, and waved back in response to my frantic waving.

It was some time, though, till she made her way down the cliff and back up the shore to where I was now painfully engaged in my drawing. At first I was angry, though I had no right to be, and so was she—but she dispelled it with a mischievous twinkle, and I said, "See what I've made for you." I had drawn her face on one of the nymphs who was dancing on the grapes.

"Now wine was being crushed from under the grape-blooded feet of dancing vintners' daughters, now steaming seas gave birth to coin-sheathed monsters . . ."

Eventually the work was done, and I felt that I had begun to fulfill my commitment, though to whom or to what I was not sure. To myself, probably.

"Twenty, thirty yards or more the nymphs and dryads and summer founts sprang up in unraveled hieroglyphs. And the sand in the dying light was the color of molten copper on which was now slashed a message that any man in any time might read and savor down the years. Everything whirled and poised in its own wind and gravity."

Now I was ready. Ahead of me lay one thing and one thing only. The filming, as far as I knew then, was finished. The sand mural was done. The contracts were signed, and the checks from Warner Bros. were coming in. I was ready now to begin what for four long years I had been fighting and struggling for the opportunity and the right to do—and for the next entire year I would be totally submerged in it—the animation with which I intended to make my first loud sound as an artist. And for that whole year of 1968 I was like a joyous explorer in a new world of exhilarations and perils, for which everything seemed daring and untried. And for that whole year Marla the sea sprite was to be dancing and fighting and laughing and loving along beside me on that seashore of the imagination which is so much more vast and beautiful and terrifying than any on earth.

31

1968—Doing the Animation

DAVID DOUGLAS DUNCAN CASTELLARAS 53
MOUANS SARTOUX
A. M. FRANCE
Phone: CANNES 902453

29 December, '67

Dear Wes:

Your fine letter was here when we got in from New York, to spend the
Christmas and New Year holidays. We are so excited by your news . . .
but, maybe even more, we are proud of your determination to see the
film through to its realization. Now, in looking back, you'll probably
wonder where you found the energy and optimism to continue—when it
kept blowing up in your face. Bravo! Naturally, when you phoned from
Cannes, I would have liked to have helped you in any way possible—but
by that time you already understood that you were in the ball park on
your own . . . you'd reached the stage where there was no help that I
could deliver.

Anyway, your film is under control, it sounds as though it has a good
cast, Bradbury may have told you that he once came to my place in Rome
and read me the same story which now is your script, Bourguignon is, of

271

course, talented and respected (he used to court the girl across the street, here in Castellaras, so Sheila saw him around numerous times)—and I *know* what to expect from your animation, having seen those first samples of your idea and work right here across the room from where I'm knocking out this letter while seated beside the fire. Don't worry, that little rascal, Lump, is sawing away under his blanket beneath the dinner table—curled in his basket hoping I'll forget, tonight, to take him down to the road before we turn in. He's in great shape—better than ever. My God, Sheila just got up from where she'd been reading beside the fire—and I see that Lump was stretched out, lizardlike, at her feet, damned near in the fire. But he *is* sawing away—and assuredly hating the soon-to-arrive moment when he'll have to open his eyes and go outside.

And Sheila? Lovelier than ever! Because of the Con Thien story, I returned from Viet-Nam much earlier than first anticipated. Once Stateside, there was plenty to keep me busy regarding new ideas for future stories. They delayed me long enough to bridge the time to these holidays. They have seemed very special, as you may imagine. Now, immediately after the New Year, I'll return to Saigon and head toward the DMZ, and other places, to poke around and see what I can uncover. I'm glad you saw the ABC show, and that you liked the *Life* essay. Naturally, I felt that it was a good return to straight magazine shooting, because the editors really opened up every available page, and then let the story run in a low-key vein. Considering the fact that all ABC technicians were on strike, and that it was my first TV effort (excluding promo appearances for *Nomad,* etc.) I thought the "Scope" effort was okay. Next time we'll do it better—faster cuts, more voice from the boondocks, smoother camera work . . . yet it was an honest film and a good start. Now, I want to shoot an essay on refugee kids, another on the Marines in the Monsoon mud, and one on MacNamara's DMZ "Barrier"—it's impossible. And won't that raise hell when I prove it! And, one more story—of which I never speak . . . and won't until it's done. But, now—we are thrilled for you . . . and so very proud of you! Come back. Lump and Sheila and our home send

> Happy New Year!
> signed/Dave

Never had I known that feeling of doing what I had been born to do as I had during the entire year of 1968 while working on the animation of *The Picasso Summer.* The William Morris Agency had negotiated a beautiful

272

contract for me with Warner Bros., and through their office I received weekly checks that enabled me to feel free of mundane worries. This, of course, did not prevent my being plagued by certain domestic problems that finally came to a head toward the end of the year, but above and beyond anything, I was *doing* what I had so long dreamed of doing— realizing a goal that I had worked so long and hard to attain.

Before this, I had been like a bird confined to a small enclosed room, and now suddenly let free, I was soaring over mountains and valleys and plains I had hitherto only imagined.

The three sequences to be animated were "War and Peace," "Erotica," and "The Bullfight"; and although by year's end I had animated over 35 minutes of film, these were edited down to the three sections of approximately seven minutes each. Warner Bros. had offered to hire any amount of assistants I might need, but I insisted on working alone, just as one would work alone on a *painting*, and so I did every frame of the animation myself, including the selection and keying of every square inch of color for the inking and painting of the cels, which were traced over the drawings, and which numbered in the thousands.

And frankly, when the titan Michelangelo set the example for all lesser artists to come, by painting that cosmic ceiling entirely alone, dismissing all assistance offered, one cannot help but emulate, even in one's own *tininess*, the law set forth by this god of art. However, Rubens and (more recently) the great Mexican muralists Orozco, Rivera, and Siqueiros employed assistants and yet in no way diminished their own creative individuality. So, one has a choice of Olympian examples, and in this case I chose the former rather than the latter, if for no other reason than that it would have been impossible to explain to an assistant the imagery of rhythm and movement that was swirling in my head.

Michel Legrand scored the music for the animation after I finished, by timing and watching it on the screen, and he did such a superb job that the picture was enhanced beyond my wildest dreams.

Although I loved equally every moment of the work, like an archaeologist making discovery after discovery, I found myself reaching the most dazzling inner heights through the animation of the "Bullfight" segment, especially in the swirling, sensuous, ever-changing rhythms of the Flamenco dancers that animate organically from the silhouettes of a bullfight in progress, and evolve with ever-growing power to a climax of movement and metamorphosis. For this sequence I did much research, and attended, as a sketching observer, the Flamenco classes in the home of the beautiful Spanish dancer, Luisa Triana.

And yet, when I look at this animation today, I see it almost as a *kindergarten attempt*, compared to that of which I know I am now ready and capable. That was the bird's first flight (allowing a slightly melodramatic but accurate analogy!)—newly exploring, at times undisciplined, at times

273

stiff and clumsy—but at least *flying*. Yet I feel once again like that bird confined to the small enclosed room; only now, having tasted the joys of flight and freedom, the room is smaller and more confining than ever before.

Soon I hope to begin a new film, this time on the life of my hero, Beethoven; a live-action feature with the animated segments appearing in certain musical portions of the film, and here I will be in full flight, not just as a bird soaring through the air, but this time (once more that tinted but truthful analogy) as a rocket in full command of every turn and maneuver, showering fire and sparks through every region of space!

There was so little continuity in the footage Serge Bourgignon had given us, so little resemblance to Ray Bradbury's script, that our editor, Bill Dornisch, and his assistants found it impossible to work with. So Serge was fired, and was replaced by Robert Sallin, who headed a highly successful television-commercial studio on Sunset Boulevard named Kaleidoscope. Bob had shown great directorial talent, and his company was the recipient of many awards. Furthermore, he was an old friend of both Bruce and myself, with a thorough understanding of what was needed.

A new group of writers, headed by the genius of Ed Weinberger, were assembled to add additional dialogue and continuity. So while I was laboring lovingly on the animation, Bruce and Sallin returned to Europe with Albert and Yvette to shoot the necessary footage required to put the film back in shape. Albert, who was not all that thrilled with acting anymore, and hoping to eventually do some directing of his own, drove a hard bargain. Not at all eager to reshoot so much of a film he had already completed, he agreed to it only on the condition that he receive one hundred thousand dollars upon release of the film. With Campbell, Silver, Cosby's back up against the wall, they had no choice but to agree. This time I was spared the agony, and spent the whole time in Los Angeles, happily engaged in that work which I had fought so hard to achieve, while the whole company went back to Europe to get the additional footage needed.

Upon their return Bruce filled me in on all that had taken place, and I was glad to have been locked away in my ivory tower! One bit of information that both amused and surprised me, however, was to hear that Bruce and Christine had been involved in quite an affair, and that Christine was now madly in love with Bruce! He had promised to send for her, to come to work for him at Campbell, Silver, Cosby—which would have been marvelous—but this, unfortunately, never came to pass.

Instead, while I tried to complete my animation without interference and interruption, Bruce and Roy and Bob Sallin, upon their resumption of editing the film (with the new and old footage combined), now became very "antsy" and impatient and opinionated about my work and a great many very unpleasant battles ensued, mostly regarding the editing—not only of the live aciton, but the animation as well!

Odious and presumptuous as the comparison may be, and intending to be neither, I could not help but remember Irving Stone's account in *The Agony and the Ecstacy* of the incredible feats Michelangelo had to undertake whenever he desired to produce even one sculpture; for he himself went with the workmen of Carrara to locate the exact chunks of marble he wanted; and then proceeded to extract them from the mountain, directing the work himself and actually performing most of the heavy labor required. This sometimes took weeks or months of incredible physical endurance, but it was the only way that Michelangelo could be sure to get precisely the proper material he wanted for his work.

Only by fantasizing that there was some common agony linking all artists, great and small—the constant and unnerving struggle, the *battle* involved in merely making creation a possibility—helped to get me through some otherwise very ugly days.

The editing room in Beverly Hills became the scene of several violent quarrels between me and Bob Sallin, who felt that he could exercise his rights as director of the live action to include the entire film—that is, the animation! To me it seemed a violation not only of our friendship (for long before the film had become a reality, Bob and his wife Sandy were in awe of my persistent efforts to bring it about), but even more so of what I considered to be a sacred trust I had conferred upon myself—to bring this new art in animation into the world. How *dare* he attempt to cut three, four, five, or more minutes of that work which I had achieved through one long year of love and sweat and labor? What about those endless scenes of Albert and Yvette riding through the French countryside on their bikes?

One final argument that began in the editing room was continued on the street; and in the heart of Beverly Hills the quiet evening was shattered by the awful sounds of raging and heartfelt obscenities and slanders that Bob and I literally roared at one another, while Bruce and Bill Dornisch and several others were trying frantically to keep us apart and subdue us, lest the police arrive and take care of the matter themselves. To say I won the argument would be less than true, although I was led to believe that I had. However, the editor (via the director) always has the last word, and much of my animation ended up on the proverbial cutting-room floor, and was, in several instances, pieced savagely together and mercilessly chopped, at least to my ultrasensitive eyes. This, I felt, was a betrayal; but the end result, overall, was satisfactory enough, and achieved somewhat the result I had hoped for.

One afternoon while I was chatting with Sandy Kaplan in the piano room at the Campbell, Silver, Cosby offices, Michel Legrand burst in, wearing his heavy wool-knit sweater, face aglow.

"I think I have it!" he cried.

Sandy and I looked at each other wide-eyed as Michel sat down at the piano and began to play, pouring forth the lushest, most voluptuously romantic sounds imaginable. We listened as in a trance, spellbound in the knowledge that we were hearing for the first time the main theme for *The Picasso Summer!* All the anxieties and hopes that I had been nurturing for this music during that period when I knew Michel was still in the throes of composition were now relieved, surpassing all my expectations for it; instantly we recognized that this was to become a classic—a "standard" in the repertoire of contemporary music—as it has since most assuredly become. With the beautiful love-lyrics later written by the ingenious team of Marilyn and Alan Bergman, it has come to be known as "Summer Me, Winter Me" and has been recorded by innumerable artists—near-great, great, and super-great, including the plaintively romantic rendition by Barbra Streisand.

Now, when this sudden and spontaneous moment comes unexpectedly to mind, it is with the thrill one feels when seeing sunlight burst through an opening in the trees as one drives mindlessly along, and thereby illuminating an otherwise wearisome journey.

Equally thrilling to me was the music that Legrand scored for my three animation sequences, in which he captured with sheer musical genius both the rhythm and color of the animation and the feel of each individual subject. This has since been released on the Warner Bros. label in an album titled, unbelievably, *Summer of '42—Michel Legrand!* Then, in smaller print on the lower part of the album, are the words: "Composed and conducted by Michel Legrand—including his *Picasso Suite.*" The reason for this is that *The Picasso Summer,* never having been released theatrically, might not have sold the album. And yet—the music from *Summer of '42* occupies only the first band on the first side, totaling three minutes and fifty-one seconds, and the first band on the second side, totaling one minute and forty-seven seconds, with the entire remainder of the album devoted exclusively to the score from *The Picasso Summer!*

There was at least this: in the tiniest print readable, at the bottom of the backside of the album jacket, we are told the following:

Augmenting the music of "Summer of '42" is the score of "Picasso Summer," also the work of Michel Legrand. His music, "The Picasso Suite," was evoked by the film, which required a great deal of orchestration. The score for this movie, in fact, represents what is quite possibly Michel Legrand's finest work.

And, let me add this: Legrand has managed to capture in this score, and most especially in that dazzlingly evocative main theme, the full sweep of all those romantic dreams and high hopes of adventure which were so much a part of those days of magic in the land of Picasso!

276

32

The Picasso Summer—*Live Action in Pictures and Prose*

GEORGE AND ALICE SMITH, PLAYED BY ALBERT FINNEY AND YVETTE MIMIEUX, are a young San Francisco couple. George is a successful architect, discontent with what he feels is the menial and uncreative work in which he is involved. His restlessness comes to a head when he and his wife Alice attend a wild art opening at a posh San Francisco art gallery, heralding the work of a "new master," a young local artist whom George sees as a snobbish phony. His works consist of a series of inane paintings—each an elaborately conceived letter of the alphabet!

That night, after the party, George and Alice lie in bed, and Alice is trying in vain to seduce her husband; but George is "turned off"— disturbed about the shallowness of the art scene he had witnessed that evening, and about the absence of outlets for his own creativity. The walls of their bedroom are covered with colorful reproductions of the work of Pablo Picasso, and when George finally falls off to sleep he dreams that Alice is wandering through Picasso's home, through an endless maze of the master's marvelous works. When he wakes in the morning and looks about him, he seems to have awakened in more ways than one. Leaping from bed he stands in front of a wall covered with colorful Picasso prints. He looks feverishly at his confused wife and cries, surprised at his own impulsiveness: "Let's go see him, Alice! Let's go to France and see the *real* master!" Alice, stunned, replies, "Picasso? *Now?* Surely you must be joking!"

And so, leaving behind the San Francisco effetes of the night before, George and Alice are off to southern France in search of the real thing. Once arrived, George's enthusiasm is without bounds, and he is overwhelmed by the knowledge that he is in the very corner of the world in which Picasso himself lives and creates. "We're here, Alice!" he cries.

277

George and Alice Smith (Finney and Mimieux) at a wild, noisy party in San Francisco (shot in Melvin Belli's apartment) heralding the "coming out" of a "new master." (COURTESY OF WARNER BROS.)

In bed after the party George is turned off to
everything, including the teasing advances
of his sexy wife. He feels that the whole San
Francisco art scene, and his own career and
life, are, after all, nothing but a sham.
(COURTESY OF WARNER BROS.)

The following morning, after his surrealistic dream of Alice, an inspired George stands beside his own prints of Picasso's works and says, with surprise at his own impulsiveness, "Let's go see him, Alice! Let's go to France and see the *real* master!" (COURTESY OF WARNER BROS.)

Alice, stunned replies, "Picasso? *Now?* Surely
you must be joking!" (COURTESY OF WARNER
BROS.)

"We're *here!*" George cries, as the train roars
through the southern French countryside.
(COURTESY OF WARNER BROS.)

Alice, seemingly unimpressed, sits across from George on the train. (COURTESY OF WARNER BROS.)

George and Alice ride through the countryside on rented bikes in their search for Picasso's villa. (COURTESY OF WARNER BROS.)

(Courtesy of Warner Bros.)

(Courtesy of Warner Bros.)

"We're actually here in Picasso's domain! Look at it, Alice! *Look!* It's all *Picasso country!* All of it!"

After checking into the Carlton Hotel in Cannes, they rent a couple of bicycles and start out on a beautiful journey through the lush countryside of Provence, to the equally lush music of Michel Legrand's beautiful *Picasso Summer* theme. All along the way they inquire of the local inhabitants as to the whereabouts of Picasso's villa. Each encounter seems more amusing and fruitless than the one before, but they ride on with joyful optimism.

Eventually they find their way to the small, ancient village of Vallauris, where Picasso had lived for awhile in the 'fifties,' transforming the tiny village into commercial solvency by turning out thousands of works of miraculous ceramics and pottery, which the artisans of Vallauris henceforth took on as their own trademark; for continuing in the example set by the master they were able to capitalize on his creations, just as he wished them to do. And, as if this were not enough, he donated to the village of Vallauris a larger-than-life-sized bronze statue of a man carrying a lamb, which now stands in the public square. This magnificent symbol of pastoral nobility is twice the miracle for having been sculpted by Picasso in *one day!*

A short way from this statue stands the village chapel, the Temple of Peace, in which Picasso saluted the town even further by decorating its walls with the now-famous murals entitled *War and Peace*. This, then, is the village in which George and Alice now find themselves, totally unaware of what they are soon to discover.

They enter the chapel in hushed reverence, overcome by the awe-inspiring power of the murals. They examine the walls with a spellbound intensity, and all the while Michel Legrand's music seems to be telling us that something new is about to take place; and sure enough, two dancing figures in the *Peace* mural suddenly spring to life, metamorphosing their very shapes to the rhythms of the music! And thus begins the first of the movie's three animated segments, *"War and Peace."* Each of these segments is approximately seven minutes in length.

The second animated sequence, "Erotica," takes place after George and Alice have returned to their hotel, weary after a long day's searching. As they lie in bed, Alice tries to compose a letter to Picasso, but is playfully interrupted by her amorous husband. As they begin to make love, Alice is slowly transformed into a multicolored figure of ecstasy, as this second animated sequence begins its explosion of color and motion, of familiar Picassoid shapes in continuous transformation, again to the rhythms of Michel Legrand's sensuously magnificent sounds.

The next day, they fare better—after another series of hectic encounters they come upon a gathering of tourists and locals atop a plateau of the observatory, and it is through the public telescope that George discovers Picasso's home. "How do you know that's Picasso's home?" asks Alice. "Because," George replies in a half-whisper, the blood drained from his wide-eyed face, *"I saw him!"*

Walking through the village of Vallauris.
(COURTESY OF WARNER BROS.)

George window shopping in Vallauris.
(COURTESY OF WARNER BROS.)

George and Alice, beneath Picasso's famous statue *Man Carrying a Lamb* in the square at Vallauris, are approached by a pair of friendly German tourists (played by Stephen Scott and Bee Duffell) who ask George to snap their picture beneath the statue. They tell him about Picasso's great "War and Peace" murals in the chapel nearby. (COUR-TESY OF WARNER BROS.)

Inside the chapel George and Alice reverently view the awesome "War and Peace" murals of the Master. (COURTESY OF WARNER BROS.)

(COURTESY OF WARNER BROS.)

293

The murals themselves. (COURTESY OF
WARNER BROS.)

(Courtesy of Warner Bros.)

(Courtesy of Warner Bros.)

296

George and Alice Smith, dwarfed by the
mighty Picasso murals.

(COURTESY OF WARNER BROS.)

298

Alice in bed, unsuccessfully trying to compose a letter to Picasso. (COURTESY OF WARNER BROS.)

The next scene finds Albert and Yvette standing at the gate of Picasso's home in Mougins, Notre Dame de Vie, atop a hill amid beautiful greenery and trees that shade the light of the southern sun. George rubs his hands with nervous anxiety, trying to get up enough nerve to ring the bell. "What'll we say?" he asks, "Picasso, we love you?" "Why not?" Alice responds, with a smile.

The postman arrives on his bicycle just then to deposit the daily load of mail from all over the world for Picasso. "Go ahead, ring away!" he says sympathetically. "He won't answer. He never answers. He locks himself

George and Alice at the gate of Picasso's home in Mougins. "What'll we say?" he asks, "Picasso, we love you?" "Why not?" Alice responds, with a smile. (COURTESY OF WARNER BROS.)

away all day and paints!" And as the postman rides off on his bicycle he looks back at them with a shrug, gesturing as if painting in the air with his hand. "He *paints!*" the postman cries. "He paints! He paints!", disappearing over the hill.

That night, at dinner, there is visible tension between George and Alice. Alice is tiring of the game, and wants to see the rest of France while they

"Go ahead, ring away," says the postman sympathetically. "He won't answer. He never answers. . . . He *paints!*" (COURTESY OF WARNER BROS.)

can. "It was fun at first," she tells George. "Let's go find Picasso!' and all that. But now—" "Let's go back to his villa!" George says, trying to rekindle Alice's enthusiasm, but in vain. "No, you go," she says. "I'm going back to the hotel."

And so, late into the night, George keeps a lonely vigil at Picasso's gate

George keeps a lonely night-long vigil at
Picasso's gate. (COURTESY OF WARNER BROS.)

While Alice, alone in the hotel, stares sadly into the mirror. (COURTESY OF WARNER BROS.)

The great matador, Luis Miguel Dominguin, leading his ranch hands for a roundup
of a herd of his bulls. (COURTESY OF WARNER
BROS.)

while Alice sits at the dresser in her hotel room, staring sadly into the
mirror. All seems empty now.

George, meanwhile, has found his way to a local saloon, and there by
chance makes the acquaintance of a Spaniard who had once worked on the
ranch of the great matador, Luis Miguel Dominguin. Realizing that
Dominguin is one of Picasso's dearest friends, George obtains Domin-

Left to right: Yul and Doris Brynner, Lucia
and husband Miguel, and Albert Finney.
(COURTESY OF WARNER BROS.)

guin's address from his Spanish friend. The next morning the two men
stagger arm in arm into the hotel room, and George wakes Alice up to tell
her the good news. He introduces her to his equally drunken friend, and
joyfully proclaims that through Dominguin he is sure to obtain an
introduction to Picasso!

George is told that he must learn to fight a bull—if he really wants to meet Picasso. Of course, it's all in good fun—just a "baby bull" and Dominguin always close by. Although stiff with fear, George manages to muster the courage to see it through. (COURTESY OF WARNER BROS.)

"Come on, Alice!" he cries. "Get up! Pack your things! We're off to Madrid!" Alice, however, has *had* it, and is disgusted both with George and his disheveled friend.

George takes a spill. (COURTESY OF WARNER
BROS.)

And so it is a sober and dejected George who leaves for Madrid and
Dominguin, undaunted in his almost Quixotic quest to meet his idol,
Picasso.

Once in Madrid, George rents a jeep and drives to the outskirts where
Dominguin's massive ranch is located. Seeing a man atop a horse in the
distance, George parks, and walking toward the man to ask directions, he
panics as the man waves frantically for George to get out of the way—of an
oncoming herd of stampeding bulls! There follows a wild scene in which
George runs madly for his life, finally jumping off a bridge into a stream.
The man on horseback rides up and laughingly rescues George by
offering him a pole (his bull-prod) to grab onto, pulling him soaking wet

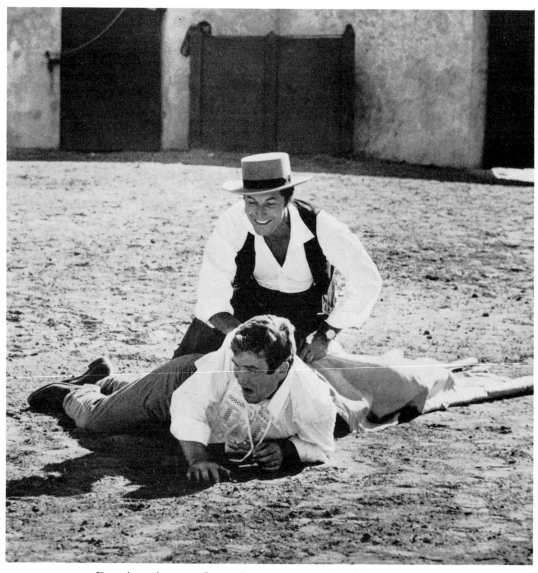

Dominguin comforts George, assuring him
that all is now safe. "He wasn't supposed to
do that," says George, spitting out a
mouthful of dirt. (COURTESY OF WARNER
BROS.)

from the stream. And so, in this way, George and Dominguin meet for the
first time. In the film, Dominguin plays himself. This sequence appeared
in chapter 26.

In the next scene, George is sitting outdoors at a long table talking to his
new host, Dominguin. At the table are also seated Dominguin's wife Lucia

While George is visiting Dominguin, Alice
strolls along the streets of Provence. (Courtesy of Warner Bros.)

(Courtesy of Warner Bros.)

and Yul Brynner and his wife Doris. Dominguin asks George why he wants to meet Picasso, and George explains earnestly his many reasons. Dominguin offers to show George several works of Picasso inside the house. "Yes," says George, "but I want to meet the real Picasso!" "Ah," responds Brynner reflectively, "but this *is* the real Picasso!"

Dominguin smilingly tells George that if he really wants to meet Picasso he must learn to fight a bull, as a show of good faith. George is shocked, but when Dominguin, still smiling, assures him that, yes, it is absolutely necessary, George (calmly terrified) takes a deep breath, and sighs, "All right, then. I'll fight a bull!" Even though it is a "baby" bull, and all in good fun, with Dominguin standing close by while he coaches the stalwart George, it is nonetheless a frightening experience. George, however, does very well, and looking proudly to Dominguin for approval sees instead a look of alarm on the matador's face as he cries, "Look out! The bull!" George finds himself running in terror, but the bull catches up to him, ramming him from the rear and sending poor George sprawling. After coaxing away the bull, Dominguin kneels beside George's prone figure, lying face down. He laughingly shakes him gently by the shoulder, telling him that he can get up now—that all is safe. George leans himself up on one elbow and wags his finger at the now far-off bull. "He wasn't supposed to do that!" he says, spitting out a mouthful of dirt.

Meanwhile, Alice, sad and very lonely, wanders the picturesque streets of Cannes and eventually happens upon a painter and his wife. She watches the painter at work for a while, and soon discovers that the painter is blind! She befriends the couple, who take very kindly to her, and accompanies them to their home for dinner. There, a charming scene follows, and the old blind painter offers Alice some warm words of wisdom.

George and Dominguin, too, have now become quite good friends, and the matador shows George his precious collection of ceramic plates on which Picasso has painted a series of bullfight pictures. Soon Dominguin begins to explain to George the almost mystical relationship between Picasso and the Bullfight, and as he talks the scene dissolves to an actual bullfight with Dominguin, and the camera brilliantly choreographs the breathtaking footwork and virtuosity of this great matador. To add to the excitement, this life-and-death ballet is accompanied by the Flamenco guitar of the great Carlos Montoya. This sequence appears in chapter 27.

The head of the bull is suddenly transformed before our eyes, as the music also changes into the rich sounds of Michel Legrand's score, and we realize that we are about to see, in *animation*, Picasso's many-sided interpretations of the bullfight!

Dominguin, ultimately, is unable to help George achieve his dream of meeting Picasso, for Picasso's phone rings unanswered.

Disappointed, George returns to France and Alice, where, reunited,

Along the way, she encounters an adventure
of her own. (COURTESY OF WARNER BROS.)

they decide to take one last swim, and one last walk along the beach before
returning home, while George recounts his Spanish adventures to Alice.
While they stroll along the beach they are oblivious (as George chats away)
of the drawings in the sand they are walking past—and in some cases,
walking over!

The camera cuts back to a long-shot of George and Alice walking
away in the distance, while in close-up we see a hand drawing in the sand
with a long, sharp stick. The urgent sound of a flute from the background

Alice, awaiting George's return from Spain, sits atop a low stone wall that overlooks Cannes and the Mediterranean, spreading far below into the distant horizon. (COURTESY OF WARNER BROS.)

music tells us something special is taking place: then, from another view, we see who is drawing in the sand with that stick—a familiar, short, stocky old man, bald, with white hair around the ears. *Picasso!* The music picks up in intensity. George and Alice are disappearing further and further into the distance, and we are witness to an unbearable irony, accented by the ever-growing buildup of the music.

Eventually Picasso tosses down his stick, and, in long-shot, we see him run, open-armed, to a small group of friends who are sitting nearby on the beach. The sun is setting, the music is swelling, and the camera pulls back to reveal the awesome spectacle of that massive fresco Picasso has created in the sand, as seen from far above: an endless variety of fauns and satyrs and nymphs and children and centaurs, dancing and loving and playing in a celebration of life.

As the setting sun burns the sky with its dark red glow, the waves from the tide begin to wash away the first of these figures in the sand, and the music has reached those glorious, sweeping sounds that carry us away in an ecstasy of bittersweet emotion.

33

The Three Sequences of Animation

"Art in the blood," said Sherlock Holmes, "is liable to take the strangest forms."

—A. Conan Doyle, "The Greek Interpreter"

The "War and Peace" Sequence

GEORGE AND ALICE SMITH ENTER THE CHAPEL OF THE PRIORY IN VALLAURIS in hushed reverence. There are only two or three other visitors, carrying candles with which to view the Picasso "War and Peace" murals, which cover the entirety of the walls of the chapel. It was Serge's idea to use the candles, in order to imbue the scene with a sense of awe. Though the chapel is adequately lit, Picasso, in fact, has himself said that he almost wished they did not light it, so that visitors would carry candles as they walked along the walls (in the manner of prehistoric grottoes), for then the candles' light would dance upon the figures as they were approached one at a time.

In any case, after obtaining written permission from Picasso himself to take over the chapel for the filming of this scene, we were free to do as we wished. This letter of permission, with Picasso's large signature of "d'accord," remains in the possession of Bruce Campbell as one of his most highly prized treasures.

So there they are, Albert and Yvette as George and Alice, walking quietly among these powerful wall paintings, lighting each section as they approach with their burning candles. And as Picasso once envisioned, the

315

Alice (Yvette Mimieux) near two larger-than-life dancing figures of the "Peace" section in the Chapel of the Priory in Vallauris. (COURTESY OF WARNER BROS.)

The painting of the two girls suddenly
springs to animated life. (COURTESY OF
WARNER BROS.)

Young girls with hands clasped during dancing around the slender, maypolelike tree. (Courtesy of Warner Bros.)

Doves linked in brotherhood. (COURTESY OF
WARNER BROS.)

A horse is felled by a spear. (COURTESY OF
WARNER BROS.)

Fig. 1   The dancing girls in their peaceful idyll are threatened by warriors in black silhouette emerging from behind large clouds against a darkening sky.

Fig. 2   Guernica in flames—peace is no more.

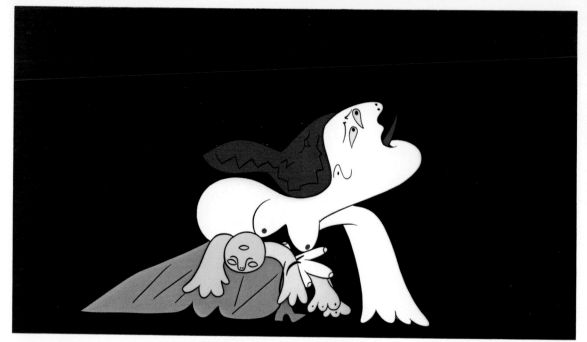

Fig. 3   These four cels depict a woman with
children in her arms fleeing in panic, crying
tears of blood.

Fig 4

Fig. 5

Fig. 6

Fig. 7   Picasso paints his *Guernica!*

Fig. 8   An ancient Sabine woman is being raped . . .

Fig. 9 ... and the entire ancient city is in
panic before the invading warriors.

Fig. 10 The large, red star of the night sky
has finally assumed the shape of a Minotaur
as he kneels beside the bed of the sleeping
maiden.

Fig. 11   Animated erotica within the imagination of our animated Minotaur.

Fig. 12   Explosive scenes of Picassoid
splendor . . .

Fig. 13 . . . and sensuality!

Fig. 14 Satyr and girl in wild, bacchanalian dance

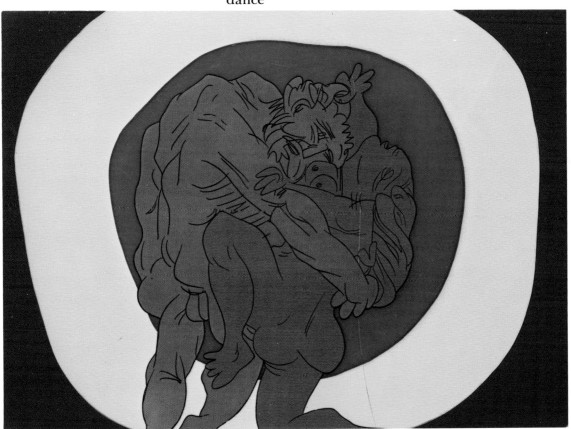

Fig. 15　Musicians and acrobat about to metamorphose into a smiling satyr.

Fig. 16　From Poussin's *Triumph of Pan*—to Picasso's artistic celebration of the liberation of Paris—to Herschensohn's celebration in animation of them both.

Fig. 17   The bullfighter in prayer beneath a
cross, traditional before the onset of the
corrida.

Fig. 18   The shapes flow rhythmically . . .

Fig. 19 . . . to become . . .

Fig. 20 . . . a picador atop his horse . . .

Fig. 21   . . . in confrontation with the bull.

Fig. 22

Fig. 23 The multicolored madonnalike
face of one of Picasso's spectators.

Fig. 24 The wildly sensual gyrations of the
Flamenco dancer.

Fig. 25   The Flamenco dancer performing
by candlelight before a seated matador and a
hooded old woman with the face of Death.

Fig. 26   The room begins to swirl . . .

Fig. 27   . . . the shapes begin to transform . . .

Fig. 28   . . . and flow . . .

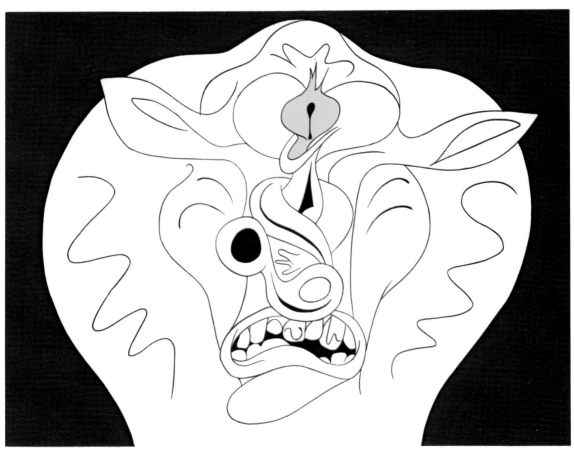

Fig. 29   . . . into the head of the bull—

Fig. 30   —glowering menacingly at the audience.

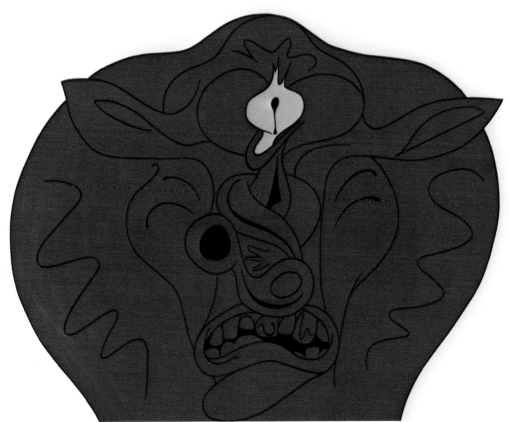

Fig. 31 At the precise moment when this highly stylized bull is lanced by the accompanying picador . . .

Fig. 32 . . . the tandem is suddenly thrust to diminutive proportions—allowing one to take in the entire spectacle of the corrida.

Terror is everywhere. (COURTESY OF
WARNER BROS.)

The warrior appears on horseback. (COUR-
TESY OF WARNER BROS.)

light did indeed dance upon his painted figures as the candles made their quiet discoveries, one at a time.

As Alice nears the section of the "Peace" mural portraying two larger-than-life dancing girls, they become aglow with the light of the candle, and the music takes on an anticipatory tone, signaling to the viewer that something—*something*—is about to take place.

And that "something" happens when the painting of the girls suddenly springs to life, or in this case into *animation* (by way of a closely matched dissolve) as the music simultaneously bursts into a joyous variation of the main *Picasso Summer* theme. The figures are a pale yellow against a solid field of dark blue.

The girls *swing* and *flow* into startlingly new shapes, matching the lively rhythms of the music with rhythms of their own as their forms swell and diminish in pulsating arabesques of motion. The two figures merge into one, and then return again to two as even more astounding metamorphoses take place. They dance and sway, bending their heads from left to right, left to right, creating visual rhythms that challenge the tempo of the music itself, as the hands become hand-wings that all but carry the two off in flight, in the ecstasy of Dance.

As a personal touch, I gave the girl on the right the face of Marla, and I knew that Picasso would approve wholeheartedly.

Next we see a group of young girls dancing with clasped hands in a circle around a slender tree, while to their right a group of picnickers, the adults, relax on the grass. I used these two groups as counterpoints to one another, using different types of movement for each of them. While the girls dance round the tree, the forms of the picnickers are also in constant motion—not the "practical" motion of eating, drinking, or talking, but rather the "poetic" motion of continually changing form, as if each figure is part of a flowing river that connects all of them in a common current of endless change.

We cut from close-ups of each group to a view of a dove with wings spread open, and around which a chain of hands are linked in brother-hood, each hand changing color in turn, from white to brown to yellow to red—the colors of mankind. The sky behind this group is a restful light blue. The dove in the center of this encirclement of hands gracefully flows from one version of its shape to another, in continuous variation of its own image.

This idyll of peace is suddenly threatened when, as we return from a close-up of the dancing girls, we see that the picknickers are *gone,* and the hill upon which they sat lowers itself to give full scope to the terrible apparition that now appears from behind a large cloud to the right of the screen.

It is a large group of warriors in black silhouette against a darkening sky, and they are brandishing their cruelly shaped knives in a rhythmic arch of movement at what remains of this peaceful idyll (Fig. 1).

We cut to a window bursting open, from which the head of a terrified woman emerges, extending her arm, lamp in hand, upon the night; as below her the city, the city of Guernica, is in flames (Fig. 2).

A horse is felled by a spear. Terror is everywhere. Women with children in their arms flee in panic, crying tears of blood (Figs. 3-6). The warrior appears on horseback. *Picasso paints his "Guernica"!* (Fig. 7)

We see an ancient city plundered as the Sabine women of another time, another war, cry in protest at their own rape (Figs. 8 and 9). Then, after many scenes of the horrors, sorrows, and devastation of war, a man suddenly beholds the vision of a dove shimmering in the golden air above him; he rises toward it, becoming himself a personification of Hope, merging into the light of the dove, the two becoming one. The profile of the man, now transfigured, gradually blends into what we eventually begin to see is the formation of the leaves of a tree, behind which the sun sends its glowing beams. This is the tree that stands outside of the Chapel of the Priory, and the camera pans down from the leaves to the ground below, where we see George and Alice Smith mounting their bicycles, and we hear once again the main theme of *The Picasso Summer*.

And so, the young couple are once again on their way, in search of Picasso the man.

I was delirious with joy while drawing this first of the animated segments, because I knew that I was doing something, for better or for worse, that had never been done before: not "cartoon" animation and certainly not "painting in motion"—but *movement* and *rhythm* of form itself, the essence of the medium for which animation was named!

Nor was it the abstract movement of the animation computer that is now in such enormous demand for TV commercials and the like, but purely and simply *drawing,* in the ancient and time-honored tradition of the art of interpreting the human body in all its aspects. This to me was of the utmost importance, knowing full well that the computer, in the hands of really fine artists, will one day decorate the very skies above with holographic wonders of color and movement, certainly in the century to come. But here, in my animation, was my own bid for the continuation of the drawing tradition, as old as the caves—to do more wonders with the human form than the most beautiful of computer abstractions.

Music, by its very nature, *must* be abstract, for it it were to sink to the mere imitation of everyday sounds it would cease to be music. Whereas visual art, by *its* very nature, would be a mere imitation of music were it to echo *only* the laws of music without retaining its inherent capacity for interpreting the infinite possibilities of the face and form of mankind. This is the responsibility of visual art. And, just as music reaches our souls and our hearts, so can animation—by adopting its own rules and laws of rhythm and motion, with infinite variation of form!

Ironically, perhaps the closest example of this kind of animation with its own rules of rhythm would be the very earliest films done in this medium, though they are of an entirely different nature.

I speak of the incredibly masterful works of the great Windsor McKay, whose cartoons in the second decade of this century were wonders to behold! Wonders of movement and drawing! This was before the development of the "cel" (for celluloid), the transparent sheet upon which the characters are inked and painted, allowing various levels of a scene to be overlayed, so that a background drawing could stay in place while the figure drawings could be photographed on these transparent cels, over the painting of the background. Therefore, before this development, the animator was compelled to *duplicate* his background on every drawing along with his characters—a *monumental* undertaking! This, Windsor McKay actually *did,* without help; and in my opinion, these early efforts have never been surpassed for sheer invention of movement and drawing.

Later came the magnificent "Betty Boop" and "Popeye" cartoons of Max Fleischer, in which music played an integral part of the animated movement. *Everything* moved, danced, even "boogied" to the rhythm of the music; buildings, trees, flowers, cars, clouds, hills—the characters virtually *danced* their way through every scene of these magical creations. The same was true of Walt Disney's "Silly Symphony" cartoons and some of the early Mickey Mouse films. With *Snow White* and *Pinocchio* on up to *Fantasia,* the immortal Disney made a "lady" out of animation in the way George Gershwin is said to have made a "lady" out of jazz. These films all have a mystical quality to me. There has never before been a magic of this kind on our weary old earth and there most probably never will be again.

I was lucky to grow up on the mystical magic of the later "early" Disney and Fleischer, and the equally joyous newspaper comic strips such as George Herriman's "Krazy Kat," Billy de Beck's "Barney Google," Cliff Sterrett's "Polly and her Pals," E. C. Segar's "Popeye," Floyd Gottfredson's "Mickey Mouse" strip, and so many others, which to me, in their visualization of that strange realm of the truly comic, always had an aura of deep, deep mystery. That realm of innocence and eternal morn, where bright colors and odd shapes were the rule; and deep chords were struck forever in all of us travelers who ventured early into this marvelous, marvelous land.

Interestingly enough, one of Picasso's greatest pleasures in the 1920s and '30s was to receive, regularly, the Sunday comic page from America featuring Rudolph Dirks's "The Captain and the Kids." So many things, really, go into an artist's pie that you can never be sure just what will be coming out of his oven. Sometimes there seems to be no connection between what an artist takes and what he gives.

But what Picasso has *given* us! In his final great testament to painting—the more than 200 oils he exhibited on the walls of the Palace of the Popes at Avignon in May of 1970, again in June of 1972, and later, posthumously, in May of 1973 (Oh, that I had seen these pictures before animating *The Picasso Summer!*—he has strained the boundaries of painting to the limits, from which, to continue in its forward thrust, Art *must* now explode into the new medium of animation. Picasso, in these paintings more than any before, has given us the ground rules of motion and color and visual joy with a *ferocity*, with an intellectual, emotional, and spiritual *savagery* that tears at the boundaries of finite logic and defies the possibility of art remaining in further confinement within the borders of a canvas! The structures of art should tremble, and the foundation of painting should rumble and shake before these testaments of a Master who has taken us through almost an entire century of exploration and adventure—through the most outrageously impossible recesses of the human imagination in order to teach a world how to see!

And yet, while the art world should have been celebrating these ferocious glories on the walls of the Palace at Avignon, the critics who had applauded him ceaselessly to this point in his incredible career, have (with the possible exception of, notably, Rafael Alberti) *condemned* or dismissed these works as simply the sad, repetitive dribblings and doodlings of an old man who had *nothing more to say!*

As for myself, I have a mental picture of Picasso at work on this orgy of paintings, which he did largely in the year 1969, as a man who was virtually ravaging that continent beneath the ocean of his imagination, in order to spew up all his treasures upon the shore of mankind, and himself emerging wearily upon that shore with his eyes now nothing but empty sockets and his inner fire reduced to ashes. But Picasso, nearing ninety, had the endless capacity for self-renewal and went on painting to the very end—the inner fire still burning, the smoldering coals that were his eyes still blazing with unquenchable vision.

The "Erotica" Sequence

The animation for the "Erotica" segment began first as a depiction of mythology, and I did more work—that is, more animation footage—on this than the other two segments. Halfway through we decided to feature mainly the Picasso *erotica* and changed the title accordingly. The mythology footage was still pertinent, however, since most of the Picasso mythology (fauns, nymphs, satyrs, etc.) is essentially erotic and certainly sensuously *joyous*, and (like the music of Beethoven) bursting with the sap of good health; it was therefore incorporated into it.

The live-action segue into the animation begins with George and Alice in bed in their hotel room after a fruitless day-long search for Picasso. Alice is attempting to compose a letter to Picasso, and George is trying in vain to make telephone contact.

"How do I begin?" asks Alice. "Dear Picasso? Dear *Mr.* Picasso? That doesn't sound right!"

George hangs up the phone and begins to take amorous notice of his fetching young wife.

"George!" cries Alice, teasingly resisting her husband's advances. "George, how do you expect me to write a letter to Picasso when you're—when you're—"

Then George, with quiet intensity, embraces Alice and shifts her to a more accessible position. With her head on the pillow he envelopes her with his body and kisses her tenderly on the lips. "Knowing Picasso," he says, "I'd think he'd like the idea of somebody writing him a letter [kiss] while they were [kiss] actually—making—love!"

And with that, the music begins, and we cut to close shots of Alice and George locked in amorous embrace; and then a close-up of Alice's profile in semisilhouette, head thrown back upon the pillow in quiet ecstasy. There follows a series of animated silhouettes of every conceivable color rising, one by one, from the live silhouette of Alice, like spirits leaving her body toward Paradise, as she succumbs to the throes of this ecstasy.

Then we open on a totally animated scene in which a young maiden lies sleeping in her bed beside a large, open, arch-shaped window. Her bed is draped by a transparent veil, and in the night sky a large red star blinks as if in recognition. Then the star begins to glow in intensity and we realize it is coming closer, and soon it lights up the maiden's room as it enters through her open window. The star then goes through a series of metamorphoses, flowing from one shape to another with an ease and grace that matches the accompanying music.

It assumes odd shapes: the form of a man, a goat, then a bull, and so on, until at last a full-blown Minotaur (the body of a man with the head of a bull) kneeling beside the maiden's bed in admiration. Throughout all this, our celestial visitor has retained his fire-red color. Then, with his left hand he gently lifts the drape of her bed and extends his other arm outward in a gesture of pleased astonishment (Fig. 10). The camera then moves in for a closer look at the now fully exposed young beauty, and as it does so, the screen bursts into a series of explosive scenes of erotic Picassoid splendor! (Figs. 11-13)

After seven or so minutes of these sensuous fireworks, we return once again to our bedroom idyl, where the Minotaur is still kneeling beside the maiden's bed, his left hand still holding the veil, revealing her splendid nakedness, his right arm still extended outward in astonishment at what he has just beheld.

Then he gently lowers the veil, begins his metamorphic series of changes, this time in reverse, from Minotaur to bull, to goat, to man, and so on, becoming once again a glowing red star, which floats quietly back through the window to return to its position in the sky. The scene ends where it began, with the star blinking as if in recognition, as the music comes to a plaintive conclusion and the scene fades slowly to darkness.

We do not return to the live-action bedroom scene with George and Alice, but continue the movie's forward thrust with a live-action daylight scene of the following day.

Now, as to the "Erotica" animation itself. Oh, we had fights! Furious arguments about the cutting of this sequence. These disagreements generally had little to do with the actual content of each scene, but rather with the length of some, and the flow of one into another.

The original understanding was that the animation was to be entirely my domain (one would suppose this should have gone without saying), and that the others were to oversee strictly the live-action portions of the movie. The others were, of course, Bruce Campbell as co-producer, Roy Silver as executive producer, Bill Dornisch as editor, and Bob Sallin as director (after Serge Bourginon's dismissal from the film). I failed to see where this could be any of their business; and though I definitely listened to their suggestions, accepting many of them even with relish, where the animation might be enhanced by my so doing, I refused to allow anyone to alter the flow of the animation itself, once completed, by the cutting or chopping of the editor's splicer!

And more than one sequence was ruined in this way, both by cutting and intersplicing, after I had been assured that this would not take place! When I realized, *too late*, that I was merely being *placated*, I was heartsick—more upset by the end result than I was, even, by the betrayal of my friends.

However, since no one who saw the end result knew what should have been otherwise, the sequence was applauded loudly, and received all around with a degree of excitement for which I had dared not hope.

But here is an example of the cutting:

I had animated the faces of a couple making love. All we see are their faces against a black background, but it is obvious they are making love, for both faces are in the constant flow of ecstasy, continually changing (in color, size, shape, and even in design), but never losing the singular identity of either lover. When the woman climaxes, her face enlarges to enormous proportion, with her lover's face diminishing correspondingly in size in a rhythm of acknowledgment, and the woman's face goes through a swift orgy of color changes. The same thing happens, conversely, when the man climaxes.

The important thing about this scene, the thing that made it my pride and joy, was that it was a continuous flow of constantly changing shapes, *pulsating* always to its own rhythm from beginning to end, lasting one full minute on the screen. But after my scissors-happy friends got through with it, the flow and continuity was constantly being interrupted with intercuts of *other scenes* as if to punctuate the eroticism of the love-making with other fantasies of love! Consequently, those "other scenes" that were interspliced with this one were *also* chopped up when seen in their turn, or in some cases, completely left out of the remaining portion of the "Erotica" sequence.

It was, in that sense, ruined; and by the time I was aware of what had happened, it was too late—the finished print had already been sent to Warner Bros.

Long afterward, however, to my delight, I realized I had *anticipated* Picasso by one or two years in this scene, for when his exhibit of paintings were hung on the walls of the Palace of the Popes at Avignon in May of 1970, there was a series of embracing couples devouring one another with lustful kisses that closely resembled my ravaged animated couple, which I had created as freely based on Picasso's work in general.

In another scene of the "Erotica" sequence I animated a huge smiling satyr entering the screen as if coming directly from the viewer's vantage point. In his arms he held a girl, and upon arriving at the center of the screen he whirls her round and round in a wild, bacchanalian dance (Fig. 14).

Now, I had given this girl Marla's face, with her broad, pagan, wholesome smile and short brown hair falling to one side across her face. And Roy objected to that! Bless him, he was a man of multiple talents and imposing personality, none of which had anything to do with animation. Of course, the others joined in (bless them all, too), siding with Roy who said the girl should have long, flowing blond hair that whipped in the air with each whirl of the satyr's body. Sure, that sounds terrific, but I wanted the girl to have Marla's face because Marla was herself a live nymph of Antiquity; she belonged in those joyous gatherings of those marvelous creatures of mythology, and it was both my prerogative and my privilege to put her there.

The arguing and the bickering became so loud, and Roy and the others were so adamant that only the long blond hair would be "true Picasso," that in order to save myself for more pertinent victories I added blond hair on a separate cel layer, leaving the original cels intact, and Marla's face as well, so everyone was satisfied. Yet I still regret having done it; although by doing so, precious time was saved in putting an end to the incredible bickering.

But could you imagine a group of executives standing behind a painter at his canvas, directing his every brush stroke? And yet this was one of the unbelievable obstacles I had to deal with, though I must say I allowed no obstacle to hamper or interfere with the joy I felt in the creation of this work.

One last word on the cutting, however. I had animated a lively scene of three figures. On the left a semiabstract figure plays a long flutelike instrument. On the right a fluidly designed dancer gaily plays a pair of cymbals that could well be his own hands. While in the middle an acrobat does a dance on his hands. Two white clouds dot a brilliant blue sky above a

Waxing and waning in climax . . .

... and the reverse. (BOTH COURTESY OF
WARNER BROS.)

A procession of Spanish ladies and matadors
preceding the corrida. (COURTESY OF
WARNER BROS.)

Matador and bull do battle in silhouette.
(COURTESY OF WARNER BROS.)

grassy terrain, upon which our three figures perform their little ballet (Fig. 15). Suddenly, without any really extreme or drastic change, they converge inward upon one another to form a perfectly recognizable face of a smiling satyr! This was one of the few metamorphic scenes I had actually planned long *before* starting the animation in 1968, and I felt rather fatherly toward it. But when it was seen in the film's final cut (and I say "cut" advisedly), we are shown barely a split-second of the satyr's face when formed by the converging figures, so that the audience is in no way even aware of the metamorphosis having taken place, for this is barely enough time for the image to register! An insignificant oversight of the editor's, perhaps, but very frustrating and disappointing when so much thought and work went into the creation of the scene.

Perhaps the most dramatic case of a metamorphosis in *time*, was in a colorful bacchanalian scene with a history of its own.

In the year 1638 the famous French painter of mythology, Nicolas Poussin, created a masterpiece known as *The Triumph of Pan*, an oil that now hangs in the Louvre in Paris. It portrayed a large number of beautiful men and women having a happy time in a clearing in the woods, with plenty of food and fun for everyone. To the left a man is sounding what must obviously be a festive note on a long horn-shaped instrument; a woman bestride a goat reaches behind her for some fruit upon a tray that a young man holds upon his head. Another man is carrying a young goat, for whatever reason we cannot, or dare not, guess; a Satyr and nymph frolic playfully. And so forth!

On August 25, 1944, Picasso, painting in his Paris studio, had great cause for celebration. For this was the day that Paris was liberated from the Germans, and the streets were mobbed with cheering crowds, crying tears of happiness, and singing songs of joy. Picasso celebrated in a way that only Picasso could. He took out a reproduction of Poussin's *Triumph of Pan*, and began to paint it, in his own way. This was to be the first time that Picasso translated an old master into his own idiom, the *variation-on-a-theme* idea, which composers of music had been doing for ages. Instead of oils, as Poussin had used, Picasso painted this large picture in watercolor and gouache. The result was pure Picasso, and is probably one of the greatest "remains" of a celebration in history!

So, it was only natural that from Poussin's oil, to Picasso's watercolor, this bacchanal should complete its metamorphosis in "time," to the medium of animation (Fig. 16). This time, however, the celebration was not for the liberation of Paris, but for the liberation of form itself, from the confines of its ancient prison, the canvas.

The "Bullfight" Sequence

The bullfight that Dominguin staged for the movie, over which we played the fabulous Flamenco guitar music of Carlos Montoya, was so fraught with excitement due to the incredible footwork of Dominguin, the camerawork of Vilmos Zsigmond, and the editing of Bill Dornisch, that an *animated* bullfight sequence following this brilliant display of tauromachian fireworks seemed at best, redundant, and at worst, totally unnecessary!

In actuality, however, it worked like a Picassoid charm. For just as the defeated bull begins his descent to the ground, filmed in a close-up head shot in stop-motion photography, the screen goes completely red as we hear the first marvelous chords of Michel Legrand's music for what is to follow.

Then, in animation, the large head of a bull in profile, drawn as an organic part of the Spanish soil in which it is partially submerged, animates back into the ground, which is in constant motion in the manner of some mysterious lavalike force.

There follows a series of classically adorned Spanish ladies and matadors who fade on and off screen one at a time, occasionally overlapping, and who stand in motionless profile as the Spanish earth swarms and rumbles restlessly at their feet. Suddenly, as the music (which till now was low and mysterious) sweeps to a crescendo of sound as from the moving earth, there bursts forth a beautiful Maja with a rose in her hand. The camera swoops in to a close-up of the rose; and then, with the bugle calls announcing the entrance of the picadors into the arena, we cut to a large group of yellow figures over a bright blue background. These are the picadors on horseback with their entire entourage, animated as if to appear moving forward while actually performing a fluid, rhythmic ballet in place. And thus, the animated corrida begins!

In terms of the "new kind of movement" I was battling to create, I feel that this segment, the "Bullfight" segment, was in an overall sense the most successful. It was done after the completion of the other two segments, and I had learned a lot by that time.

In particular, there were three sections of continual metamorphosis. The first, in black silhouette against a deep purple background, begins with a bullfighter in prayer beneath a cross, which is traditional before the onset of the corrida. These shapes then flow rhythmically into the silhouette of a picador atop his horse in confrontation with the bull. Reproductions illustrated here (Figs. 17–22) represent a color variation of this segment, which appears later in the sequence.

These shapes animate into several variations of design, and then proceed to animate still further into the silhouettes of the matador with his cape in combat with the bull. At one point the bull and the matador animate into the silhouettes of two Flamenco dancers, male and female, black figures against a brilliant yellow background, who (as they dance) pulsate, *alternately,* to tiny and huge proportions, giving the effect of one dancer receding to a great distance as the other dancer comes forward

335

toward the viewer—all in a constantly alternating flow and pulsating rhythm. They then animate gracefully back into the matador and bull, as the yellow background melts back into deep violet, and the bullfight continues in uninterrupted flow. As accompaniment to all this, Michel Legrand composed some of his most brilliant and exciting music.

This section ends with the bull tossing the matador into the air, and we cut to a close-up of a multicolored madonnalike face of one of Picasso's spectators (Fig. 23), as tears pour down her cheeks in response to the tragedy.

The second section of length features a female Flamenco dancer in wildly sensual gyrations against a background of yellow flames and red sky (Fig. 24). Part of this section shows her in black silhouette, and in another portion we see her in full detail, long black hair whipping about as she spirals and flows from left to right in orgiastic abandon.

In the third section of length we return to the animation of the bullfighter at prayer and go through the entire metamorphosis once again, all the way to the bull tossing the matador into the air—but this time with a difference: the whole thing becomes a *fugue*, for when we get just a short way into it, we begin *again* with a transparent overlap (called, technically, a *second pass*) with the bullfighter in prayer, and so on, but continuing with the first pass simultaneously. After we are a short way into the second pass we begin a *third* pass (transparent overlap) and continue that through, while the first and second passes are still going through their own metamorphoses.

And so on, and so on, layer upon layer, but *each time in a different color,* so that eventually we are watching a spectacle of multicolor and multimotion of this same choreographic bullfight overlapping transparently again and again, but each layer at a *different* point of the choreography, *and* in a different color. In other words, a visual "row, row, row your boat," where each singer takes up the tune at a different point—but, I hope, to a more spectacular and sophisticated degree.

Then, appearing in shorter duration, between and around the three above-mentioned longer sections, are many other little metamorphoses depicting different aspects of the corrida and Flamenco themes.

In one of these, a scene in which is portrayed a Flamenco dancer performing by candlelight before a seated matador and a hooded old woman with the face of Death, it animates, in its entirety, into the head of a bull, which glowers menacingly at the viewer (Figs. 25-30).

At still another point we see a highly stylized bull with the picador atop his horse, and at the precise moment in which the picador lances the bull, the entire group is suddenly thrust down to diminutive proportions where, seeming now to appear at a great distance, they are enveloped by the entire spectacle of the bullfight arena, cheering crowd and all; and they continue their combat, unabated by the transformation in size and place (Figs. 31-32).

I also included a more finished version of a short scene from my four-minute sample animation of an agonized matador (in close-up) whose entire head and neck are revolving like the spiral of a screw, making complete revolutions, to convey the effect of great torment and anxiety. These head turns are intercut with quick flashes of the glowering bull's head we saw earlier.

Ad infinitum, almost! What I have portrayed here verbally is in no way intended as a definitive description of the three sequences of animation, but only a few samplings of some longer sections from each sequence. But I really had fun animating the bullfight stuff; Flamenco dancers of almost every description, including one who performs with a savage ferocity as she stomps out the sensuous beats with her high-heeled shoes (which I animated to gigantic proportion, to heighten even further the emphasis on the beat); and guitarists, crowds, majas, toreros, Dons—virtually the entire cast of bullfight characters and environs.

The sequence ends with an animated Dominguin waving his hat in triumph to the wild crowd, and animating slowly into the face and form of Albert Finney, and dissolving from this animated Finney into the real-life Finney, whom, we now see, has been fantasizing what we have just witnessed. He is waving his hat, but slowly, and with a tinge of melancholy, to an imaginary crowd, as he stands beside the real-life slaughtered bull in the arena from which Dominguin has recently made his exit.

And so, too, the animation makes its exit.

34

Post Picasso Summer

IN APRIL OF 1969 *The Picasso Summer* WAS READY TO BE PREVIEWED BEFORE an invitational audience at the Academy Theatre in Beverly Hills. Realizing that there is a fine line between immodesty and pure braggadocio, I hesitate to report the entire evening's events, without simply saying "the impact upon the audience was overwhelming—in short, folks, *I'm terrific!*" I have friends who hate me to be apologetic about this sort of thing and who would seethe at reading this; these very remarks in themselves smacking of a false modesty, which I myself seethe at reading—after all, the very act of writing an account of one's own adventure can hardly be attributed to the *shyness* of the author.

But, damn it all, it was a great reward for all the years of sweat and agony that went into the making of the film—and practically the one and only reward we were to know! My family was glowing with joy and anticipation as the audience filed in, studded with show-business celebrities and many good friends, but mostly faces I had never seen before. I was accompanied by Diane Baker, whom I had met a week or so earlier, when, having seen her on a television production, I fell in love with her and contacted her agent to make a luncheon date with her, on the half-pretense of discussing a business venture. Well, it paid off and we became good friends, and she looked beautiful indeed on this, my evening of evenings.

The audience simply could not have responded more enthusiastically, and after each animation sequence there was thunderous and lengthy applause. At the film's end the lights went up and I looked at Diane, who was covering her face in her hands. "I'm shattered," she said. "Stunned."

And she kept her face covered for a long while, then finally removing her hands to reveal a look of devastated emotion.

Then an old friend, Marj Dusay, ran up and sat down beside us to offer her congratulations; it is difficult to conjure up a vision more breathtakingly beautiful than Marj, and needless to say I was in a state of egocentric bliss. Then my parents and my sister Vi and her husband Mort came over and I was submerged in a beauty of the most blessed nature; I needed no more acknowledgment than this to be flung to the farthest reaches of rapturous contentment. But more was yet to come, as face after shining face appeared with words of appreciation beyond all expectation. And when we finally reached the lobby, Yvette Mimieux ran over and threw her arms around me saying that the animation was a masterpiece, and all eyes were upon us.

Well, it was as short-lived a glory as anyone has known, for the film was never to be released. We did, however, have one more invitational preview several weeks later at the same theater, at which I received a compliment I refuse to omit from this testament of modesty. Bruce Campbell brought a young girl over to me who was accompanied by a husband or boyfriend, as I was standing in the lobby of the theater, after the screening. She had asked to meet me so that she could *touch* me! Damn, why did the glory end no later than it had begun? For I could never have guessed, on evenings such as these, that the adversities I had faced in getting this film on the screen were but a *preamble* to the adversities to come! Enjoy ye, while ye may!

In mid-May of 1969, with *The Picasso Summer* now behind me, and unaware of its death throes still ahead of me, I was looking for some new outlet in which I could utilize my new animation concept, while preparing a film on the life of Beethoven, a long-cherished dream.

Through an article by Kevin Thomas in the *Los Angeles Times* I was drawn to the offices of Sandy Dvore, a dynamic young man who was mentioned in the article as "the most acclaimed creator of title sequences since Saul Bass." The article went on to say that Dvore utilized special optical effects for his film titles, and occasionally animation. I figured we could both do each other some good.

I showed him a 16mm print of my Picasso animation, and in attendance also was his pretty little assistant, Susan Retsky. Dvore liked my film and told me that he would keep me in mind. Several nights later I had dinner with Susan, who was also a highly talented artist, and she told me that Dvore had said privately, after I had gone, that I was a genius and should be locked in a room and made to do nothing but animate. This delighted me, for I figured I would be a shoo-in, should any animated titles be requested of Sandy Dvore's company.

Sure enough, a few weeks later, Susan informed me that Sandy had been given the title-job for a new film called *De Sade,* and that some imaginative animation would be required. I was elated.

However, as time went on and Dvore never called me, I began to wonder, and Susan discovered eventually that he had given the job to a company of professional title animators, and that he had sent them a storyboard of sketches that looked suspiciously like the silhouette segment of my "Bullfight" sequence in terms of technique and style, and his instructions to the animators, beneath the various sketches, were literal descriptions of the type of movement in my work! In this way, Dvore himself would be credited with the animation on his *De Sade* titles.

When *De Sade* was released, Dvore had a large display in the lobby of the Hollywood theater in which it opened—featuring the storyboard of sketches in my style, with much bombast about Dvore's new approach to animation. And I was furious.

I sat in a rage of anticipation waiting for the film to begin; to watch a title sequence in a technique of animated movement stolen from me, in this film that was to be seen long before the release of *The Picasso Summer*—so that *I* would be the one who was considered the thief.

My fears, however, were quickly allayed as I watched the titles unfold on the screen. The animators who had followed Dvore's instructions had created a stiff and jerky succession of angular movement, with absolutely no fluidity, no continuity of movement, no flow, and absolutely no inner rhythm. I was exhilarated with relief, for the kidnap had not come off, and my baby was still safe in the crib.

In October of 1969 David Douglas Duncan was back in the United States, plugging his new book, *Self-Portrait: USA,* on national and local television and radio stations throughout the country. This book was his great photographic essay on the presidential election campaigns of 1968.

When he arrived at the Beverly Hills Hotel he contacted me, and I rushed over, looking forward enthusiastically to seeing my friend and mentor once again. He was waiting in the lobby, and in his arm he held a copy of his large new book. Grinning broadly, he handed me a copy and I opened it eagerly to read the inscription that, he told me, he had written before I arrived. It read:

13 Oct. 69
Beverly Hills

For Wes—
    Bless Picasso for bringing you to our door—

Saludos
Dave

Duncan was to appear that night on the "Bob Grant Show," at a radio station on Wilshire Boulevard, and I had offered to drive him there and sit in on the broadcast. I was once again impressed, as I had been watching him on the national talk shows, at the way he instilled a sense of awe and respect in all those with whom he came in contact, including toughened professional interviewers and TV hosts of all types. He had a ruggedly quiet, no-nonsense way of talking that discouraged any false airs in whomever he was with: that rare combination of direct, down-to-earth honesty and worldly elegance that somehow set him a notch above the crowd.

Afterward we went to the coffee shop at the Beverly Wilshire Hotel where Dave had his favorite nightcap—a chocolate sundae. I told him of the state of the film, and how it was still "just sitting" on a shelf at Warner Brothers; and he lamented once again about what a shame it was that he and Picasso had been temporarily on the "outs" when I met him that first time in Castellaras, for they were now once again on the old intimate terms. Things would have been different, he assured me, and Picasso would have participated in the animation from the start, without the necessitation of a live-action film accompaniment. Nor would there have been any such nonsense as the Dominguin-Doris Brynner tryst to louse up his participation.

"Anyway," said Dave, "Sheila and Lump and I are pulling for you to get that film off the shelf and into the theaters!"

In late spring of 1970, from out of the blue, I received a surprise telephone call from New York.

"Hello!" said the cordial voice at the other end. "This is Peter Max!"

Of course, needless to say, I was quite surprised, for I had never met Peter Max; but his posters and wildly colored designs were, especially at that time, all the rage. One could say, in fact, that he was the "superstar" of the pop-art world, especially with the younger set.

After expressing my delight and surprise, he explained the reason for his call.

341

"I'm coming out to Los Angeles in a couple of weeks for the Kinney Shoe people, to give a big send-off to my new Peter Max shoe designs, which will be on the market in June. Well, I've heard from several different sources about the remarkable bit of animation you've done on your Picasso film, and I thought I could kill two birds with one stone and have a look at it."

"Of course," I said, "I'd be happy; have you something in mind regarding animation?"

"Well, in fact, yes," he replied. "That's what I'll be wanting to talk to you about—after I see your work. And besides, I'm always interested in seeing what my fellow artists are doing!"

A couple of weeks later I received a second call from Peter Max, informing me that he was in town and staying at the Beverly Hills Hotel, where he was to speak before an assembly of Kinney Shoe salesmen from all over the country. The subject of the talk was Kinney's new line of Peter Max shoes, for which the salesmen were all congregating to be indoctrinated. Apparently the Kinney people regarded this new line as something so big and sensational that it called for the presence of the creator himself to fire the enthusiasm of the entire sales personnel.

It was arranged that I would screen my animation for him on the morning of his talk, and then afterward I would accompany him to the Beverly Hills Hotel while he gave his speech. He arrived at the screening with a pleasant Los Angeles couple, a husband and wife, and a young lady, who were long-time friends of his.

Never had my animation received such an enthusiastic response, for Peter could hardly find his voice. "You're my man!" he cried. "You're the man I'm looking for—*no one else* will do now!" It seems that he was planning a full-length animated feature based on his designs, with a story written by himself. "But with your type of animation!" he said. "It's more than I dared even hoped for! You can fly with it—do your own thing, but following my designs."

As his enthusiasm mounted, he began to envision a whole series of animated features—he would form his own animation company, which I would head as producer, director, and animator of all his films!

"It would be here, on the West Coast," he said, "where it's all happening."

Peter had a very imposing face, and as his ideas caught hold and drove him to a pitch of great intensity, he seemed to radiate an aura of almost visible energy. In fact, with his long (shoulder-length), black hair, parted in the middle of his forehead, his black beard and moustache, and his black eyes burning from behind a prominent, slightly down-curving nose, he gave the impression of a benevolent young Rasputin. Only his agreeable New York accent and mannerisms took the edge off this otherwise hypnotic impression.

The large assembly room at the hotel had what must have been a couple

342

of hundred chairs set up for the talk, and the surrounding walls and tables were covered with Peter Max posters and artifacts.

Peter spoke for over an hour, and his subject was Peter Max, Peter Max, Peter Max. I was astounded at the ingenuousness and frankness with which he spoke about his greatness, but it seemed, after all, to work: for, within the first five or ten minutes, he had these conservative, straitlaced businessmen in the palm of his hand, and they were fired up with an enthusiasm that unleashed itself in wild cheers and applause, as well as with laughter at Peter's off-the-cuff brand of humor. He showed a short film dealing with himself and his work, which punctuated his talk perfectly, and at the finish he received a furious standing ovation.

The shoes themselves—that is, the Peter Max shoes—were of an obvious transient and faddish nature, with wild colors and designs such as huge smiling teeth painted on the heels and so on, and though in themselves intended as a short-lived but super-camp fad, were to act as a virtual breakthrough in the "anything goes" variety of shoe design, or in fact, for clothing in general.

After his brief bout of handshaking, autographs, and scattered congenial conversation, he walked over to me, and, taking me by the arm, said, "Let's talk." We went into one of the sitting rooms near the lobby where there were several large trays of refreshments upon an elegantly decorated table. Peter walked over to the center tray, which was filled with small pieces of hard candy, and took himself a handful. Suddenly a female voice boomed out with imposing authority: "Young man, don't you dare touch that candy with your hands!" At first thinking it a joke, we turned, smiling, to face the accuser, but found, to our surprise, and Peter's sudden humiliation, that it was indeed not a joke. For walking toward us, her face encased in a scathing frown, was a tall, beautiful woman—apparently some sort of hotel hostess.

"What do you think *I'm* here for?" she continued her scolding. "We do *not* touch public food with our hands!" And so saying, she took a large, sterling-silver serving spoon and, scooping it into the tray, doled it out into little plates that she handed to us. "If you want anything hereafter, please ask me. That's what I'm here for. Do you want me to lose my job?"

The absurdity of this whole scene, coming so fast on the heels of the overwhelming adulation Peter had just left in the adjoining room, and then walking out as if straight into his childhood once again to be chastised by a grown-up for being such a naughty boy, somehow set the scales right, and we suddenly doubled over in an uncontrollable fit of laughter.

Sitting at a small table, we were joined by Peter's friends and fell into a warm and cordial conversation. We came to the conclusion that working together would be a highly productive and happy enterprise, for we had each arrived at a harmonious understanding of the other's goals and personal dreams for what he wished to attain in that limitless world of art.

343

However, once Peter returned to New York, the usual troubles started. To make an otherwise very long story short, it turned out, much to Peter's unhappiness (and certainly to mine), that Peter's manager thought the whole idea far-fetched and impractical, and he was, in fact, militantly opposed to it. The closest I came to getting him to give in a little was his proposal that I come to New York to work for Peter's company, where we might eventually work things out and finally get the enterprise going. This was highly unsatisfactory to me, and Peter expressed his profound regrets, explaining that he could hardly go against the wishes of his business manager, whose wisdom had thus far proved almost infallible.

I leave this little episode—without comment.

Shortly after Warner Bros. saved the day by buying *The Picasso Summer* for over 1.7 million dollars, the Hymans relinquished control of the studio to a new organization, headed by Ted Ashley, with John Calley in charge of production. This new regime promptly shelved fifty pictures that had already been bought and paid for by the old regime, including *The Picasso Summer*. This was the decision of John Calley, a young "hip" executive who decided that "nobody would be interested in a film about Picasso." I argued heatedly with him by telephone, not being able to get in to see him in person (!), and he insisted that he would not release the film, and that personally he did not give a damn for Picasso.

After so many attempts to convince Calley to release our film theatrically, I was not entirely pleased to learn that the studio was planning to lease the film to CBS for two showings on television. I needed help. I needed someone to talk about the film, to publicize it.

In early March 1972 I decided to turn to Rona Barrett, the famous Hollywood columnist and television personality, with whom I felt an instinctive rapport whenever watching her on TV. I called her and told her of my plight with Warner Brothers and asked her if I could show her *The Picasso Summer* in a private screening. She immediately acquiesced, and I arranged for the screening one night a few days later.

She showed up alone at the designated time, and I was immediately impressed by the quietly powerful aura emanating from her tiny frame. Her eyes had a bright, amused look that had an incongruous mixture of directness and shyness, and I knew from watching her on television that she was capable of a bold and headstrong spunkiness that in no way detracted from her femininity. We hit it off immediately, and I was glad that I had followed my impulse in calling her.

We sat alone in the elegant screening room, which was located in an office building on Sunset Boulevard in Beverly Hills, and I filled her in

344

briefly on my dilemma before signaling the projectionist to start the film.

When it was over and the lights once again went on, she turned to me with an enthusiastic smile that delighted me and filled me with hopeful anticipation. First she expressed a ravenous enthusiasm for the animation and then said that she felt that what she had seen were two separate films, and that the animation could stand alone without the live action (a comment similar to a remark Mort Sahl had made to me after the second screening at the Academy Theatre, when I bumped into him later that evening outside the all-night market on Pico and Robertson). "But," she continued, "your animation is unlike anything I've ever seen before. And I intend to herald your art!"

She promised to do all she could to help me by publicizing my dilemma on her nightly syndicated television show. She was true to her promise, and a day or so later, on March 13, while watching her show I was surprised to see stills of my animation suddenly appear on the screen behind her, as she looked into the camera with that familiar bright look and said the following:

Inside sources revealing Wes Herschensohn's Warner film, *The Picasso Summer,* has now been bought by CBS to air as a late night movie.

However, the pic's 7-minute "Erotica" sequence has been removed for TV viewing, with CBS apparently feeling it's a little too much for the tube. We're told real reason for removal of the sequence is that Warner is keeping it for use in a pilot presentation of an anthology series called "Man & Woman" produced by Fred Coe.

Anyway, since *Picasso Summer,* starring Yvette Mimieux, was never released to theaters, this makes it the most expensive film for TV ever made, at $1,600,000. Herschensohn saying "After 8 years of pregnancy, my baby is finally born, minus an arm, but at least it's born."

This is Rona Barrett in Hollywood.

Michel Legrand's superb score for the film was being constantly played on radio and television, and the song ("Summer Me, Winter Me") had been recorded by dozens of top recording artists, including Barbra Streisand. Warner Brothers leased the film to the CBS Television Network for two showings—the first to be seen Friday, August 4, 1972, and the second on the following December, for the 11:30 P.M. time slot, which had previously been occupied by the "Merv Griffin Show," in competition with Johnny Carson's "Tonight Show."

I was horrified to find, however, that over *one-third* of the film had been cut! My objection was not to the fact that it was cut, for such is the necessity of television, but rather to the crude and arbitrary manner in which it was done.

The story, as shown on television, had absolutely no semblance of continuity, so that even I, who had been with the film since conception, found it difficult to keep pace with what I saw on the screen, and the animation was chopped barbarically. The "Erotica" sequence was spared all this, for this segment was dropped altogether for the TV showing. This was partly due to the fact that Fred Coe, who had produced many important films for television, as well as "Night Watch" for Broadway, really wanted to incorporate the "Erotica" sequence into a pilot for a prospective television series called "Man and Woman," featuring stories (dealing with the relationship of the sexes) by such men as Hemingway, Fitzgerald, Faulkner, and so on, and felt that the "Erotica" animation would make a good change of pace.

In my outrage, I placed the following ad in the *Hollywood Reporter* and *Variety* a few days after the first TV showing of *The Picasso Summer*:

THANK YOU, CBS

for the massacre of my movie,

THE PICASSO SUMMER

shown Aug. 4 on the 11:30 "Late Night Movie" slot.

You sure as hell wouldn't have bought the movie if what you first saw was your own version of it.

You cut virtually one-third of the film, including the Bullfight, the whole story continuity, the entire animated EROTICA sequence, and chopped up the WAR AND PEACE animation at the precise moment of transition from WAR to PEACE. Brilliant. How did you do that?

I understand you plan a second showing. Do us both a favor, and forget it.

Love,

WES HERSCHENSOHN

The response to this ad was overwhelming in terms of letters, phone calls, and personal accolades, and the ad was even reprinted verbatim in several columns. To my delight and surprise, I found that in spite of the indiscriminate, arbitrary editing, the picture had made a profound effect on many people, and the *Hollywood Reporter,* in their review of the film, although they disliked what they could glean from the live-action portion, said that the film "contained some of the most dazzling animation since *Fantasia.*"

Most gratifying was that great body of people who told me that before seeing the animation they neither understood nor cared for Picasso's work, but after seeing the film, understood Picasso as if they had learned a new language of vision; and they looked forward to viewing his works in order to relate them to the ideas of motion and rhythm in which they were presented in the animation.

Although I received many calls and letters as a result of the CBS showings, I would like to quote one letter that gave me particular pleasure and gratification; it came from a young lady whom I had met briefly only once, during the time I was just beginning work on the animation:

August 5, 1972

Dear Wes,

How can I describe the effect on me of the new world that was opened up to us all, as I watched in a state of shock, your animation last night on my television screen? I sat thinking I was watching a nice, very pleasant movie, when suddenly these dancing forms exploded before my eyes, and I knew I was witness to a new birth of art, unlike anything I had seen or imagined before!

Like a revelation of my own subconscious mind, these forms, like *thoughts visualized* in a stream-of-consciousness surge, unfolded, ever-changing, merging into one another to form new images—it was a visualization, for the first time, of the workings of the inner mind! Whether this was your intention, I don't presume to know. Most probably I have yet to learn much, as to what it was you were telling us!

Will this be the first and last time we are to be privileged to view this new world? It would be like hearing only one symphony in a lifetime—how sad if this were the case. These shapes and colors moved *organically,* as if part of one great whole, a living organism, not representative of anything but its own self, and yet reminding us how glorious the experience of life and thought can and should be!

I can only thank you for what you have given us, and pray that this is just the beginning. The world needs you as it has always needed its artists to push us forward toward the only real progress that matters to mankind, by opening our eyes to the magnificence of creation and the human mind and spirit.

Lee

One day Jim Byron called to tell me that Sam Arkoff, head of American-International Studios, had screened a print of *The Picasso Summer* at his home for himself and his family, and told Jim that he thought the "Erotica" sequence was the most *truly* sensual art he had ever seen, without being laughable or vulgar, and that he had no uneasiness whatever about his children seeing it.

347

This pleased me immeasurably, for my aim had been, indeed, to be as erotic as possible without being offensive. Therefore, upon hearing this from Jim I tried to approach Mr. Arkoff about my new idea for the Beethoven film, but was never able to see him. Life goes on!

Jim, however, was desirous of becoming my manager through his firm, Destiny, Inc., which at that time he was heading in partnership with Yvette Mimieux. He thought it would be a real coup to make for himself a new public-relations package of three totally disparate clients: an astronaut, an Olympic champion, and an artist. He had already obtained the former two and wanted me to complete the "package." However, this never came to pass, though for a long while Jim never failed to come up with other new and spectacular ideas in an attempt to sensationalize my particular brand of animation, trying in vain to invent a special term to describe it—in the way that Disney, in 1941, had coined the term *Fantasound* for his new theatrical stereophonic sound system that was used for the first time, in limited theaters, for his *Fantasia*.

35

Epilogue—A Tape

AS I APPROACH THE CONCLUSION OF THIS BOOK, HAVING WRITTEN IT TO THE best of my recollection and by the perusal of endless notes, all of which I deemed pertinent to the telling of my story, I decided to check with Bruce Campbell about certain things I may have forgotten or skimmed over incorrectly. He agreed to a taping session, and we spent a couple of hours together one afternoon, at which time I quizzed him and let him say whatever came to his mind.

The following are some interesting and unedited excerpts from these tapes. "B" is Bruce, and "W" is me:

W: I'm trying to remember the name of that hotel we stayed at in Paris.

B: Sure, I still have an ash try I took (*shows me the ash tray*)—the Hotel Plaza Athené! When we got to Paris, we had been up for two days, plus that, hadn't had any rest! That was the trip where we went to see Dominguin, and then to Truffaut.

W: That's right, then that night we went to our hotel, when was it, what night was it that all the hotel lights were out?

B: Well, we had been out to dinner—that night club where we almost got arrested. And I was all for just seeing how far we could push them. And you kept saying "No no no no, *remember Truffaut!*" We had that appointment to see him the next morning. "*Remember Truffaut!*" you'd say.

W: So—it was, what, around two or three in the morning when we got back to the hotel and found all the lights out?

B: Oh yeah, at least! It must have been four. So ridiculous—this luxurious hotel and they turn the lights out—all the lights—and we had to find the way to our rooms by lighting matches!

W: Yeah, I forgot to mention that. What hotel at Madrid did we stay at? I left the name blank. I have to go back and fill it in. Was it the Paláce?

B: Well the one you and I stayed at together, and the crew, in Madrid, was the Ritz. Or was it the Paláce? Excuse me, it *was* the Paláce. I still have one of their bath mats. The red and white one. Marvelous old hotel—I loved Madrid! Those little phones—of course, that was there *and* in France. Remember the conversation I had with Pedro?

W: Yeah?

B: The telephone rings, "RRRGHH!" Just enough, y'know, to frighten you alive—it was a very expensive hotel room, and a very beautiful setting. And these ancient telephones. And then when you got him on the phone it was like *forty years ago!* They invented it, put it in immediately, and never changed it.

W: All those European hotels are like that. Now—jumping—remember that time in San Francisco that we shot the. . .

B: I want to talk more about the telephones.

W: (laughing) The house in San Francisco where we shot the scene. . .

B: You mean where we shot the party sequence?

W: No, I'm talking about the "gruesome threesome"—remember the guy who carried the little baby in. . .

B: That was done in Burlinghame or San Mateo County somewhere. That was where Yvette was wandering around the estate. Right? I didn't go to that shoot. I'd love to get hold of that footage, too! Boy, would I love to get hold of all that footage and remake the picture. I wasn't there, my brother was in charge of that shoot.

W: Oh yeah, Jim. Now, the Melvin Belli apartment. I wonder if there was anything interesting I may have left out of that—stuff I might not have been in on or remembered.

B: There was a funny incident. Serge wanted to have the shot open on the bridge [Golden Gate] through the bay window and pull back into the Belli apartment, and there's a grand piano—somebody playing a baby grand piano. Well, Melvin Belli had no baby grand piano, and he was up on a hill, so they had to hire a crane—I've still got shots of it—of them lifting that piano—at probably extravagant cost, I'm sure—several hundred dollars, a thousand dollars, to lift that piano into the apartment. *But*—that's movie making!

W: Yep!

B: By the way, I had a horrible time with Roy Silver on the roof at Belli's place, and we almost ended our relationship.

W: No, really?

B: Oh, *yeah!* I had a horrible fight with him the night before where I broke down and screamed "How dare he treat me that way!"

W: Really?

B: Oh yeah, next time he was *absolutely unglued.* I remember him coming to the set with Bourgignon, because I told Bourgignon he could have *everything*—I didn't know, then, the brutality of the man—because Roy was very good about that. Anyway, we paced back and forth on Belli's roof, and we had just gotten the contract from Coca-Cola for a million dollars for Bill Cosby—I remember him waving that around—he was very pleased. The picture had almost come to a crashing halt—but it didn't. Conditions got better.

W: What happened? What *had* the conditions been?

B: Well, the conditions were that Roy was going stark raving out of his mind! After what had all happened, and so forth, that Picasso wasn't *there,* and all. . .

W: That's right, this was *after* all that. . .

B: *And* money was—the banks were closing in—we were teetering on the verge of bankruptcy. We had seven hundred thousand dollars of corporate funds in that picture all borrowed mostly, or stolen, somehow.

W: And this was *after* that whole European thing.

B: Yeah, this was coming back; we were in San Francisco. It was nip and tuck, that we weren't going to be able to finish the picture—or stay in business, for that matter!

W: So when you got the thing from Coca-Cola, the million dollar contract. . .

B: Yeah, that of course buoyed his spirits. But anyway, I had a big fight with him that night. It's the only time we ever fought.

W: Regarding what?

B: Regarding the fact that it really wasn't all going to plan, so well. And we were having tremendous problems, and we were saddled with a maniac—Serge—and Roy kept wanting me to make it better and there was no way to make it better. Hopefully, we would gallop to keep up with Serge, so that we could survive in it all so that we could finish. But to make it better, it wasn't gonna be. And—uh—I had been taking that from Roy for a long time. Y' know: "It's *your* fault! *You* got me into this!"

W: Oh, no!

B: Oh, yeah! That went on and on and on.

W; And isn't it also true, didn't you once tell me, over there, that he was afraid I might assassinate Picasso to make a name for myself, or some such nutty thing?

B: Yeah. He was really very angry. He was very upset that it hadn't gone—and then it all came to a head at Melvin Belli's. . .

W: Did he think it was your fault? Or my fault?

B: Uh—he really—he was just—terribly upset. He was a little kid from the Bronx who never did anything, and all of a sudden he's got himself a million dollar talent—a *ten* million dollar talent by the name of Bill Cosby, and I have it all in San Francisco. (*We both laugh*)

B: "Just because I listened to you!"—he was giving me that for a long time. Finally, on that night I said "That's all!" He should hope to God—y'know—we *have* this! Making pictures is a very death-defying venture. It really is. I lost two friendships—*three* friendships—totally destroyed. A marriage out of *Johnny* [Bruce's second film production *Johnny Got His Gun*, with Dalton Trumbo, who subsequently became his father-in-law]. I mean totally destroyed. Bankruptcy—long-time friends! Bob Sallin and I *do* not speak! Anyway, as *you know*, it's a death-defying business!

W: Yeah, right.

B: And—uh—*Picasso Summer* was a classic example of that, because we were really reaching for something that was daring just to *think* about, let alone—I'd tell people, I'd say—we walked around saying we were going to take the Michelangelo of our time and make him *move!* Wes Herschensohn's concept. Everybody said "Get *out* of here! You're crazy! *That*'ll never happen! Have you got the rights?" I'd say "No," and they'd say "Get *out* of here!" They used to say "First of all how dare you mention it when you don't even have the rights—get *out* of here!" I remember Sammy Weisbord at the Morris office: "You fools, you'll never get that off the ground!" (*laughter*) "Oh, yeah? (*fantasizing our reply*) That's *just* what we like to hear! Never get it *off*, huh? We'll—soon—see—about—*that!* Give us a couple of plane tickets to Madrid! *We're* going to see Dominguin!" (*much laughter*)

W: How about the writing of the script—I mean, the story discussions, at the Bel Air Hotel? Serge insisting on the Bel Air. . .

B: Oh, he drove us up the wall! That Bourgignon is a whole book unto—he's at *least* a chapter in your book. He won't be, but. . .

W: No, he won't be—but he's in there.

B: —In terms of making the film, because—you do have him directing from the horse.

W: Yeah.

B: I remember the day I'm driving with Albert and Yvette from the hotel in San Francisco down to the location at the Union Carbide building—whatever it is—the big—the Alcoa Building—where we shot the bedroom sequence.

W: Yeah, we used it as a sound stage. It had just been completed, mostly still vacant, and it had that great view of. . .

B: Serge shouts, "We have no bedroom! There is no bedroom around! We must build a bedroom!" Serge says. So we built a bedroom. He wanted the room in the Alcoa Building because of the *view* and so forth, and then we didn't even see any background movement because he shot it at the time of day when there was no background movement, so it could have been a *drop!* *(laughter)*

B: *(continues)* Anyway, we're driving down the street, Albert and Yvette and I, and I see some *horses* ahead from the Police Department, and I shout "Oh, he's here! Serge is already on the set, ready to direct!" *(laughter)* Well, that was probably my best line in the picture—Albert and Yvette thought it was very funny, very spontaneous, everybody laughed.

W: That was funny.

B: *(seriously)* I thought, today, Wes—before you came over—and maybe this should be in the book—

W: Yeah?

B: That—in order to tell you what I would have to say about *my* side of the experience coupled with—not that you were just somebody off the street coming and saying, "Tell me about your experiences with *The Picasso Summer*," but you're the man who invented it, and who *(laugh)*, in a strange kind of a way—through your brother's intervention that day when he called me and said, "Come to lunch at Carolina Pines"—that I thought today before you came over, that to *tell* this—my side—would take a lot of sessions. We're going to do it in one afternoon in about an hour and a half; well that's ridiculous, because there are a lot of stories, and the stories take a little time just to have them come out.

W: Sure. I know.

B: But there's an enormous amount of material, how can we possibly— what is there to talk about? I can go on *(laughs)* on *my* coloration, the way *I* phrase things—I could go on talking about some of these things—as I said—some of my best moments on that picture have been, when all of a sudden for some reason it'll come out at a gathering, or maybe a couple of people sitting around, they want to know about it, and so forth—and *marvelous* stories!

W: I know, I've heard you tell them.

B: I mean, are you gonna put in the fact that the *reason* that we didn't get Pablo Picasso to appear in the beach scene was because Dominguin was making love to Yul Brynner's wife?

W: Oh yeah, it's in there.

B: I mean that's the *reason!*

W: *(laughs)* It's in there.

B: That's how it all started!

W: You mean that's how it all *ended.* That made the cover of *Confidential* magazine! Which I've still got a copy of.

B: Now—your book is about making the picture.

353

W: Well, the book is about making the picture, right. But most of the book is what happened *before*—

B: Getting you into it.

W: Right. That's really the story I'm telling. And now *this* part is the "production" part—and environs.

B: Right. Shoot!

W: Well, let's see—okay—was *Picasso Summer* part of Roy Silver's demise, or—he seemed to survive that pretty well. I mean his *Rainbow Club* on the Sunset Strip, and. . .

B: Oh, *yeah!* No, *Picasso Summer* got us a five-picture, twelve-million-dollar deal. See, my strategy in making that original move with you to try to get the picture done was that here we were going after something that was very *audacious;* this kind of project—we could have done almost any kind of film we wanted to. So, it didn't work out, but we also got a five-picture deal for twelve million dollars from Warner's, we got back our 750,000 dollars, plus another eight.

W: So his antagonism toward you and me should have been completely washed over then because of all that. I mean, he had to know from the beginning that there was an element of risk, just like. . .

B: Well, at that point we were in a lot of trouble when I talk about the Belli situation. To this day he feels that the picture went close to knocking us out, and that we were on the hook for an unbelievable amount of money. So that hurt. And in the overall, had the company succeeded, meaning had Mr. Cosby hung in, because we were right on a straight line, it would have been a wash. But because, based upon what we were doing—we were making so much money, because we had a lot of things going—the record company [Tetragrammophone], deals with NBC, etc. It really wouldn't make any difference. In other words, the point really wasn't *proven.* Yes, we got the five-picture deal for twelve million dollars, but we *never got it to make!* And the fact that we went over, reaching for this. Again, in the grown-up way of looking at things—the more sophisticated way of looking at things—that's the nature of the motion picture business! We certainly weren't the first people ever to go over on a motion picture—whether it be a little one or a big one, it happens all the time. And, I'm sure to this day most of it was paid off—that's why I would love to see the picture go out!
was paid off—that's why I would love to see the picture go out!

W: Yeah!

B: Maybe make a little noise—which I'm sure it would. At a time when they're really hurting for pictures, I can't understand Warner Brothers not at least *attempting* to do something with it. It's ridiculous. They don't want to pay Finney that additional one hundred thousand dollars, per his contract deal upon release of the film, so they let the picture lie stagnant. I don't see how it couldn't be worked out—Jesus Christ, they could work something out with Finney's agent!

W: Oh, of course. Well—we'll see. You never know.

B: By the way—off of that—my brother does a wonderful imitation of Serge Bourgignon yelling to you from his camera on the hilltop when you were drawing on the beach, trying to beat the oncoming waves—you drew a faun and he wanted a—"*No,* Wes! A *dove,* Wes! A *Dove!*" Jim does it beautifully. "Wes! No! *No!* Ohhh, *merde!*" (*We both roar with laughter*)

B: And, are you going to tell about the man who picked up five Emmys in 1975, Ed Weinberger, for *Mary Tyler Moore* and *Rhoda,* and all those things he does, and very successfully—once one of the other writers on our film, finally?

W: Forgot about that.

B: Oh—are you going to tell about the time I came very close, toward the end of the picture, to trying to convince everybody into changing the title of the picture from *The Picasso Summer* to *The Duke Fishman Story?* Are you going to tell that story?

W: (*laughter*) Oh, of *course!*

B: Or, my other idea—was to have, right at the very end of the film, when the music swells up, and the seagulls are flying and so forth—and we fade out, and we fade in real quickly on a picture of Picasso, and he winks at us? In animation?

W & B: (*much laughter*)

★   ★   ★

And so the final result of my efforts and my testament in animation was, ultimately, no more tangible than that massive fresco I had drawn in the sand, in Picasso's absence, to be washed away by the waves of commercial bickering, in the tide of mindless conformity.

All one can hope is that when those waves return to the sea from which they came, they carry with them some memory of those images on the shore, and in some immeasurable way affect the mysterious current of that otherwise unalterable, unchanging sea.

Index

356

357